Harvard Studies in Cultural Anthropology, 4

The Harvard Studies in Cultural Anthropology is founded in the belief that answers to general questions about the human condition may be discovered through the intensive study of other cultures. The series will publish books that elucidate and interpret cultural systems in order to contribute to comparative understanding.

NATURE AND SOCIETY IN CENTRAL BRAZIL

The Suya Indians of Mato Grosso

Anthony Seeger

HARVARD UNIVERSITY PRESS
Cambridge, Massachusetts
and London, England
1981

Printed in the United States of America

Library of Congress Cataloging in Publication Data

Seeger, Anthony.
Nature and society in central Brazil.
(Harvard studies in cultural anthropology; 4)
Bibliography: p.
Includes index.

1. Suya Indians. I. Title. II. Series.
F2520.1.S89S43 980'.004'98 80-18682
ISBN 0-674-60485-7

For Elizabeth Mapalu Seeger
so that she may understand her names
and
for those whose names she bears

Acknowledgments

NO WORK OF THIS KIND can be completed without the aid of a large number of people and institutions. My debts are especially numerous because of our long stay in Brazil and the great kindness with which my wife, Judy, and I were treated by persons whom we are honored to call friends.

My graduate training at the University of Chicago and two of the years that we were in Brazil (1970-1972) were supported by a departmental grant from the Training Program in the Behavioral Sciences (USPHS GM 1059). An additional year of support at the University of Chicago (1973-74) was extremely beneficial. My parents also helped with generous gifts in times of need. Our 1976 field trip received travel assistance from a Ford Foundation departmental grant. Further field research in 1978 was financed by Ford Foundation research grant 739-0817-SS-16 and a Financiadora de Estudos e Projetos (FINEP) departmental research grant.

Following our arrival in Brazil we had to wait eight months before beginning our fieldwork with the Suya because of certain developments in Brazilian Indian policy. Many people helped us through that difficult time, but none so much as Dr. Henrique Fix and Dona Fanny Fix, their daughter Dora and her husband, Alessandro, their son Alexandre and his wife, Sýlvia, and their daughter Célia and her husband, Ruy. Knowing them and living with them was an experience we can only repay with gratitude.

Among the many others who helped us were Major Samuel Schneider Netto of the Brazilian Air Force and his wife, Bella, and Dr. David Fringer of the Peace Corps. They complemented their immense practical assistance with warm friendship. We also owe much to Garret and Dede

Bouton, Stan and Coleen Nicholson, Morris and Leslie Blachman, Steve and Suzanne Quarles, Sandy Davis, Ken Brecher, and Roberto and Celeste Da Matta.

Miller Hudson, then science attaché to the U.S. Embassy, Dona Marina Muricy, representative of the National Institutes of Health in Rio de Janeiro, and members of the U.S. Embassy in Brasília, especially Mary Marchany, were of assistance. To the many others who helped unravel the skeins of bureaucracy, I am extremely grateful.

My colleagues in Brazil were most supportive of my project. Among them were Amadeu Lanna, Roque Laraia, Júlio Cezar Melatti, Lux Vidal, Alcida Ramos, Manuel Diégues Júnior, Roberto Da Matta, and the faculty and students of the Department of Anthropology of the Museu Nacional.

Our debts to all these people and to many others are so extensive that it is difficult to express our gratitude. I can only say that the eight months we spent in Rio de Janeiro, São Paulo, and Brasília—as well as our fieldbreaks and my semester at the Museu Nacional in 1973—were not lost time. We met many fine people and learned a great deal from them.

We also owe much to people associated with the Xingu reservation (Parque Nacional do Xingu), in which the research was done. We were transported several times in the planes of the Brazilian Air Force (FAB) which at that time provided the only means of entering the region. Of the non-Suya in the Xingu reservation we shall be forever grateful for the kind reception given to us, our researches, and our music by Cláudio and Orlando Villas Boas, who created one of the brighter spots in the otherwise dim history of Indian policy in the Americas. We were also much aided by Mairawë, the Kayabi in charge of Diauarum in Cláudio's absences; Marina Villas Boas, Alvaro Villas Boas, and others working at the reservation headquarters in São Paulo; Dr. Roberto Baruzzi and his colleagues at the Escola Paulista de Medicina; and the late Dr. Noel Nutels. Dona Cida, nurse at Diauarum during the first ten months of our stay, and Olympio Serra, for several years the director of the reservation after the retirement of the Villas Boas, were also of considerable assistance.

Without the kind, generous, and patient cooperation of the Suya, the efforts of these people would have been in vain. I owe a great debt to their general perseverance, linguistic ingenuity, humor, honesty, and willingness to admit a lack of knowledge rather than fabricate responses. I wish to thank especially the following men who gave so much time and effort to making sure that I understood as well as possible: Kuyusi, Tewensoti, Kogrere, Robndo, Wetagü, Peti, and Bentügarürü. (I have used their real names here; in later discussions I have used pseudonyms for ethical reasons.) To Botko, my fishing companion of many months on the clear waters of the Suya-Missu River, and to Ntoni, a companion of the hunt, special thanks are due. To Soi, Gaiso, Gaisari, Tàkuru, Wekwoiyi, and all the other women in the house in which we lived, many thanks are due for the food and companionship they shared with us both. We and the Suya had good times and tough times together.

Special thanks to my teachers at Dalton, Putney, Harvard, Cornell, and the University of Chicago. Professors Victor W. Turner and Terence Turner, for many years my advisors, taught me that the study of anthropology should be undertaken with dogged attention to detail, with humility, and with humanity. From them, too, I learned some rollicking good songs.

The transformation of a dissertation into a book is a long and difficult process. I am indebted to Professor Judith Shapiro for her close reading and detailed comments. The department of anthropology encouraged my efforts by nominating my dissertation for the Marc Perry Galler Award in the division of the social sciences—an award it later received. Above all, the metamorphosis of this work was made possible by the invitation to teach in the graduate program in social anthropology of the Museu Nacional in Rio de Janeiro. My position at the Museu Nacional allowed me to return to the field to clarify and enrich my data and analyses; the support of my colleagues and students was invaluable. I am especially grateful to Roberto Da Matta and Eduardo Viveiros de Castro, who helped shape and stimulate my thoughts. David Maybury-Lewis, whose undergraduate course first interested me in the Gê, has been a constant supporter.

My wife, Judy, and I learned much about each other while we learned about the Suya. She sometimes saw me return at the end of a long hungry day with no fish; returning I sometimes found no manioc *beiju* prepared. Her good humor and freedom from the obligations of field research were particularly attractive to the Suya. She grated tons of manioc in companionable discussion with the Suya women; in an informal way she gathered much of what I know about them. In the elaboration of this work she has been a companion, proofreader, colleague, scholar—and patient throughout. In the field we shared sickness, hunger, and depression and health, repletion, and ecstasy. In the middle of hundreds of miles of moonlit forest and swamp, under a sky filled with unfamiliar stars, we sang together in harmony and peace. Without her contributions this would be a far different, and inferior, work.

For the variegated contributions made by these people, and by others whom I have not mentioned by name but whose anonymity does not detract from my gratitude, I proffer my thanks and in this book some concrete results of their assistance.

Contents

Tables

Figures

Nature and Society in Central Brazil

Guide to Pronunciation of Suya Words

No attempt has been made to reproduce the phonetics of the Suya language in this book. In the pronunciation of Suya words and phrases used in the text, consonants should be pronounced as they are in English. Unaltered vowels are similar to those in Spanish or Portuguese.

a is pronounced as the *a* in father
à is pronounced as the *u* in up
e is pronounced as the *e* in men
i is pronounced as the *ee* in see
ï is pronounced as the *i* in hit
o is pronounced as the *o* in open
u is pronounced as the *oo* in shoot
ü is pronounced as the *oeu* in boeuf
˜ indicates a nasalization of a vowel
ñ is pronounced as the *ny* in canyon

Syllabic stress accents have been omitted for simplicity.

Introduction

Of all the sciences, [social anthropology] is without a doubt unique in making the most intimate subjectivity into a means of objective demonstration.

—Claude Lévi-Strauss, *The Scope of Anthropology*

THE COLLECTION OF DATA in anthropology is almost always the result of a fieldworker at a particular point in his life and theoretical formation and under certain circumstances of health and situation, working with a social group at a certain point in its own processes of change. The contact is usually difficult for both parties. If anthropology can claim any validity from the contingency of the fieldwork on which it is based, it is only because of the hard work and dedication to a theory and a method on the part of the fieldworker and much patience on the part of the group with which he is working.

Every fieldworker, by virtue of his individuality, must have a different approach to his subjects and a different work style. These are often dictated by particular circumstances. When he finally leaves the field, every fieldworker has had an intense personal experience and, one hopes, collected data that are theoretically interesting. His experience and his data are not completely unrelated. Increasingly we must ask to know more about how a person worked in order to collect the data. Did he work for long periods or short? Did he use the native language, interpreters, or a contact language? Was there one informant or many? Did he use surveys or self-selected informants? How a person worked and what he did have a profound effect on everything he writes.

All fieldwork is to some extent a violation of the society studied. Anthropologists must ask difficult and sometimes unpleasant questions. Even in terms of the allocation of his time an informant must choose to answer questions instead of doing something else. A fieldworker may place other hardships on the community by eating food from its gardens, by demanding watchful care through his ignorance of social forms and natural dangers, or by insisting on clear answers on subjects where ambiguity is preferred. The second group of questions about a person's fieldwork must include, Why were they so patient? What made them put up with him? Why was it worth their while to answer his questions? What was he to them?

I intend to answer these queries with respect to my own fieldwork among the Suya Indians in northern Mato Grosso, Brazil. In my own case, however, I shall begin with the first vague formulation of the project in order to explain why it was the Suya that I studied. My experience in Brazil before I was able to reach the Suya was important. When, after considerable delay, I was finally able to enter the field, the delay had some far-reaching consequences. My life and work in the field itself was a process, not a static situation. It was a process that terminated only with my last departure. It was marked by certain consistencies in approach and method. It was at once idiosyncratic, because it reflected my own personality and choices as well as certain contingencies in the field situation, and replicable, because of my training in theory and method in anthropology as I thought of it between 1970 and 1973.

I wanted to go to central Brazil for two primary reasons, one personal, the other theoretical. Central Brazil seemed to me a fascinating place ever since my fifth-grade geography class. The bizarre animals, the teeming insect life, the small-scale societies were fascinating. I prefer small groups of people and become uncomfortable in large crowds. I was able to pass many months in a remote area more content than I would have been doing participant observation of attendance at football games, for example. There is an element of self-selection in all fieldwork.

On the theoretical side, I became interested in the comparative study of Gê societies in college. My first exposure to the intricacies of Gê social organization was from Professor David Maybury-Lewis in 1966. The Gê seemed to raise many of the most interesting questions in anthropology and to provide an ideal area for comparative studies. I continued to study lowland South American tribes, especially Gê-speaking ones, during my graduate study at Cornell University and later at the University of Chicago.

The outlook for comparative study of the Gê was rapidly improving as members of the Harvard-Central Brazil Project completed their researches. The works of Terence Turner (1966) and Joan Bamberger (1967) on the Northern Kayapo, Jean Lave (1967) on the Krikati, Júlio Melatti (1970) on the Kraho, Roberto Da Matta (1971) on the Apinaye, David Maybury-Lewis (1965, 1967) on the Shavante and Sherente, and Christopher Crocker (1967) on the Bororo were important contributions to the ethnography of the Gê and of South American Indians in general. Other studies, notably those by Amadeu Lanna (1967) and Lux Vidal (1973), also contributed to the growing corpus of material on Gê-speaking societies.

Some important features of culture and social organization seem to appear in all the Northern and Central Gê groups, for example those of subsistence and residence. The comparative analysis of institutions and beliefs in an area such as central Brazil can lend validity to a hypothesis raised in the context of any one of the groups because the hypothesis can be tested in other closely related societies. I believed this to be a great improvement over the traditional practice of constructing a hypothesis from a single case and then skipping directly to large-scale cross-cultural analysis characterized by users of the Human Relations Area Files. In the interests of participating in the comparative study of the Gê-speaking societies I resolved to study the Suya.

When I was drafting my proposal in 1969, there were both pros and cons to any proposed study of the Suya. The Eastern Suya had been visited for two months in 1960 by an ethnographer who published an article on them in the *National Geographic Magazine*: "Brazil's Big-Lipped Indians" (Schultz 1962). Harald Schultz saw the Suya only in a temporary camp, and apparently he could neither make himself understood by nor understand the Suya. Although in the *National Geographic* article Schultz makes much of the similarity between the Kraho and Suya languages, implying that he could converse with them, in a more scientific article (Schultz 1960-61) he describes his inability to communicate with anyone besides a resident Trumai who himself could not speak Suya. Schultz's reports indicated that the Suya were an amalgam of Upper Xingu and Gê cultures and that they were suffering the consequences of extreme depopulation. The only other published work on the Suya characterized them as "a society in ruins, in which the size itself limited the scope and interest of the analysis" (Lanna 1967, p. 68). I was assured by Terence Turner, who had met a Suya boy visiting the Northern Kayapo while he was doing his fieldwork there, that the Suya were probably not as disarranged as Lanna believed. It was not all clear, however, what the state of Suya society would be. This was a clear disadvantage to any precise formulation of field research among them.

An interesting new development had occurred, however. The warlike Beiços de Pau, or Tapayuna, who were then being "peacefully settled" on the Arinos River, were said to speak a language virtually identical to that of the Suya. Their population was described as large and dispersed in as many as twelve villages. This discovery of a new group of Suya made the project more interesting. I intended to begin my fieldwork by studying the Eastern Suya on the Xingu River where I would learn the language. Then I planned to visit the Arinos and study the other villages. This would have allowed me to study parts of the same "tribe" that had been separated for a fairly short period of time. It would have been an ideal study of micro change. With this in mind I wrote my proposal to study the myth, ritual, and social organization of the Suya in order to investigate comparatively the nature of the relationship of myth and ritual to aspects of social organization and the general coherence of symbol systems. In November 1970 my wife and I arrived in Rio de Janeiro, intending to enter the field in January 1971.

Brazilian Bureaucracy and Indian Politics

We expected our entry into the field to pose no special problems. Many anthropologists had worked in central Brazil, and all had told us stories about the bureaucracy and that it had taken them two or three months to obtain permission from the various agencies supervising the Indians and all research carried out by foreigners on Brazilian territory. In our case, though, it was not two or three months but eight months before we arrived in the Xingu reserve to begin our fieldwork.

Frustrations and agonies filled the months devoted to obtaining the necessary permissions. Our first application was denied without practical foundation, and in spite of our maneuvering we were unable to obtain a reconsideration of our proposal. Only in April 1971 did we discover that a new road, BR-080, was cutting through the Xingu reserve not far from the Suya village. Part of the network of roads then being constructed in the Amazon basin, BR-080 was shown on highway maps as passing to the north of the Xingu reserve. It became clear that the real reason for denying us permission to study the Suya was a desire to keep the new trajectory of the road a secret until it could be passed off as a *fait accompli.* Upon completion of the road, all land north of its crossing of the Xingu River was confiscated by the federal government, and all the Indians living there were told to move south into the new boundaries of the Xingu reserve. The Xingu reserve was accessible to anyone by road, and the conflicts and disease that have resulted from the contact of ranchers with the Indians who refused to move south form another tragic episode in a story that began with the discovery of the Americas by the Western Europeans.

Fortunately, the Suya village was unaffected by the new road, which passed forty miles to the north of the village, and equally unaffected by the disappropriation. With considerable support from a variety of sources we were finally able to obtain our permission to enter the Xingu reserve from an unsmiling secretary to the president of the National Indian Agency, hereafter referred to by its Brazilian acronym, FUNAI (Fundação Nacional do Indio).

I often wondered toward the end of our battle to obtain permission whether it was not absurd to spend so much time waiting. No one we spoke to could believe that it would take so long, and we were always urged to try another source of influence. Each wait was only for "a few weeks more" while we tried something else. The long months were a huge drain on our energies and resources, but we met many kind people, our command of Portuguese improved, and we did some touring. Above all we made some fine friends.

There may have been some unintentional benefits of our long prefield stay in Brazil. But it had an important effect on my fieldwork. After eight months of waiting, if the Suya turned out to be unsatisfactory or impossible to work with, there was no alternative other than to stay. I had already lost so much time that the thought of trying to change tribes was most unpleasant. I had cast my lot with the Suya. We boarded the plane in São Paulo bound for the Xingu at the end of June 1971.

A Musical Entrée

When we boarded the Brazilian Air Force DC-3 that was to take us to Posto Leonardo Villas Boas (figure 2.5), it was our good fortune to have as a fellow passenger Cláudio Villas Boas. Cláudio was then in charge of the northern part of the Xingu reserve, where the Suya live. With his brother Orlando, he was a candidate for the Nobel Peace Prize. We hardly exchanged a word on the noisy, vibrating flight. We sat sideways along the sides of the unpressurized plane with its cargo of rubber balls and cloth (to attract certain hostile Indians and to keep others friendly), rice, beans, and greens (to supply Air Force bases in central Brazil), and the odorous carcass of a recently slaughtered ox to supply the Air Force base in the Xingu, Jacaré.

Posto Leonardo is a fairly large cluster of houses which include a small hospital, a guest house, residences for the Villas Boas, and a large cooking and dining building. There are also a number of smaller houses for workers. Posto Leonardo always seemed to us like a city, for there was electricity for a few hours at night and the roofs were of tin or tile rather than thatch. On our first evening Cláudio Villas Boas remarked that he had heard that we sang and asked whether we would like to sing that evening. We fetched and tuned our banjo and guitar and began an evening of song that continued for some hours. We were instant hits, not only with Cláudio and Orlando Villas Boas and the Brazilian[1] workers at the post, but also with Indians visiting the post who had come from their own villages some distance away.

The next morning Cláudio descended the Xingu to Diauarum in a small boat, promising to speak to the Suya and tell them of our coming. He spoke to them. We did not learn the details of what he said until many months later. He told the Suya that we were musicians, that my father was an important man, and that we were coming to learn the Suya language and music. The Suya could ask us to sing any time and we would sing. If they did not like us, they were to tell him and he would send us away. Near the conclusion of my fieldwork I discovered that he had also told the Suya that we would eventually write a book. When we wrote it, he would read it. If the Suya had not told us the truth, if they had not taught me well, he said he would be angry with them. The Suya greatly respect Cláudio Villas Boas, and the result of his enthusiastic recommendation to the Suya was a favorable reception for us.

We spent more than two weeks in Posto Leonardo waiting for an opportunity to go to Diauarum. We passed the time visiting several tribes whose villages were not very distant from the post and solidifying our reputation as singers. We were asked to sing almost every night, and visiting Indians learned our songs and listened to our stories. One day we went to witness a ceremony among the Yawalipiti, a tribe close to Posto Leonardo and perhaps the wealthiest in terms of trade goods. We were invited back the next day to sing for them in exchange. As we sang, a Yawalipiti brought a small cassette tape recorder from his house and recorded our singing, just as we had previously recorded his. Later we learned that he took the machine to other villages and played our music for them as well. On every subsequent visit to Posto Leonardo we were always asked to sing to a large enthusiastic audience. It was most flattering.

At last we were given space on a boat to Diauarum. We arrived jointly with a group of doctors who had flown there to vaccinate the Indians in that part of the Xingu reserve against smallpox. All the Suya and the Juruna and many of the Kayabi were congregated in Diauarum, sleeping in their temporary houses which most of the year stood vacant. They crowded the river bank as we arrived. The Suya men were evident among the crowd, standing silently with their arms crossed, set apart from the others by their large red lip disks. They were looking us over. Walking into a new situation cold is never easy. The first time was certainly the worst. Neither the Suya nor I knew what to expect of each other.

The Raising of an Anthropologist

A week or more after we arrived at Diauarum we were finally paddled to the Suya village, located some two and one-half hours from Diauarum on the Suya-Missu River (figure 2.5). Cláudio Villas Boas had asked the Suya to build us a house, but they had not done so. When I was asked by Niokombedi (105),[2] one of the chiefs, where we would like to live, I replied that we would prefer to live in a Suya house because we did not like being lonely. He invited us to stay in his large house in which lived some thirty-five people in one open room. At first we slept in a corner of the house, which resembled a large tobacco barn. Later we were invited to sleep closer to the middle of the house. Our hammocks were slung, a rack was made for our luggage, and we settled down to live.

Three difficult problems had to be solved. The most immediate was what we would eat. The second was how we would manage our gifts of trade goods, and the third was how I would collect the data I wanted. The first was the most important to us in the short run; the second was the most important to the Suya; the third was the most important to me in the end.

The Suya experience with visitors prior to ourselves had been short visits by people who brought their own food and either ate it alone or shared it with some of them. Because of drastic weight limitations on the Air Force plane we had not brought anything except some milk, protein supplement, sugar, and a few dehydrated soups in case of illness. After a week there came a day when we were given only one nut to eat all day, though the season was one of plenty. I decided that something had to be done, and I spoke to Niokombedi, who was the male head of our house. He told me that Judy could take our gourd or plate to the single cooking hearth and be given food by one of the women doing the cooking. Then began the rather subtle training of the anthropologist as fisherman and hunter.

We were given less and less food from the common cooking pot until I went fishing. Then we were given more, but again the amount diminished as I occupied myself with concerns other than subsistence. After a while it was clear that in order to stay and survive, I would have to participate in the food-gathering to an extent that I had never imagined. I took part in nearly every collective hunt and fishing expedition during the first ten months. I also went fishing myself, usually as the companion of a ten-year-old boy who was a far better fisherman but who suffered from convulsions and needed a companion to keep him from falling out of the canoe into the water. We were both monolingual at first, and since fishing and hunting are a serious, not a chatty, business, I would come back to the village exhausted and cursing the day that I had decided to work with a group that did not have a money economy. I felt as though I was accomplishing nothing. My long days on the river and in the forests ultimately contributed a great deal to my understanding of the Suya, but this was not evident in the early months of our stay.

Upon my request through the chief, the men cut a garden plot for us and we planted it in September with manioc, corn, sweet potatoes, yams, peanuts, bananas, and sugarcane. After an initial distribution within the house most garden products are brought in small quantities from individual gardens and eaten by their owners. Without a garden of our own it was merely good fortune that we received any of this food. The Suya were not maliciously starving us, but we did not fit into their preconceived ideas of non-Suya foreigners, and we did not belong to their food-sharing patterns. In addition, we were a couple. Nuclear families are important economic units. As a single man I might have been adopted into a family and fed, but as a couple we were expected to be more independent. In the first four months I lost thirty pounds.

Another difficulty whose extent we understood only later was the significance of our possessions and trade goods. I had brought a quantity of trade goods to the Suya and had given perhaps half of them to the *capitão,* or chief who acted as an intermediary between Brazilians and the Suya, for distribution to the village on the day we arrived. This was the usual procedure in the Xingu reserve, and one established by the Villas Boas brothers. The rest of the goods I kept for later trade. The Suya wanted the goods, but they did not know how to get them. I did not know what the respective worth of the various items they wanted to trade was to them. Furthermore, a trade is not something haggled. One is ashamed to ask for more than is offered even though one may be disappointed. It seemed important to distribute goods, but it was also important to have more on hand to maintain interest in our presence. The problem of distribution was settled on the first trip by trading things for a collection of artifacts. I never traded anything directly for either food or information, but I gradually became more generous and allowed those with whom I worked regularly to have anything they asked for.

The Suya were especially sensitive to our supply of trade goods because only witches (*wayanga*) hoard things for themselves. It is a tribute to the cultural relativity of the Suya and to their patience that they never accused us of being witches. After the first large distribution of presents that followed our return from every fieldbreak, exchange was the norm. The Suya did not beg or consistently ask for things. They said that if they were always asking for too many things or taking things, I would not come back with more presents. They were very astute, and I did my best to encourage that belief every time I returned to the village.

In addition to bringing gifts, we brought and administered medicines. Cláudio Villas Boas supplied us with some other medicines that we had not brought, and we treated any health problem that the Suya brought to us. This saved the family of the sick person a trip to Diauarum, and often we were able to treat infections or attacks of malaria before they became serious. If the patient did not improve, we learned to rely on the Suya judgment of when he should be taken to Diauarum for more advanced treatment than we were equipped to give. The giving of herb medicines is not prestigious among the Suya, and they did not consider exchanging anything for our treatment. They appreciated our efforts nevertheless. As with hunting and fishing, medicating was a difficult task which made the Suya more receptive to our presence and more interested in my work.

The third problem, that of data collection, was also solved with time. There were only three Suya men who spoke Portuguese fairly well. Several other men spoke a little, and the rest, including all the women, hardly any. The first months were an agony of frustration, for I was not able to speak Suya, nor was I able to accompany the Portuguese speakers during the day. There was no obvious way of arranging regular hours for language work or using interpreters. Hunting, fishing, and family support are of paramount importance. Only a few adult men had to support a large number of women and children (see table I.1). Those few individuals with whom I could communicate were busy and could not spend all their days with me. In a money economy one can give money for tedious work such as language instruction, and the money can be used to buy food. Among the Suya nothing could buy food, and as a result my language work during the first four months was sporadic. To complicate my first visit, many families took extended dry-season trips to hunt and fish some distance from the village.

I was disappointed in another way during the first field period, from July through November of 1971. Unlike the other Gẽ, the Suya appeared to be ritually sterile. No major ceremonies of any kind were performed, with the exception of a very short garden-burning ceremony and sporadic singing of songs from other tribes. Nor could I discover any moieties. The very subject I had wanted to study was apparently not operating.

In November we left the Suya in order to visit our families over Christmas. We were thin, weak, and discouraged. I had collected a lot of straightforward observations: garden size, village plan, food distribution, census, some linguistic transcriptions, and answers to a wide range of questions that I had asked mostly in Portuguese. The answers were

Table I.1 Sex and age distribution of the Suya

Age	Male	Female	Total	Percentage of population
			Eastern Suya	
0-4	8	8	16	17.75
5-9	12	11	23	25.50
10-19	10	8	18	20.00
20-29	7	9	16	17.75
30-39	2	7	9	10.00
40-49	2	1	3	3.30
50+	–	5	5	5.70
Total	41	49	90	100.00
			Western Suya	
0-4	4	3	7	16.50
5-9	4	9	13	30.00
10-19	5	4	9	21.00
20-29	2	7	9	21.00
30-39	1	1	2	4.60
40-49	1	–	1	2.30
50+	2	–	2	4.60
Total	19	24	43	100.00

generally inconsistent and unintelligible. I read *Notes and Queries,* an outline of topics that travelers and anthropologists should investigate in the field, and decided that I had asked all the right questions but that the Suya did not know anything. Amadeu Lanna was apparently right about the disorganization of Suya Society. Yet with the time and commitment already made, I had no choice but to return to the Suya in January. I did. It made all the difference. Although the first four months were important and are probably part of the process of fieldwork anywhere, my work really began in January 1972. After that there were peaks of activity and lows of frustration, but the material was always more interesting. It continued to improve through my last visit, when I realized that far from being shallow, Suya ideas are so complex that they often eluded my grasp. The further I investigated any matter, the greater its complexity and richness became. The early Suya answers to my queries were like those to a child; simple. The more I learned, the more they taught me.

Our very return to the village in January was a sign of commitment to the Suya. Few visitors enter the Xingu region during the rainy, mosquito-ridden, malarial months from November through March. We returned with presents, including specially requested presents and things that I had not known the Suya would want on our first visit. We arrived in January to find our garden full of corn ready to harvest. From then on we were able to share our garden products with other families and set up food exchange networks. We always received more than we gave, but at least there was an exchange. Exchanging food also strengthened my relationships with my best informants.

The Suya began their name-giving ceremony, the mouse ceremony, just a few days after our return. For the first time I began to get consistent data on naming practices and ceremonial groups. I discovered that our first visit had coincided with a period of comparative ritual inactivity. I continued to fish and hunt, and I continued to find it onerous. But since I was rapidly becoming conversant in Suya, it was easier to find someone to talk to when I wanted to work. I was no longer limited to the few men who could speak Portuguese.

We arrived in mid January 1972 and left the field again at the end of April. We spent some time in São Paulo working and shopping; then we returned to the Xingu in mid June and remained in the village until early September when for various reasons—the most immediate being the complete lack of chloroquine for the treatment of malaria—we went to Posto Leonardo. I spent the next two weeks there working on my data and writing field reportss. I could eat rice and beans kindly supplied by the administrators there and devote my entire days to reading my notes, organizing them, and preparing new areas for investigation. Meanwhile Judy flew to São Paulo, completed a whirlwind shopping spree, and flew back to the reserve in two weeks. We returned to the Suya in early October and remained until the beginning of February when our health was weakened by repeated attacks of malaria. In those final months I hunted and fished less and did more anthropological work. I eventually became weary of my role as manipulator-of-conversations, eavesdropper, gadfly and dependent, though. We left the field in the beginning of February 1973. From March through June I gave a course with Professor Roberto Da Matta at the Museu Nacional in Rio de Janeiro. Judy returned to the Suya from April to May and checked on a number of questions that were central to my thesis.

In retrospect I realize that the Suya raised me. When we first arrived they treated me like a child—which I was. I could not talk. I could not see as they saw. It took me months, for example, to see the shadow or the ripples of a fast-moving fish in the water and to shoot well enough to hit it with an arrow. I could not distinguish the sounds that the Suya heard; I did not understand or know. At first they did not let me out of their sight. I never went out in a canoe alone. I never wandered unaccompanied in the forest, although I walked around in the gardens. I learned to step exactly where they stepped to avoid putting my feet on stingrays, spines, and into ants' nests. I learned slowly where it was good to fish and how to fish. It was not worth the time of an adult to teach me, so they sent me out with boys who were better than I was.

The Suya taught me to speak with the same patience with which they taught their children. Bemused by my ability to write things down and still fail to remember them, they kept quizzing me. They also used the technique of saying an obscene phrase very rapidly for me to repeat and then bursting out laughing when I said it. They would tell me things in the dark as fathers tell their children. They took an interest in making sure that I understood. I was almost always referred to the person who knew the most about any given subject, be it a myth, song, house name, genealogy, or history. I was instructed not to work with women or young men because they knew nothing. Whether or not all their care actually resulted in my understanding them should not reflect on the honest attempts of every Suya to make me understand.

They were treating me like a twelve-year-old boy by the time we left. I could paddle, fish, and hunt about as well as a twelve-year-old. I could talk adequately but without the flair and control of image and metaphor employed by adult men. Above all, young men are supposed to listen and learn. In some ways I was an ideal twelve-year-old.

The women supervised the raising of my wife. She learned to cook our food, weave, speak Suya, and gossip for hours. She progressed from a scraper of manioc tubers to the owner-controller of entire batches of manioc flour and manioc drink. The women taught her their language so that they could ask her all kinds of questions, and she reciprocated with her own. She often gave me important data, and sometimes she alone witnessed an event. Only women may be present at a childbirth, for example. In some ways Judy could enjoy her life with the Suya more than I was able to, for she was not obliged to be an anthropologist. She could interact with the Suya as a sympathetic human being, while I always had to remain a social scientist as well.

Why did the Suya put up with us? I have suggested that the answer is not simple. At the start it was no doubt because of the introduction of Cláudio Villas Boas. But in January 1972 he left the Xingu and never returned to Diauarum during our stay. Our music may have been part of the reason, and our presents were also important. At times the shipment of supplies to the reserve by FUNAI was halted, and we were the only sources of bullets, long pieces of fishline, small fish hooks, and other such items. The Suya appreciated our medical aid. The Suya women liked my wife and enjoyed her presence. There is a lot to laugh about in a pair of blundering adults who act like children. The Suya like to laugh. They also respected my interest in those parts of their own society that they found interesting—ritual, song, stories, kinship, and ideology. I was an excuse for the performance of rituals: to teach me so that I would know and record them.

When we left the village in February 1973, the Suya said with more drama than truth first that they would all die because we were not there to treat them, second that they would have no trade goods because we would not be there to supply them, and third that the men would not spend as much time in the men's house because I would not be there with them. They invited us to return and said that if I had any friends who wanted to learn about their language and their music, they would be happy to teach them as they had taught me.

In fact we did return, in December 1975, to find them in excellent health and spirits. They welcomed us enthusiastically and immediately incorporated us into their activities as if we had never been away. While they were as strong as ever, I was out of shape after two years in front of electric typewriters and blackboards. I was not able to paddle as long, run as fast after monkeys disappearing through the trees, and sing as hard on top of little to eat as I had been before. It took the Suya and myself some time to realize this, and the field period ended abruptly after about two months, when I left with pneumonia. I was able to improve my command of the language significantly, however, and to resolve some of the questions that had arisen when I wrote my dissertation.

Living in Brazil and working at the Museu Nacional between 1975 and 1980 has made the contacts we have with the Suya more varied. I returned for a brief visit in July of 1976 and was on my way in July 1977 when a malaria attack made the trip inadvisable. Instead, a Suya who was in São Paulo for medical treatment visited us in Rio. I had the satisfaction of being something of a native. When the man who visited repeatedly lost his sense of direction in the streets I said to him, "Remember how I was when I first arrived in your village? I didn't know anything. If you lived here for a long time you would learn." He agreed that it takes time to learn. I can imagine some of what he said about us when he returned to the village. He was obviously scandalized that we slept in a different room from our infant daughter. I am planning another trip to the Suya to talk with them in more depth about their music—a topic which I was able to develop considerably in 1975-76 (Seeger 1977a, 1979).

One of the difficulties of an anthropologist is deciding when to stop working with a group. When I left the field in 1973 I arbitrarily gave myself five years to finish my major work on the Suya in order to turn to other topics and other societies. This book is an important step in that process.

Field Methods

My daily routine was designed to maximize overhearing the Suya converse among themselves, opportunities to ask questions, and observation. An average day during a nonceremonial period would begin between 4:30 and 5:00 A.M. when everyone would take a bath in the river, which was much warmer than the predawn air. Then, if I did not go hunting or fishing, my wife and I would both go to every house with our box of medicines to see whether anyone wanted treatment. It was easier to go to the other houses because some people did not feel at ease in our house and because when Suya have malaria they do not leave their hammocks. When we went around in the morning, we were not called on for the rest of the day unless there was an emergency. Visiting every house enabled me to see who was around and what people were doing. We would talk a little in each house. If people were well, our medical rounds would take only a few minutes. If there were many colds, lung infections, and malaria, they would take over an hour. Then I could work, if nothing came up, writing in my journal or asking questions of people who had stayed in the village. Those who had gone out hunting or fishing would come back around noon if they had been successful. Then we would have the first food of the day. There were no fixed meal times in the village; we ate whenever food came into our house. One of my wife's important contributions was that she could manage to be in the house and store some food for me if I was somewhere else when food was being distributed. The heat of the day was usually spent sleeping or writing. Early afternoon was a good time to find people for asking questions, and then I would write again in my journal. In the late afternoon we would make another round of the houses, treating people who were sick if necessary and often obtaining a little to eat on the way. In the rich light of the setting sun families would gather in front of their houses, talking and playing with their children. We usually joined them.

At dusk the men would congregate in the center of the village plaza and talk, or sing, or ask us to sing. The women would gather in front of their houses to talk. When we sang, they would come into the center as well. Since I brought no light source other than the candles we used for night medication and emergencies, I did not work at night. Instead I would join the men in the center and listen with increasing comprehension to their talks. Sometimes I learned things. Often I learned nothing. The men volunteered information when there was enough moonlight for me to write, and occasionally I would check on a point that I wanted to make sure there was a consensus on. I was rarely the center of attention at these gatherings, which were usually devoted to long hunting stories, political talk, and oratory. When the older men would go to bed, anytime between 8:30 and 10:00, I would retire also. We left the plaza to the young men who pursued their amorous adventures in the night hours and slept more during the day than either the adults or the anthropologist. Our house was often quite active at night, but I slept soundly and missed much of the surreptitious coming and going. The Suya would often wake us when some public event was occurring, such as a child birth, an eclipse, or a meteor shower, which was another advantage of living in a house with them.

The systematic performance of fieldwork was difficult under the circumstances. My work was always somewhat sporadic, which had a detrimental effect on my data and prolonged my stay. I always carried a small notebook with me and wrote down everything of interest. On long days of fishing I would think about what I had learned and write down questions to be asked. I would arrange questions into lists on a given topic. Equipped with these general lists I would look for any person who could answer any one of the various groups of questions. In the first months I observed a lot and learned the language. I put aside questions that I could not ask or understand one month, and I would be able to work on them the following month.

The search for people to answer my questions was always difficult. I did not like to impose, and when they felt imposed on, the Suya were masters of the cursory answer. When they were hungry, they were not interested in giving long answers to questions. When they were full, they were likely to be sleeping. There were certain times when neither of these was the case, and I used those times to the best of my ability. Some days no one that I wanted to talk to would be in the village, and the next day I would be out fishing myself. Sometimes, on the other hand, everyone would be in the village, and I would have pages and pages of material.

I did not use structured interviews. The lists of questions that I carried were only a framework. It is extremely difficult to get a response to an abstract analytic question. I would make brief notes during the interview and then write them up as fully as I could. I used a tape recorder only for oral narrative, music, and some descriptions of ceremonies that I was unable to witness.

I did not use only a few informants. I used almost everyone in the village for various things. There were some individuals, however, who were specialists in certain areas and whose ideas always supplied the greatest detail. Each of these major informants had a specialty, something that he was particularly good at or knew particularly well. The Suya were extremely consistent in the information they gave me. While some would know more about a given subject, they rarely conflicted. All important points I checked with several informants, especially in the beginning. This became more difficult later because everyone would agree that the person who told me the first time knew the material best. People would often say that they knew something badly and refer me to another person.

I found that the Suya think very contextually. My general questions during the first four months elicited confusing and shallow answers. However, at the time of the name-giving ceremony the Suya were all thinking about naming and the important relationships involved and about the ceremonial groups that appear in the ceremony. When a person died, they were able to give me rich data on death and the afterlife. When witchcraft accusations occupied everybody's thoughts, they were all interested in talking about witches. I found it most productive to investigate in depth anything that was happening in the vilage at the time, using various informants and getting information from my wife about what the women were saying.

Another tactic I learned to capitalize on was the haphazardness of the process in which I would discover new and previously unsuspected things. I tried to ask all the questions I could think of. But there were some things that I learned only by chance. I did my best to maximize chance, especially after I could understand what people were saying to one another. I would overhear something, write it down in my pocket notebook, and find the person later to ask him more about it. I learned many interesting things in this way. One man commented to another that he would have good luck hunting because he had dreamed a good dream (which introduced me to dream symbols). On a different occasion one man asked another, "Did you turn into a bird and fly up to the sky with your grandmother?" (which introduced me to fever visions). Living in a large house with thirty-five people, as we did, helped immensely in this respect. I also spent many hours listening to conversations in the men's house and in the men's councils at night.

The Suya occasionally volunteered information that they thought I should know. They would sometimes say, "Did you know such-and-such?" They often asked such questions in the dark, and I would struggle to remember central points to write down or follow up the next day. One important topic was raised in this manner by a woman who sat down next to my wife's hammock one evening and said "Do you know . . ." and gave us a list of indirect affinal reference terms that I did not suspect existed. Listening to conversations of Suya among themselves was important because when the Suya spoke directly to me, they often simplified things as they did when talking to a child, and they used vocabulary they thought I knew.

The accidental discovery of areas previously unsuspected continued through the last weeks of my stay. I terminated my fieldwork not because I believed I knew everything but because I thought I knew enough about those areas that interested me. I did some systematic investigation. I used photographs of everyone in the village to discover how people addressed and referred to each other. I checked most points with several informants. If something more interesting or noteworthy than what I was working on came up, I always dropped everything else to pursue it. But in the end it was the systematic questioning coupled with careful listening that provided the data for this work. My personal experience with the Suya was important. But as with all good anthropology, my experience was an aid rather than an impediment to collecting richer data.

Data Obtained and Data Unobtainable

I was able to obtain some kinds of data and other kinds were impossible to investigate during my stay with the Suya.

For historical reasons the Suya were not living as they thought they should. Residence, male initiation, and ceremonial life were all deeply affected by depopulation. Suya ideology did not entirely agree with the practice that they had followed since their severe loss of population. The ceremonial life was also affected by the absence of a number of men who were away on a pacification expedition, at the request of Cláudio Villas Boas, during much of my stay. The Suya keenly felt the lack of these men during ceremonial periods. It was impossible for me to witness certain rituals. Some of them had not been done in decades. I have made every attempt to note the changes that have occurred in Suya society, but this work is not a historical reconstruction.

The material I was unable to obtain on social organization and defunct ceremonies was just what I had hoped to get from the Suya groups reported on the Arinos River in 1970. It was only after ten months with the Suya in the Xingu and nearly two years in Brazil that I was certain that there were no more Suya groups to be studied. I did my best to offset the shortcomings of my data with extensive interviews with survivors from the Arinos who had been moved to the Suya village, but this work suffers from my inability to visit a second group of Suya.

Although I have good material on witchcraft accusations during my stay, complete historical data were nearly impossible to obtain. In general the Suya responded to all questions, but they were reluctant to repeat any of the "bad speech" of witches in the past. I was unable to collect rich social dramas because most social dramas revolve around witchcraft accusations. Only witches speak bad speech, and even to repeat it is bad. The Suya also declined to sing two songs because they considered the very act of playing them back on a tape recorder a threat to the village: they would be attacked by enemy Indians as a result. Chants that harmed only individuals I was allowed to record in the deep brush, far from the village, as long as I did not play them while I was in the Xingu.

The Suya taught us as much as they could. They were fine companions, and we had many delightful times and some hard times together. They were patient, generous people who trained me to be an anthropologist and something of a Suya. They took pride in our progress and were concerned when we were ill. The teaching was often in two directions: I sometimes answered as many questions as I asked. And I discovered from embarrassing experience how easy it is to say "We do it that way because that is the way we always do it" when a difficult explanation defeated my linguistic abilities. I learned to empathize with my informants. We learned each other's songs, and we sang them. From the notes I took, the field reports I sent to my advisor, and from the exhilaration of singing for fifteen hours without stopping this book developed. It is an attempt to translate what I believe to be the fundamental dimensions of Suya society and cosmology into terms that can be understood by non-Suya, without doing unforgivable injustice to the things the Suya tried to teach me with such care.

1

Suya Cosmology

THE NATURE OF THE INTEGRATION of different parts of a society has been a recurring question in the social sciences. This integration may take the form of the relation between base and superstructure as in Karl Marx, or between religion and social organization as in Max Weber, or between social morphology and perceptual category as in Emile Durkheim and Marcel Mauss, to mention only a few. At issue is the relationship between the interaction of human beings and their conceptualization of themselves and their universe. This investigation of the social organization and cosmology of the Suya Indians of central Brazil was stimulated by these questions and is meant as a contribution to their discussion. No attempt, however, is made to lay them to rest.

The object of this book is to reveal the principles that underlie most of the important domains of a lowland South American Indian society, the Suya, and to show the way in which these principles are used and manipulated in different social contexts. The intention is not to display a crystalline structure—although conceptual structures do appear—but to show the way in which members of a given society regularly apply a limited number of principles to the many and varied aspects of their lives.

One dynamic principle of Suya classification underlies their classifications of space, time, animals, food, their bodies, and themselves. The principle is expressed in their villages, their body ornaments, their myths, their curing chants, their perception of political process and ceremonial effectiveness. Concerns that seem very different are organized by the Suya in basically the same way. The use of the principle is both dynamic and creative; they apply it to new experiences such as the coming of the whites and the first visit to the city as well as to reinterpret former situations.

Marshall Sahlins has argued, without exaggeration, that much of anthropology can be considered a sustained effort to synthesize an original segmentation of its object, an analytic disjunction of the domains of society made without reflection, on the basis of Western society (Sahlins 1976a, p. 205). Too often, societies have been considered conglomerates of economic systems, political systems, and religious systems, which are then analyzed independently. Or one domain is reduced to a direct expression of another. This segmentation of human societies on the basis of a folk classification of our own has obscured the nature of the integration (or lack of it) of the society as a whole. By limiting our analyses to certain domains, we prevent ourselves from seeing their unity.

The escape from the blinders imposed by our own society might be called "cherchez la native category." Instead of analyzing arbitrarily defined domains, the analyst should follow native categories and native ways of thinking about their society, wherever they lead. Certainly not a new idea (Durkheim and Mauss 1903), this approach to other societies has been advocated in a number of important and recent publications (among others Schneider 1972; Geertz 1973; Sahlins 1976a). Such a tactic has been used here, with an important modification. It is difficult to present a society in terms of its own categories without making excessive demands on the reader, who must always relate what he is reading to his own experience. Nor does every reader necessarily want to make the effort of entering such an analysis. Therefore I have organized the chapters around themes that have traditionally been separated (time and space, kinship, politics, the life cycle). But the argument throughout is that the domains are organized on a similar logic. I have chosen this course because anthropology must be as much a comparative endeavor as an interpretive one, and the presentation of the results of one's studies to members of one's own society must be made as accessible as possible without doing undue damage to the materials and the theory.

Throughout the book I have attempted to show how the Suya define and use their own categories and concepts in specific contexts. Similar concepts appear in different domains, clarifying the analysis and the relationship among them. The discussions of body ornaments and animal classification help clarify the nature of leadership and the power of chiefs, but only because native concepts are consistently used to analyze other concepts and practices.

Neither the attempt to demonstrate the operation of common principles in different domains nor the use of native categories in analysis is new in social anthropology. They have a venerable history in the discipline (Fustel de Coulanges 1864) and may be found in the classic works (Radcliffe-Brown 1922; Malinowski 1922), in the work of E. E. Evans-

Pritchard (1940), as well as in more recent studies (L. Dumont 1966; Levi-Strauss 1966c). What distinguishes this treatment is that within a single work several quite different domains are analyzed and their relationships demonstrated. This is not a book *about* politics, or kinship, or cosmology, although all these appear in it. The question is rather how these aspects of Suya society are related. It is a book about the underlying principles and their relationships, about the specificity of each domain. It is an analysis of the social and cosmological organization of a complex, though technologically simple, society.

The interrelationship of the domains of lowland South American societies has been obscured by the tendency of recent authors to concentrate on a single one of them. Claude Lévi-Strauss's *Mythologiques* (1964, 1966, 1968, 1971), endowed with incredible comparative breadth, are above all concerned with myth and cosmology. Joanna Kaplan's recent study of the Piaroa (1975) concentrates on kinship, marriage, and political organization alone, as does Peter Rivière's work on the Trio (1960). Jean-Paul Dumont's book (1976) on the Panare is specifically a "cultural" study that focuses on the relationship of native categories in different symbolic domains but does not discuss their operation in the context of social and political action. Gerardo Reichel-Dolmatoff's description of a Tukanoan cosmology (1971) also largely divorces the cosmology from the society that believes in it. Although each of these authors contributes to a particular debate, they leave many questions unanswered. A reader interested in something other than the central topic feels like a person confronted with a jigsaw puzzle with some of the crucial pieces missing.[1]

Analyses of belief systems independent of their contexts often appear exotic, static, and scarcely credible. Clifford Geertz has succinctly expressed the reservations of many readers: "Nothing has done more, I think, to discredit cultural analyses than the construction of impeccable depictions of formal order in whose actual existence nobody can quite believe" (1973; p. 18). By revealing the workings of given principles in a variety of contexts I have tried to make the formal order that I present both more believable and more dynamic. I have also tried to show that the native concepts are not simply idle cerebrations but important facts to be considered by any scholar studying any domain such as politics, or kinship, or metaphor. No social scientist can afford to ignore the perceptions, concepts, and their use by the peoples studied, regardless of the kind of society involved.

Certainly one of anthropology's most important contributions to the understanding of human societies has been to show that other societies, taken on their own terms instead of judged by our own, have organized social relations (albeit differently organized) and a logic of their own (albeit a different one) and that they are always changing (sometimes in ways that we do not perceive as change). If our analyses of lowland South American societies, or of any other, make the societies seem exotic and incredible, then we have failed in one of our important tasks. We may use the greatest methodological rigor, but it is a *rigor mortis* if the result is unbelievable, because few people can check what we have affirmed. The Suya, with whom I lived and worked, are living, breathing, eating, laughing, conniving, manipulating, singing people, like all people. But the way they live, eat, laugh, manipulate, and sing is what counts, and these ways should not seem either exotic or incredible to the members of other societies. The Suya, after all, do not think of themselves as exotic, and certainly not as unbelievable.

Cosmology can be defined as the way in which the members of a society construct their universe and think of themselves and other beings within it. Thus it is an attempt to create order in the world. This finding of order is not isolated from the rest of their lives in some philosophical never-never land. Order is created in the building of a village, in the ornamentation of the body, in the use of a given kinship terminology, and in the systematic performance of certain kinds of behavior—such as joking, avoidance, sexual relations, or food exchange. It is also expressed in the classification of animals and human beings, in dietary restrictions and culinary customs. A cosmology is expressed in more than the abstract thoughts of idle minds; material things and human relations are also expressions of principles that may be expressed elsewhere as abstract thoughts (Lévi-Strauss 1966c, chap. 1).

Few cosmologies are completely integrated to form a single, consistent system. Perhaps the Catholic cosmology of the Middle Ages or that of the Dogon in Africa came closest (Griaule 1965; V. Turner 1973). In most societies historical events and new ideas continually alter the cosmology. The Suya, for example, adopted some concepts from their captives and others more recently from Brazilians. They also have their own innovators. I find too radical Victor Turner's distinction between cultures possessing elaborate and coherent cosmologies (such as the Dogon, Fon, Yoruba, and other West African cultures) and those (such as those found in central Africa) in which "order and cosmos come from purpose, not from an elaborate and articulated cosmology" (V. Turner 1973, p. 1105). Cosmologies can exist that are not as complete or coherent as those of the Dogon and Fon yet still transcend mere clusters of focal ritual symbols. Far more numerous than total, unitary, cosmologies are probably those like the Suya's, which are partially integrated, consistent within certain areas. The Suya possess more than a conglomeration of ritual symbols. Their symbols are part of a larger cosmology which appears as an organizing force in all domains of the society. Suya cosmology is not as rich as the Dogon, but it exists and has considerable force and coherence.

Nature and Society

Many aspects of Suya cosmology rest upon the fundamental distinction that the Suya make between animal (*mbru*) and human (*mẽ*). Expressed in other words, for which there are no immediate Suya glosses, these can be taken as nature and culture. I use the word "society" instead of the more frequently used "culture" to contrast with "nature" because the Suya word *mẽ* refers to living Suya, especially to the epitome of society, the adult initiated men. Also, the Suya see nature as threatening to individual human beings or to the entire social order, but not to culture in the usual anthropological sense. One must remember that nature is also culture: it is a cultural construction of the Suya. Nature as they define it is not nature as we define it. By contrasting the English words "nature" and "society," I hope to avoid confusion about what culture really is. The two domains are culturally defined and must be analyzed as they are defined by the Suya.

Nature and society are opposed and contrasted throughout Suya cosmology—for example, in the delineation of time and space, the characterization of persons, the conception of the life cycle, and the definition of illness. The distinction between nature and society always has several levels of contrast. The two domains cannot be represented as a binary column of unalterably opposed elements because there are gradations of socialness in society and gradations of naturalness in nature.

The most extreme distinction between nature and society is between the group of animals classed as strong smelling and the group of initiated men living in the men's house located in the village plaza (who have no strong odor). The former is the most natural of the natural and the latter is the most social of the social. Other contrasts are made as well: (1) Adult initiated men are opposed to women, children, enemy Indians, and animals. (2) Adult initiated men, women, and children are opposed to enemy Indians and animals. (3) Adult initiated men, women, children, and enemy Indians are opposed to animals. In each case the first element is considered social in contrast with the second element. In different contexts the contrast between nature and society rests on different groupings. Women are not natural and animal-like per se, but in a given situation women are contrasted with men, and traits that are characteristic of the natural domain are emphasized. Possession of these natural characteristics makes women less fully social than adult initiated men, but they are considered equally human and social in their joint opposition to enemy Indians or animals.

The Suya separate the natural world from the social world in a number of ways. One of the most important is the spatial layout of the village. Suya categories of space cannot be distinguished from the village structure that informs them. Even their name for themselves is related to the village: "people of the large circular villages." There are six concentric spatial domains, with the center (the most social) being the plaza and the most peripheral (the most natural) being the distant forest. Between these two lie four intermediate zones whose features are contrasted differently in different contexts, as with living beings. Time concepts, like space, also distinguish between the natural and the social.

Different features are used to identify and classify animals and human beings. Animals are classified by odor into three categories, which I have translated as "strong smelling," "pungent," and "bland" or "tasty." The strong-smelling group includes carnivorous animals and birds as well as a few animals with special physical attributes. The pungent category consists of large mammals, the macaw, and a few amphibians. The bland group consists of certain small mammals, a number of birds, and nearly all species of fish (in contrast with our own idea of fish as strong smelling). These three groups are important in food prohibitions and temporary diet restrictions. Humans are discussed in terms of faculties such as hearing, speaking, and vision and in terms of their membership in social groups. Included in these social groups are the age grades, which are also distinguished by odor.

Nature and society are contrasting principles expressed through specific attributes such as spatial relationship to the plaza or classification by odor. In space, animal classification, and other domains there is a clear gradation between the extremes of the social and the natural. In different contexts the intermediary things, such as the female sex, may be considered natural (when certain natural attributes are emphasized) or social (when other traits are emphasized). Nature and society are not fixed realms containing categories such as women, parrots, anthropologists, and jaguars. To see them in this way is essentially static. Instead, the Suya use the principles in a more dynamic and creative way. To grasp the dynamic, context-specific features of the contrast between nature and society is to see how the application of these principles by the Suya leaves room for the creation of new metaphors, the interpretation of new events, and the reinterpretation of past ones.

Nature and society are always acting on each other. Natural beings and substances can transform social human beings into animals or into humans with animal-like characteristics. Men, on the other hand, kill animals and cook their flesh for food. When the distinction between the two domains is in danger of becoming blurred, certain restrictions are imposed and certain activities are limited. For example, dietary restrictions are common in periods of ritual or social transition. Unusual events also threaten the distinction between the domains. When there is a solar eclipse, the Suya say that snakes slither across the plaza, jaguars prowl behind the houses, and caymans leave the rivers and crawl on land. To counteract this invasion of the social domain, the adult men must gather in the plaza and sing a song of war until the eclipse passes.

Certain customs must be observed in order to maintain the integrity of the village. Others are observed in order to maintain the integrity of the individual. These include hunting restrictions, diet restrictions, and restrictions on sexual activity, as well as the performance of certain collective activities. The social world must retain its social attributes to prevent its dissolution by the power of the natural entities. The tension between nature and society is expressed by the constant transformations that they perform on each other.

Transformations

Transformation is an important concept in Suya life. The transformation may be either from natural to social or in the reverse direction. An example of the former is the processing of food. The Suya must eat animals and products of forest and garden to live, but they do not eat them raw or indiscriminately. The natural product must be transformed before it can be eaten, with the exception of certain gathered fruts, insects, and honey. No less than food, human beings are processed by society. A child is not considered a fully social being at birth. The Suya describe the life cycle as a process of transformation that begins at birth, when the newborn child is picked up by some relative, through naming, walking, initiation, parenthood, and old age. The close initial ties to the natal family and the naturalness of the child are attenuated by giving names, by ties of ritual relationships, and eventually by marriage. The human body is also transformed. The ear, the organ that is the locus of morality, is socialized by the insertion of a large disk in both men and women. Men also wear large lip disks that alter the shape of their lower lips. Eyebrows and eyelashes are plucked. The body itself is socialized, and bodies that have not been so treated are considered animal-like. Bearded, bushy-browed Brazilians are always compared with monkeys, as I was when I went for more than two days without shaving.

Transformations may go in the reverse direction. A man may become a deer, an armadillo, or a witch (*wayanga*) by failing to maintain a sufficient distance from natural objects. Severe illness, death, weakness, and sexuality are also transformations of the social human beings into more animal-like beings.

The transformations may be inward and invisible, as in the case of a good man who becomes a witch, or they may be external and visible, as when a normal man becomes an animal (in myths) or a child becomes an adult, or when a lip or earlobe is pierced. These transformations give the Suya cosmology its dynamism and animate most of the domains of Suya society. There is a tension between animality and sociality in the domains of space, time, classification of persons, classification of animals, humor, health and sickness, politics, the life cycle, and in myths, rituals, and song. Any analysis must reveal the importance of this tension rather than obscuring it in formal diagrams.

The Reintroduction of Nature

Carefully isolated from the social world in some domains of Suya behavior, certain attributes of the animal world are incorporated into other domains. Suya songs are learned from animals. Music, a central feature of the ritual life of the Suya, is newly obtained from nature every time a ceremony is performed. Similarly, curing chants attempt to instill a particular animal attribute into a person in order to stimulate rapid growth, give strength, or cure certain illnesses. The close relationship of human beings and the natural world, described in the myths, continues in these symbolic forms. Under certain circumstances nature is reincorporated into the very core of society. Together nature and society and their transformations form a total cosmos.

Metaphor and Symbol

Metaphors and symbols are vital features of Suya life, and they are used not only to interpret the universe as the Suya perceive it but also to act on the universe and on Suya lives within it. In metaphor and symbol the domains of nature and society—clearly separated in many forms of classification—are brought together for specific ends.

A metaphor is more than a simple figure of speech in which one thing is linked to another. It is a creative and dynamic medium in which interpretation plays an important part (Wagner 1972; K. Basso 1976). Its importance lies in the specific nature of the meaning or meanings to be derived from the juxtaposition of the two different domains. In an interesting study of "wise word" metaphors among the Western Apache, Keith Basso has written: "the meaningful interpretation of metaphor rests upon an ability to discern some element of plausibility or truth in a statement that asserts implausibility or falsehood" (1976, p. 98). When the Apache say that "girls are butterflies," they mean a particular association. Basso's suggestion to one of his consultants that they were associated because both were beautiful and (from girls' clothing) brightly colored was the cause of much amusement. The consultant replied, "Maybe they are the same that way, but to us it doesn't mean anything" (K. Basso 1976, p. 105).

To *us* it doesn't *mean* anything. The point is important. Not all possible parallels between domains are important to the members of a society in a given context. In the context of "wise words" the bright colors of girls and butterflies are irrelevant, meaningless. What is important is that girls, like butterflies, sometimes act mindlessly, "chasing around after each other having a good time when they should be working" (K. Basso 1976, p. 105). What is at issue is not the total range of possible relationships but the ones that a certain society chooses and considers meaningful.

The Suya use metaphors in curing chants and in dream interpretation, in humor and in ceremony. For a child with convulsions they sing of the white cayman, called "controller of still waters" because it lies without a tremor in the still waters of the rivers and streams. Thus "stillness is a white cayman." All curing chants create a relationship between an animal with a specific trait (stillness in this case) and certain desired traits in the patient (stillness instead of convulsions). New curing chants are created from time to time, based on new metaphors.

Occasionally several meanings of a metaphor may simultaneously have validity. For example, among the Suya, women are sometimes referred to as "our game" (in the sense of hunted animal). The Suya are referring to various ways in which women and game are alike: (1) We (men) pierce both game (with arrows) and women (with penises). (2) Women and powerful game animals have the same strong odor. (3) Hunting and sexual relations both occur outside the plaza in the more natural spatial domains. All these features are relevant at once, and they make the metaphor more powerful. Indeed, perhaps root metaphors or central metaphors all condense several meanings into a single juxtaposition.

A powerful metaphor such as "women are game," shares several features of the symbol as defined by Victor Turner (1967, 1973). For Turner a symbol is an object or act that has multiple meanings, unifies in one term quite disparate *significata* or referents, condenses many ideas, actions, and relations between things in a single element (the symbol), and tends, in the case of important ritual symbols, to have two poles of meaning, one consisting of components of the moral and social order, the other of sensory phenomena (V. Turner 1973, p. 1100). The practice in analyzing symbols is thus to trace their multiple meanings and to see which of them operate in a given ceremony or social event. Like the analysis of metaphor, this is a search for meaning(s). This process is followed throughout this work.

The Suya have a word for "symbolize." It is *kodo,* and translates literally as "goes with" or "accompanies." It implies an analogic relationship between two terms and two realms. Thus when a man dreams of a desirable woman who flirts with him, he expects to have a successful hunt the next day. The woman in the dream is *mbru kodo* (*mbru,* animal; *kodo,* goes with). The Suya exegesis of symbols and metaphors usually consists of knowing the things that "go with" other things.

Many parts of Suya life are not believed to have symbolic meaning. Compared with the Ndembu, studied by Victor Turner, the Suya are not a highly exegetical people. They also dislike attempts at folk etymologies. Many things, they say, are done the way they are "because it is always this way." In these cases, as in the use of lip disk and ear disk, the search for meaning has to take a different approach. Meaning is to be found, but the analysis must use more than exegetical features of the symbol.

Power and Meaning

Any discussion of metaphor and symbol must raise the concept of power. Ritual symbols "are not merely things that stand for other things, or something abstract, they participate in the powers and virtues they represent" (V. Turner 1973, p. 1102). The same is true for metaphors, as in the case of the curing chants.

I have defined nature and society largely through their opposition. But nature may also be defined through its transformative power over society. The Suya use the domain of nature to effect their own transformation. (A similar view appears in T. Turner 1973.)

Metaphors use the natural domain, which has the power to transform the social. Nature surrounds society—literally in the case of spatial categories. Precisely by its marginal and threatening aspects, nature has power. The power is always being used, reintroduced through metaphor and symbol into the very heart of Suya culture. The power of specific features of the natural world is brought to bear on human beings to transform them—to make them well or sick, to effect a rite of passage.

Thus the apparently separate domains of nature and society are far more intimately linked than they at first appear to be. The continuous interaction between them is part of the process of Suya life. Symbols and metaphors are powerful and active. The Suya cosmology is not a dry construction with which the Suya while away empty hours; it is a framework for action and exists therein.[2]

The Body

The body, its substances, and its faculties are of fundamental importance in Suya society, not only in themselves, but also in their use to classify large parts of the universe. Kinship is based on an ideology of a physical identity shared by children, parents, and siblings. The socialization of the person is marked by alteration in the body itself. Animals are classified by their odor, as are humans, who are also classified by their hearing, their vision, and their speech. Victor Turner (1967) and Mary Douglas (1966, 1970) have suggested that the body is important as a referent throughout the world. Although this is undoubtedly true, in other parts of the world kinship is also organized around lineages (as in Africa) or marriage (as in many parts of Asia). Kinship among the Northern Gê rests on the concept of corporeal identity. Similarly, there are no gods, no creators, no concepts of grace or damnation; instead, there are moral concepts related to certain social and antisocial attributes of the human body and its faculties. The physical body and the bodily faculties thus assume even greater importance, for it is through them that the cosmos is interpreted.

The Suya in Comparative Perspective

In addition to presenting its own argument, this book is meant as a contribution to two comparative analyses of lowland South American Indian societies. These are the careful ethnographic study (in some cases, restudy) of the Northern and Central Gê societies begun by David Maybury-Lewis and a number of his students in the Harvard-Central Brazil Project, and the broadly comparative structural analyses of myths presented by Claude Lévi-Strauss in his *Mythologiques.* These two orientations inform and enrich each other and lend support to my own claims. The developments in central Brazilian ethnography give important insights into the analyses of Lévi-Strauss. His analyses have strongly influenced the recent fieldwork in the region, including my own.

In a pioneering article first published in 1952, "The Social Structures of Central and Eastern Brazil" (Lévi-Strauss 1963), Lévi-Strauss notes the theoretical difficulties that the available accounts of the Gê-speaking and Bororo tribes present to his analysis of marriage systems. One of his conclusions is that "the study of social organization among the populations of central and eastern Brazil must be thoroughly re-examined in the field" (1963, p. 130). Maybury-Lewis took up that task and worked with the Sherente and Shavante, two groups of the Central Gê. He brought the tools of British social anthropology to bear on the task and the result, *Akwẽ Shavante Society* (Maybury-Lewis 1967), is one of the best monographs on a lowland South American society. Later Maybury-Lewis organized a project that undertook the systematic study of a number of other Gê and related tribes by students. The published work of these students does not include many ethnographies (the exception being Da Matta 1976) but does include a number of outstanding dissertations that have circulated in manuscript form: T. Turner (1966), Bamberger (1967), Crocker (1967), Lave (1967), Da Matta (1971), and Melatti (1970). These writers have confirmed the earlier studies of Curt Nimuendaju (1939, 1941, 1946) which revealed a great complexity in the social organization of the Gê societies. They have also corrected some of his errors. One example of the difficulties raised by early ethnographers is Nimuendaju's claim that the *kiye* of the Apinaye were an institution based on parallel descent which regulated marriage. In fact, *kiye* have nothing to do with marriage, as Da Matta has shown on the basis of further research among the Apinaye (Da Matta 1968, 1976).

The Northern and Central Gê societies provide opportunities for what Fred Eggan has called the method of controlled comparison (1954). Instead of comparing widely separated societies, Eggan suggested local comparisons utilizing regions of relatively homogeneous culture. One advantage of this method is that it can lead to a clearer understanding of the small variations between related societies. The Gê are an ideal people for this kind of study. They all speak related languages. Many aspects of their social organizations are similar: uxorilocal residence, a somewhat similar ecological adjustment and technology, elaborate male initiations, and important naming systems. There is variation in the type of kinship terminology employed, the presence or absence of a men's house, the details of name transmission, the type of body ornamentation, and many other features. Thus every group varies in important ways from every other. Recently published monographs (Da Matta 1976; Vidal 1977) and collections of papers (Maybury-Lewis, 1979) should make some of the material available for use in comparative studies. Some interesting comparisons between the Gê and the tribes of the Upper Xingu have already been made (Viveiros de Castro 1977).

Lévi-Strauss undertook a different kind of comparative analysis of the central Brazilian societies in his later works (1964, 1966a, 1968, 1971). His completed analysis of South American Indian mythologies reveals an elaborate shared code of oppositions in the myths of a wide selection of tribes. His original intentions were these:

> By means of a small number of myths taken from certain aboriginal socities which will serve as our laboratory we hope to construct an experiment whose significance, if we succeed, will be of a general order . . . The aim of this book is to show how certain categorical opposites drawn from everyday experience with the most basic sorts of things—e.g., "raw" and "cooked," "fresh" and "rotten," "moist" and "parched," and others—can serve a people as conceptual tools for the formation of abstract notions and for combining these into propositions. (Lévi-Strauss 1966b, p. 41)

The structures of "primitive thought" that Lévi-Strauss claims to find revealed in these myths include many aspects of lowland South American tribal cultures that have never been the object of direct investigation by field ethnographers. He has taken them from the content and structure of the myths themselves, not from reports on the societies. The total effect of his work on myths is both dazzling and disturbing. The volumes have stimulated accolades and excoriation. Lévi-Strauss is an emotional as well as an intellectual issue in American anthropology, as anyone who attends sessions on his work at the annual meetings of the American Anthropological Association can testify. Many criticisms center on the nature of the oppositions that Lévi-Strauss has discovered and whether they existed in the native societies or merely in the mind of the French anthropologist. The question of where the oppositions may be found is all the more important because Lévi-Strauss claims that it is ultimately immaterial whether the Indians' thought processes have taken shape through the medium of his thought, or his through theirs (1966b, p. 58).

I regard it as quite important at least to speculate on whose thought is operating in which culture. Although it is unlikely that any form of anthropological analysis can claim to be uninfluenced by the thought processes of the analyst, there are clearly degrees of influence. Certainly one of the contributions of Lévi-Strauss's analyses derives ultimately from his extensive readings in the ethnographies of the area and his ability to see patterns in them. That is why so few others, attempting to use Lévi-Strauss's methods, have had his success.

A few researchers have extended Lévi-Strauss's ideas through a more careful use of South American ethnography and a development of structural analysis. Perhaps the most successful of the attempts is Terence Turner's "Origin of Cooking Fire" (1973) in which he analyzes a number of variants of the Gê myth of the origin of fire. Turner's analysis, which owes much to that of Lévi-Strauss, can go much further because his data are far richer. Stephen Hugh-Jones (1974) has carefully analyzed a rite of the Northwest Amazon. Jean-Paul Dumont's analysis (1976) of the Panare demonstrates the presence in Panare culture of a number of features discussed by Lévi-Strauss in the *Mythologiques* but does not give flesh to the concepts that he delineates nor carry the analysis much further.

In spite of the methodological and theoretical problems in the *Mythologiques,* Lévi-Strauss has discovered some of the most important parameters of Gê cosmology and probably of the cosmologies of other tribes as well (to judge from Dumont and Hugh-Jones). Many of his claims hold for the Suya even though he never had more than cursory data on them (Steinen 1942; Schultz 1960-61; Lanna 1967). Nature and culture, raw and cooked, the five senses, the ambiguity of honey, and other features that he discusses are indeed important in the Suya classification of the world. They are among the features that give the cosmos its order and in terms of which metaphor and symbol are created.

This book is not intended solely as a vindication of Lévi-Strauss for a group that he could not write about. I shall not list where he was correct or incorrect in the details of Suya cosmology. Instead, the analyses are carried to domains of the society that Lévi-Strauss, because of his sources, could not analyze. The concepts themselves are treated in a detailed way that he, because of his broad comparative interest, could not develop. I do not restrict myself to religion or mythology, as Lévi-Strauss and others have done. Rather, I agree with David Schneider that the system of symbols appears in many domains: "The fact is that the ultimate values, the collective representations, what I call the system of symbols and meanings, permeate the total society and its institutions and are not confined to religion, to ritual, or to myth alone" (1976, p. 208). I wish to contribute to the structural analyses of South American Indian societies precisely through the demonstration of the actual use of formal constructions in a given society and the way in which they appear in domains other than those of ritual and myth.

The mutual stimulation of Lévi-Straussean analysis and the restudy of the Gê societies is nowhere clearer than in the demonstration of the importance of dualism in these societies (Da Matta 1976). My own claims for the dual nature of Suya cosmology are not based on a theory about the human mind or thought in general (thereby contrasting with those of Lévi-Strauss). Rather, I believe that such dual structures permeate Suya society and those of the other Gê-speaking societies of central Brazil.

There are two justifications for analyzing Suya society in terms of a simple binary contrast. One of them lies within the society; the other is of a comparative nature. The pervasiveness of binary distinctions in domains such as space (two directions), ceremonial moieties (two different and complementary moieties), the idiom of relationship ("us" and "other"), and aesthetic style (the binary structure of song and chant) justifies the analysis in terms of Suya society itself. In addition, the comparative material available on the other Gê societies reveals a similar dualism, showing that it is neither unique to the Suya nor to my interpretation of them.

The first careful analysis (contrasted with description as represented by Nimuendaju) was published by Maybury-Lewis on the Shavante. He describes his monograph as "little more than an argument that Shavante society can best be understood in terms of the dichotomy between *waniwihã* and *wasi're'wa*" (Maybury-Lewis 1967, p. 295). A summary statement (p. 292) lists a series of antitheses:

wazepari'wa	*da hieba*
malevolence	benevolence
taking	giving
terrifying	consoling
ending	beginning
(death?)	(life?)
west	east
affinal place	kin place
affines	kin
wasi're'wa	*waniwihã*

He argues that dualism must be divorced from moieties and concrete institutions altogether. "Instead anthropologists might consider how far a particular dyadic model was explanatory of a given society; or to put it another way, what range of rules, ideas, and actions was rendered intelligible by the model and, equally significantly, what range was not" (Maybury-Lewis 1967, p. 298).

Other ethnographers of the Northern and Central Gê societies have discovered and developed dualistic perspectives on the societies with which they worked (Lave 1967; Melatti 1970; T. Turner 1966, 1973; Da Matta 1976).

Jean Carter Lave, in her analysis of the naming system of the Krikati, emphasizes the opposition between domestic organization and ceremonial organization as radically contrasting forms (Lave 1967, p. 294):

domestic organization	ceremonial organization
relational terminology	positional terminology
networks of individual relations	society-wide aggregates

Roberto Da Matta has discovered similar principles. According to him, the fairly flexible Apinaye domestic organization and the highly structured ceremonial organization are two basic domains of Apinaye society, "antithetical, complementary, and fundamental" (Da Matta 1968, p. 356). In *Um mundo dividido* Da Matta develops some very interesting ideas about the nature of dual organization.

Other Gê ethnographers have remarked on the importance of the dichotomy of nature and society in addition to stressing the importance of dualism. In his article on Apinaye omens Da Matta writes:

> It is the selection of certain characteristics which explains the presage. This selection operates as a function of the juxtaposition [of human and animal characteristics], which permits the humanization of the animal. More precisely, the juxtaposition creates the conditions that bring together the world of man (culture or society) and the world of animals (nature, or the world that man does not completely control) that are normally separate. (1970, p. 87, my translation)

Terence Turner, in his analysis of the myth of the fire of the jaguar, also emphasizes the importance of nature and culture among the Northern Kayapo, with this important qualification: "Culture and nature are not separate but formally parallel orders standing in static, metaphorical relationship to one another, but dynamic systems engaged in a perpetual process of accommodation and attrition" (T. Turner 1973). Although this statement departs from Turner's earlier, more sociological analyses, even his earlier work describes Kayapo society as possessing many elements of a dual organization. Joan Bamberger's analysis of the Northern Kayapo specifically mentions the important opposition of nature and society, with women as the mediating figures (Bamberger 1967, pp. 122-137).

Perhaps the most radical exponent of the importance of the dichotomy between nature and society in a Gê society is Júlio Melatti. The concluding chapter of his dissertation (Melatti 1970) is composed of thirty-three principles considered important in Kraho society. Several of them are devoted to the fundamental opposition of nature and society.

> There is a ritual opposition between society and nature . . . Even though the Kraho do not express this opposition explicitly it is impossible to give meaning to their rites without considering it . . .
>
> There is a tendency to transform all oppositions into the opposition of society/nature. Generally, in the opposition between two elements, one of them possesses a certain characteristic which more closely approximates nature than the other, making, therefore, that opposition a representation of the opposition society/nature.
>
> The oppositions man/woman, adult man/immature man, living/dead, consanguines/affines, village members/members of other villages can be identified with the opposition society/nature. (Melatti 1970, p. 452, my translation)

In addition, Melatti identifies the oppositions of central versus periphery, pairs of opposed moieties, kinsmen related to procreation versus kinsmen related to naming practices, and kinsmen versus affines with the same opposition of nature and society.

Melatti's conclusions with respect to nature and society, although quite cogent, seem divorced from the body of the work in which he presents a detailed ethnography of the Kraho in traditional terms. He adequately defines neither what is natural nor what the Kraho consider social. The socialness or naturalness of any element apparently also depends on context, since the oppositions "village members" versus "members of other villages" and "kinsmen" versus "affines" (who are likely to be in the same village) are each identified with the society-nature opposition. Melatti tends to see the oppositions as monolithic and unrelated. He notes, however, that each opposition is mediated by the inclusion of some part of the natural term in the social one. Thus the opposition men versus women appears throughout Kraho society except that a few women accompany the stages of initiation with the men in some ceremonies and the wives of certain political leaders have ritual and political status. I have already suggested that the interrelationship of the domains of nature and society is much more complex than that of a simple mediation.

All the authors just cited were students of Maybury-Lewis and were influenced in important ways by the works of Lévi-Strauss. They are also careful and conscientious fieldworkers. They all perceived a fundamental dualism in the societies they studied. It should be clear that neither the dualism of nature and society nor the terms themselves have been arbitrarily chosen for the purpose of this analysis. Instead they are the outgrowth of my own investigations among the Suya, and they are supported by the writings of other ethnographers as well as by the myth analyses of Lévi-Strauss. These analyses reinforced one another and provide a basis for the comparative analysis of lowland South American societies. This book carries the analysis further than the others because it starts with the Suya definitions of what is natural and what is social and then illustrates the usefulness of the pair in analyzing Suya society.

The Suya Indians construct their universe and interpret events according to the interaction of two complementary and opposed principles, which I have called nature and society to gloss what in Suya is the relationship between animals (*mbru*) and Suya (*mẽ*). Nature and society act on each other through mutal processes of transformation. What is social is typically unchanging unless affected by natural elements, and to the Suya it is morally good (health, moral rectitude, the status of adult initiated men, the center of the plaza); what is natural is typically powerful and transforming. Sickness and death are the direct results in the intervention of natural entities (witches); social transformation is achieved through ceremonies in which songs learned from animals are sung and the participants become something that is at once animal and human; and political power involves a central ambiguity expressed in terms of the natural attributes of chiefs. Nature and society are contrasted principles rather than concrete things. Something may be considered natural in one context and social in another. What is common in every case is the relationship of contrast and transformation. The actual entities involved vary according to context and intention.

The dynamic interaction of nature and society is not restricted to a single domain (such as mythology) nor to a few related domains. It appears as an organizing principle in many varied domains. Concepts of time and space, the body and its faculties, the natural and social world, kinship, the life cycle, leadership, medicine, and mythology all express this relationship between the natural and the social. Suya society is extremely consistent, and therefore analyzable, in terms of this basic relationship between humans (thought of in a specifically Suya way) and animals (similarly specifically defined).

It might be argued that at this level of generality all societies are alike. Nature and culture are, after all, important concepts in Western philosophy. They have also been described in many other parts of the world. But nature and society are defined differently in different places. Every society creates the nature it needs and deserves, as Lévi-Strauss (1966c) and Sahlins (1976b) have cogently argued. Western concepts of nature have changed over time. Nature and society are defined somewhat differently even among such closely related societies as the Northern Gê, although here the similarities are much greater than between ourselves and the Suya. Moreover, dual principles of this type illuminate to different degrees the societies to which they are applied. Thus the dynamic interaction of nature and society as a principle analyzes quite well many of the domains of Suya society. A similar attempt to analyze the societies of the Upper Xingu will not have the same success, although the contrast may be useful for certain domains. Jean-Paul Dumont has argued that for the Panare Indians of Venezuela a triadic scheme of nature-culture-supernature is more applicable than a binary one. This is not the case for the Suya. In Western society the dual model leaves much unanalyzed, although David Schneider (1968) has shown that parts of the American kinship system can be analyzed in these terms. Other principles of organization are probably more satisfactory analytic tools. The usefulness of nature and society as organizing principles of Suya society is not taken as a given but is revealed in the course of the ensuing analysis.

I do not claim to "explain" Suya society in historical or causal terms through this analysis of their perception and construction of themselves and their universe. I am instead suggesting that we can best understand this construction in terms of these principles and that our understanding in these terms will yield rich results in the domains that are usually considered more concrete or real, such as subsistence and politics. It is not that the Suya produce and reproduce within the limitations of the central Brazilian ecosystem that makes them interesting to me, but the specific way that they do those things. And the coherence of the specifically Suya way of life is best approached, I believe, through the principles that I have set forth in this chapter.

2

A First Encounter with the Suya

U*NTIL 1972 THE ONLY WAY* to get to the Suya Indians in the Xingu National Park Indian reservation was by air. It is still the only practical way. One takes off through the forest of skyscrapers in São Paulo, rising above the brown smoggy tangle of industry, wealth, and power, to fly for hours over carefully tended fields bounded by gray lines of asphalt. The fields lose their sharpness and the roads much of their asphalt before the plane reaches Goiânia, but cities regularly appear and are left behind. From Goiânia to Xavantina, where the plane often spends the night before flying to the Xingu, one flies over endless pastures, some quite recently cleared, and occasional clearly bounded stretches of forest. Small dirt roads cut like ruled lines across the flat terrain. Parallel tracks show where motor vehicles drive to tiny houses or corrals. Xavantina is a frontier town, established in the 1940s as a government outpost. It boasts a single hotel, electric light for a couple of hours at night, and one-room stores filled with canned goods, blankets, salt, pungent rolls of tobacco, bottles of cheap sugarcane liquor. There one eats a last Brazilian meal of rice, beans, and chicken from the backyard, makes the last few purchases, and is up before dawn to return to the air strip for the last part of the trip.

In the first light the plane flies over more pastures, but the roads, even mere tracks, soon become scarcer until they disappear altogether. Suddenly there is not a single straight line in sight. Everything curves, twists back on itself, or has circular patterns. The rivers wind tortuously, the strips of gallery forest follow them, receding lakes leave round spots of discolored vegetation, and the oxbow lakes show clearly where the rivers ran only a few years before. The eye suddenly has no fixed referent; everything undulates, following a logic of its own. After about forty minutes a small circle of what seem to be haystacks appears and disappears, identified as the village of the Kuikuru Indians, with threadlike paths leading to the lake, river, and gardens and with the smoke of morning fires rising lazily into the still air. The change is eerie: one is clearly entering a completely different world. One leaves the plane on a grass landing strip, surrounded by Indians, in unaccustomed heat. After the plane takes off again, the quiet suddenly descends, the sound of several unknown tongues falls strangely on the ears. Space, sights, sounds, and smells are different. Even the very air and water have different textures.

But the Xingu today is less isolated. In the past decade roads have sliced across virgin lands, opening them for ranching. Deforestation and the planting of dry rice, or grass for cattle, have altered much of the formerly trackless expanses. In many cases the ranches reach or invade the lands granted to the Indians. In 1976 I went to the Suya by bus: five days of rattling discomfort on a series of different lines. The twenty-three-hour trip from Rio de Janeiro to Goiânia is comfortable enough. The next twelve hours to Barra de Garças are hot and dusty. From Bara de Garças, however, the bus becomes "a mother's heart" (there's always room for one more). There may be forty seated passengers and as many standees: weatherbeaten men, women, and children with their belongings. At most bridges everyone has to get out so that the bus can cross empty, and at every settlement it stops for "water"—the men toss down half a glass of sugarcane liquor and climb back on, the women nurse their babies. The last leg of the journey, from São Felix do Araguaia to the Xingu, is made in a bus so rusted out that one can poke one's fingers through its sides. It may be filled with the bandaged survivors of the previous bus which has gone off the road, rolled over, and hit a tree. In the dry season this stretch may take as little as twelve jolting hours; in the rains it may take three days.

The last town before the Xingu River, São José do Xingu, is known as Bang-Bang because of its violence, especially when the workers cutting trees on the spreading cattle ranches come to town to drink and play. Ranch owners only come to this part of the world with their body guards. During the heat of the day it is simply a wide, dusty street lined on one side with stores and bars and eateries, populated largely by women and chickens; dogs lie in the shadows, and there is a sense of being at the edge of the world. One is taken to the margin of the Xingu River to wait for a boat and make one's way into the unaltered winding river of the Xingu reservation. The Xingu is then less a shock than a longed-for relief: the cool viscous water steeps the dust and the sweat, the vomit and the liquor out of the pores. The silence is a balm to the ears, the strangeness of the Indian village a familiarity, the coolness of the hammocks a delight after the bedbugs and fleas of tiny stifling bedrooms. Eight hours of motorboat ride up the river from the road (by canoe it is three days) and one is in a different—and more pleasant—world, but one already profoundly affected by Brazilian society.

The topography of the land through which the motorboat runs on the way to the Suya village is flat; the river winds slowly between mostly forested banks. It is a low, scrubby forest with a fairly heavy undergrowth of thorny plants, not to be confused with the high, clear-floored Amazonian rain forest.

The village itself is located on a large bend in the Suya-Missu River, in the midst of subsistence resources. There are rivers and lakes rich with fish, ample forest for hunting jaguars, tapirs, wild pigs, forest deer, and other game animals as well as for making gardens. The village is near enough the Indian post called Diauarum for medical aid and somewhat removed from the other Indian tribes in the region by being on its own river. Of these resources it is the earth that is the weakest; there is not much good soil in the vicinity. Bananas, corn, and sweet potatoes are always small and relatively scarce compared with the yields in better soil elsewhere in the region. The Suya say that game, too, is more plentiful in the higher forests where the earth is better. They sometimes plant crops in gardens as much as two days' travel from the village, and they also go on long hunting and fishing expeditions. In the steadily expanding ring of gardens around the circle of houses they plant the staple crop, manioc, which grows well even in less fertile earth.

The circular village of the Suya, with its large, hard-packed central plaza, its seven large houses, and the surrounding gardens and forest on three sides, river on the fourth (figure 2.1), presents a dramatic contrast to Bang-Bang. The village has a center and a limit; it is a social system unto itself. Its members live well on the products of garden and forest, in a cultural tradition created and refined in the place they live. Bang-Bang, its main street a dusty through road and its stores filled with goods manufactured far away, is clearly a bead on a string that stretches to Rio de Janeiro and São Paulo, to Wall Street and West Germany. Very little grows in Bang-Bang. The emphasis is on clearing, cutting, burning, and planting grass for cattle. The cultural center of Bang-Bang is thousands of miles away.

The Suya village in 1971 is also a new settlement. Stumps stand in less used parts of the plaza. Gardens crowd in on the backs of the houses. A house is under construction. But the carefully planned nature of the village is evident even to the uninformed eye (figure 2.2). Lines drawn from the doors of the opposing pairs of houses intersect just about where some logs lie waiting for the men's evening council. The trails to the gardens and the paths to the canoe-beaching area some hundred yards to the west of the village are hardly worn by the traffic of human beings.

In spite of the obvious order, the Suya present little that resembles homogeneity. The houses are of several styles. Most are built of upright

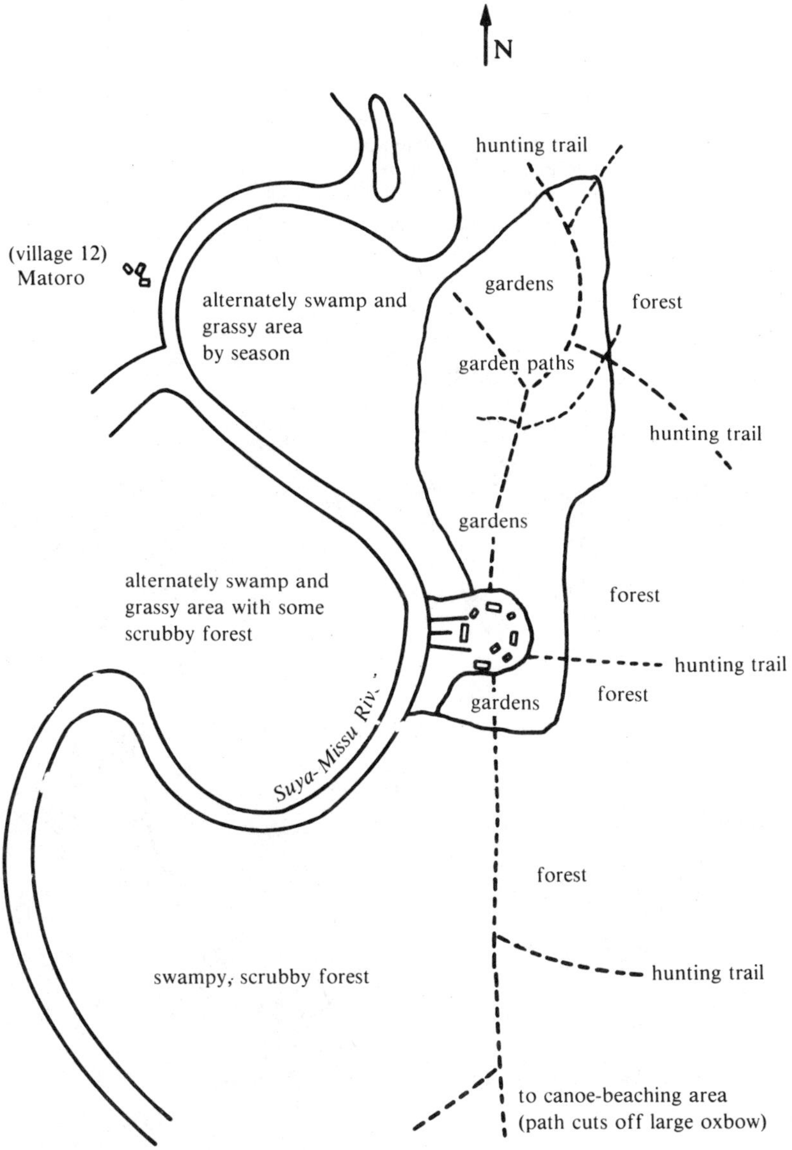
N
hunting trail
(village 12)
Matoro
gardens
alternately swamp and
grassy area
by season
forest
garden paths
hunting trail
gardens
alternately swamp and
grassy area with some
scrubby forest
forest
hunting trail
gardens
forest
Suya-Missu Riv.
forest
swampy, scrubby forest
hunting trail
to canoe-beaching area
(path cuts off large oxbow)

Figure 2.1 *Suya village and environs*

House names

1 *kikre mbrukïntà* (house where animal ceremonies are danced)
2 *kikre hrikti, kikre saka* (tall house, white house)
3 *kikre sarono* (untranslatable)
4 *kikre ngràw* (untranslatable)
5 Western Suya house with several possible names
6 *kikre saka* (white house)
7 *kikre saka* (white house)
8 never completed

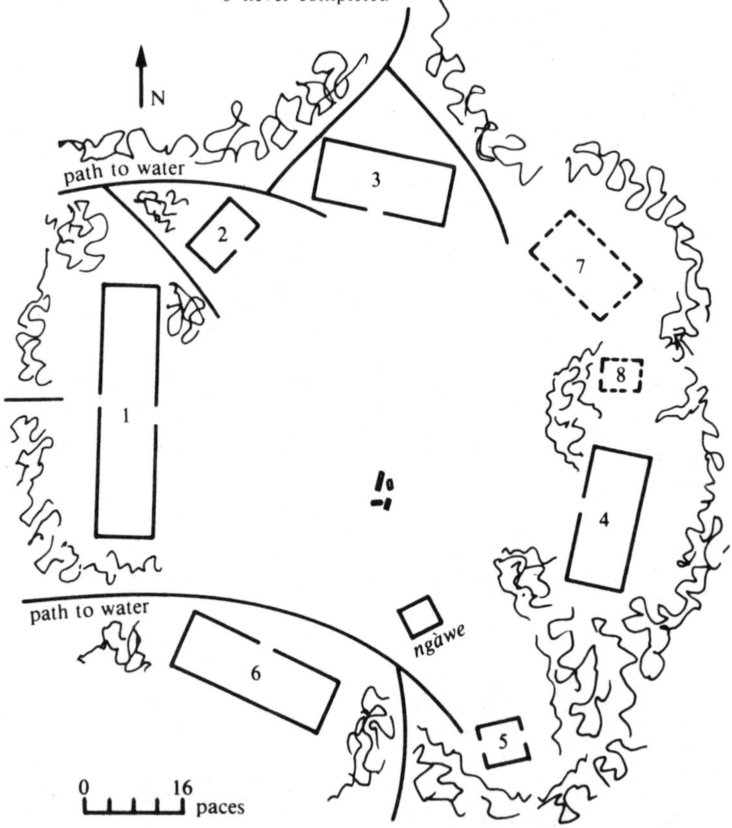

Figure 2.2 *Suya village plan*

logs and thatch like the buildings of the Indian post; one is built in the style of the Upper Xingu Indians; yet another is a rude shelter. Like their houses, the Suya are varied in appearance. Older men with long hair, large wooden lip disks in their lower lips, and empty loops of earlobe hanging and flapping carry thatch to the new house along with younger men with Upper Xingu Indian bowl-style haircuts and no lip ornaments, and others with shorn heads looking like army recruits. They wear a startling assortment of tattered shorts and shirts, are missing a lot of teeth, and speak a few words of Portuguese. More distant because of their language and sex, women work in faded knee-length dresses at processing manioc tubers. They are more uniform in dress and appearance, and they tend children as they work, talking unceasingly among themselves. Inside the houses a similar mixture of clay pots with battered tin ones, of ornamented gourds and chipped cups, of native hammocks and manufactured ones, and an occasional Gê Indian style platform bed, reinforces the impression of heterogeneity and "culture loss." It takes some time to discover that this veneer of clothing, architecture, and material culture is thin, that it is accompanied by little economic or religious intervention in the traditional lives of the Suya, and that there is in fact something importantly unitary and Suya in all that occurs.

Subsistence and the Sexual Division of Labor

Men and women spend much of their lives in different tasks. To men fall the responsibilities of obtaining fish and game for consumption as well as most raw materials for manufacture. To women fall the tasks of processing all vegetable and most animal products for consumption by the family or the village and the bearing and rearing of children. The sexual division of labor and of artifact manufacture is summarized in table 2.1. Sex roles are established early. Little girls play with miniature baskets and baby slings while little boys play with miniature bows and arrows. The children play together also, each sex playing appropriate role. The sexual division of labor is complementary, and families often relax together, talking, playing, and grooming.

The woman's domain is the domestic one, located especially in the large houses and behind them. Suya houses have no internal divisions, and are illuminated by light coming through the doorways and chinks in the walls. Although apparently without spatial divisions, there is in fact a clear etiquette of space use in which each family has its own part of the house where it slings its hammocks, where it has its own fire for the night, and its own belongings stuck in the thatch out of reach of children and pets. The house as a whole usually has the center section reserved for collective social events and other section reserved for cooking when the weather does not permit cooking outside. One or two communal cooking fires serve all the house residents. The food is cooked there and distrib-

Table 2.1. Male and Female Activities and Artifact Manufacture

Male	Female
Activities	
Hunt, fish	Cook all food brought to the houses
Skin and butcher large animals	Pick up tiny fish in crocheted bags
Cook meat in men's house or on all-male trips	Carry game up from canoes
	Prepare birds and fish for cooking
Cut and burn gardens	Bring in all garden products
Plant manioc, sugarcane (new crop), bananas	Plant sweet potatoes, cará, bottle gourds, squash, cotton, papaya (new crop), watermelon (new crop)
Poke holes for corn	Drop corn kernels in holes made by men
Gather large firewood for manioc processing	Gather small firewood for all purposes other than manioc processing
Build houses for in-laws	
Build fires from scratch	Keep fires going
Collect fruits and honey	Collect fruits
Artifacts	
Bows	Cotton thread[c]
Arrows	Hammocks[c,d]
Clubs	Baby slings of cotton thread
Baskets (all types)[a]	Children's arm bands
Combs[a]	Crocheted fish bags
All feather ornaments	Crocheted part of Manitsaua-style headdress[d]
Male body ornaments	
Beds	Manioc squeezing mat[d]
Canoes[b,d] and paddles	Clothes from Brazilian cloth[d]
Mortar and pestle[a]	Hammock-style mosquito nets using Brazilian netting[c,d]
Manioc graters[a]	
Gardens (wife's)[b]	Palm fiber waist strings
Houses[b]	Pottery, all sizes and styles[d]
Beiju turner[a,d]	Griddles for beiju[d]
Fire fan[a]	Ear disks for women, all personal adornments
Flutes[d]	
Rattles	Gourds
Necklaces of teeth or claws	Necklaces of beads and vertebrae
Palm nut rings (for trade)[d]	Dolls for girls
All major ritual paraphernalia	
Mats of palm leaves[a]	
All their own tools	

[a] Made by men for women.
[b] Made by men for their affines.
[c] Made by women for men.
[d] Learned from the Upper Xingu or other Indians.

uted to all the families. High-roofed, roomy, cool in the heat of the day, and filled with people talking and children playing, the house is comfortable and convenient. A person might be off in a corner making an artifact, but he can be present in the conversation and may shout a comment down the length of the house to a relative. The women can follow the progress of their children with their eyes and then with their ears, without having to get up and follow them around. There are always people ready to tell a mother that her child is getting into trouble—although only she is expected to do much about it.

Both sexes are involved in the collecting and processing of food. The Suya never express concern about starvation, but they know hunger. Food is always there in the forests; they say it is simply a question of more or less work to find and bring back. At different times of year different amounts of vegetable and animal foods are brought to the village. In a lean time the village is always much quieter while the men are away hunting or fishing. Women who are not processing manioc retire to their hammocks; children play quietly and occasionally fuss. The whole village is quiet except for the grating of manioc, the shrieks of parrots, and the buzzing of flies. As soon as a man or group of men return successful, the house bustles, laughter rings, and the hammocks of the families swing as they eat and drink and talk about the hunt or what happened while the men were away. There is no store of food beyond small amounts of manioc flour. What is brought in, even if it is a lot, is distributed and eaten on the same day or possibly extending into the next. Even a single small fish is boiled, the flesh and water mixed with manioc flour, and the starchy porridge eaten on manioc *beiju* by all the members of a house. At certain times a single mouthful can be important. Eating and giving food are important pleasures, and there are many delicacies—honey, for example—that delight the Suya palate and whose very occasionality enhances them.

The domestic life of the Suya continues much as it always has in spite of contact with Brazilian society. If anything, it is easier because of the steel tools, the metal pots, the fishooks and line, the guns and bullets that the Suya receive as presents from the government. The Suya produce no surplus for sale. They eat what they have and plant what they think they will need. When food runs short in the gardens or when fish and game seem scarce in the vicinity, families leave the village on extended trips, eating from the forest and using the distant richer hunting, fishing, and gathering resources. The return of these groups is eagerly awaited by those that stay behind, and a large-scale distribution of what is brought back always takes place. Wild honey, roast wild turkey, wild chicken, ducks and doves, roast fish, roast game, seasonal delicacies such as turtle eggs, and pets such as fledgling birds, tiny turtles, or baby monkeys are brought to the houses, distributed around the village, and enjoyed by all.

The year-round tropical climate is clearly divided into rainy and dry seasons which are intimately associated with the Suya diet and social life. Little rain falls from May to September. The rivers shrink between their banks and flow through dazzling white sand beaches. In September the heat builds up until the rains, in the form of violent thunderstorms, bring relief. The violent storms give way to more frequent rains in October and November; then the rivers rise, overflow their banks, and flood forest and savannah. The rain is neither steady nor necessarily daily. But there is almost always some rain to be seen falling from the ranks of clouds that fill the giant sky. From the height of the dry season to the height of the rainy season the river may rise as much as eighteeen feet, connecting the lakes and oxbows to the main river and replenishing the fish in them each year as new fish get trapped by the receding water.

The rainy season and the dry season are important to the Suya, and they differ in more than just the level of the water. Different strategies of food collection obtain, and different activities occupy people's time. Seasonal foods provide resources for community events such as rituals, or scarcity may cause the extended family groups to take long trips and leave the village ritually inactive. During the dry season, when the lakes and rivers shrink, fish are plentiful and the Suya fish with bow and arrow and fish poison. During the rainy season the rising waters make fishing less productive and they concentrate on hunting game, fattened on the ripening fruit or fresh grasses and concentrated by the rising waters, or on gathering food resources such as fruit. The larger annual variation is broken by many smaller seasons. In August turtle eggs are abundant in the sand banks. The rich, oily fruit called *piqui* is important in October and November when fish are scarce and game is not yet plentiful. In January the corn ripens, a crucial ingredient for many ritual foods. In April the new sweet potatoes can be eaten. There are yet smaller periods, when a particular fruit is plentiful, when ants swarm, when edible larvae are big and fatty within certain palm nuts.

Although diet, subsistence strategies, and most aspects of Suya life vary in important ways with the seasons, a general domestic pattern may be discerned. The Suya rise early. The men often sing in the men's house shortly after the rise of the morning star. On days without singing a man might turn on a radio at full volume around 4:30 or 5:00. The women are up, blowing the coals of their sleeping fires, nursing their babies, and leaving in the cold predawn to dig manioc or to bathe in the warm river and dry themselves by fires at the bank, bringing back pots of water on their heads. Every day at least one of the men in each house leaves in the dark or early morning, his paddle, bow, arrows, and rifle clattering lightly to his stride, his dog following behind, to go fishing or hunting in the cool of the morning. He may call quietly to a friend, and then their footsteps disappear down the familiar paths to the canoes.

Most fishing is done by two men, or a man and a boy, who either use fishline (useful for certain species) or take turns paddling while the other stands in the bow of the canoe, bow and arrow ready, to shoot fish as the canoe moves slowly through the clear water. Large fish which frequent the shallows or gather around flooded fruit and berry bushes are hunted in this way. But even when fishing, the men are attentive to the sounds of the jungle, and they may abandon their canoe to search for a bird whose call they have heard, to look for honey, to dig out an armadillo, or to go after game flushed by the dog. Occasionally men fish in larger groups, using a natural fish poison in small lakes, a frequent activity especially at the very end of the dry season.

Men hunt collectively, individually, or on family excursions. Individual hunting is usually in the vicinity of the village; even when he goes with his family to the gardens a man always takes his gun, bow, and arrows. Collective hunts of several hours or a single day's duration are joined by most of the men and their dogs. These often begin their sweep some hours from the village by canoe, and any animals that are startled are killed by the scattered men. Longer collective hunting and fishing expeditions occur at the time of rituals, when a group of men may be gone for as much as two weeks, returning laden with enough food to assure enthusiastic participation and ample time for painting, singing, and dancing.

While some are off fishing or hunting in the early morning, other men stay around and repair their arrows, make artifacts, sit and converse in the men's house, or lie in their hammocks and talk or play with their families. "Work" is a leisurely affair masking a fairly orderly arrangement whereby all the men share the responsibilities of hunting and fishing. Some take on more than others: married men are expected to do more, adolescents are not obliged to do much, boys are often off in a peer group playing or stalking minnows in the shallows or paddling canoes across the river to play and swim. The morning passes in the domestic sphere, the plaza virtually deserted. The women, in the houses or behind them, prepare manioc flour and *beiju*.

The beiju—a round, flat, white manioc griddle cake, between one and two feet across and about one-quarter of an inch thick—is the starch staple of the Suya diet. It is practically pure starch, has no leaven or salt, and at first seems very dry. It is often wrapped around fish or game, although it may also be eaten alone. Every morning the women of each house, sometimes with women from other houses, make several beijus for each family with children. They are eaten by adults and children in the village, who tear a piece off whenever they want. The hunters and fishermen often eat nothing until they return, though they sometimes take some leftover beiju or starch drink along with them in the morning. Fresh beiju is made if a large catch of fish or game is brought back, and in the late afternoon another is often made to be eaten in the evening.

The preparation of the flour for the beijus takes a lot of work and is the principal subsistence activity of the women. Usually a woman works with her daughters, co-wife, or other helper at the task, which takes much of the day. They dig up the tubers in the gardens belonging to one of the women, carry them in, scrape the skins off, rinse them, grate them, and rinse the poisonous juice out of the gratings, which are then shaped into balls of flour to dry before they are used. The juice is boiled to make a starchy drink which is ready at dusk. The sediment, pure starch, is saved to make very fine types of beiju. Each married woman processes manioc and is the "owner" of the finished products. These are always shared, but a day's work usually leaves her with enough for a day of other activities, when she spins cotton, sits in the doorway, and discusses recent events, caring for her own children and grandchildren and those of other women in the gardens or at work on the manioc processing.

Men who leave in the early morning are usually back by noon. Each house cooks on its own hearth and all the families in that house receive a share from it. After eating, families bathe together. Couples may go off to the garden in the late afternoon for conversation and sexual relations. They may also dig up some manioc or bring back some sweet potatoes or bananas or firewood when they return. One or another man may go out fishing in the afternoon. These men return before dusk and another meal is eaten in back of the houses. In the growing darkness people can be heard spitting fishbones on the ground, and there is always the steady clunk-clunk of gourd against metal as women cool pots of starch drink for their families.

In the dark the men gather in the center of the village to talk and listen to each other. Men's talk ranges from descriptions of the day's events to tales of the past and plans for the future, to comments on the strange doings of the whites, to joking and teasing. They sit around a tiny, smoldering fire from which they light their hand-rolled cigarettes of Brazilian tobacco. The women often gather in front of their houses to watch, listen, and converse.

After the older men go to bed with the farewell, "Till tomorrow," the young men stay in the plaza where their giggles and laughter can be heard from the houses. They pursue their amorous intrigues stealthily in the dark. The fires by each family's sleeping place burn low, to be stirred up occasionally and new wood added. A child can be heard crying in some house, causing comment. From any house in the village one can hear the cry of an infant, the cough of an old man, or the shrieks of a child with a nightmare. Sleep is not something the Suya do for eight hours straight. People are always up and around, moving quietly through the house and out the door. Babies are suckled, myths are told, dogs bark and are silenced, until the morning cold and plans for the day get people up in the chill predawn.

If the daily routine is fairly leisurely, it can be broken by the sudden appearance of a lot of game, or the sighting of a plane, or a domestic emergency such as a child's burn or the sickness of an adult. These bring everyone together to discuss the case and to consider what action might be taken.

Ceremonial periods are always more hectic. Larger amounts of food are sought, larger batches of manioc are prepared. Someone is usually singing all during the day, walking around the central plaza, elaborately ornamented with bright-colored feathers, new lip and ear disks, and body paint. Many men are engaged in making ritual paraphernalia. The predawn and late afternoon are marked by the low unison singing of all the men in the village. Special shouts indicating joy punctuate the usual sounds, and the whole village is mobilized in a new way. In the evening new songs are taught, or women might sing instead of the men, dancing and singing songs learned from the women of the Upper Xingu societies. The whole village is moved by a euphoria that the Suya say is characteristic of ceremonies. The euphoria (*kin*) makes them want to sing, and the singing makes them euphoric.

Suya life has not a single rhythm but a variety of rhythms. In addition to the contrast between everyday life and that of ceremonial periods there are rhythms of interpersonal relationships for each person. Every person has people with whom he or she jokes or at whom he or she hardly glances. There are people with whom food is regularly shared, and those from whom one receives nothing and gives the same. There are brothers and sisters and lovers and spouses, witches and warriors, good friends and threatening enemies. The Suya have created and live in this complex, small, and for the most part secure world. It has always been a changing world, and recent experience has taught them about new threats from the outside. They are applying their creative minds to deal with new problems whose vastness they are only beginning to perceive.

History

The Suya language belongs to the northern branch of the Gê language family. This group includes the Northern Kayapo, Apinaye, and Timbira societies located presently in the states of Maranhão, Pará, northern Goiás, and Mato Grosso do Norte (figure 2.3). The members of this group have been pushed westward by the expansion of the frontier during the past four hundred years. In addition to the Northern Gê, there are also Central Gê groups (the Sherente and Shavante groups) and Southern Gê who inhabit the southern states of Brazil.

The Gê may be distinguished from the Indians of the tropical forest by

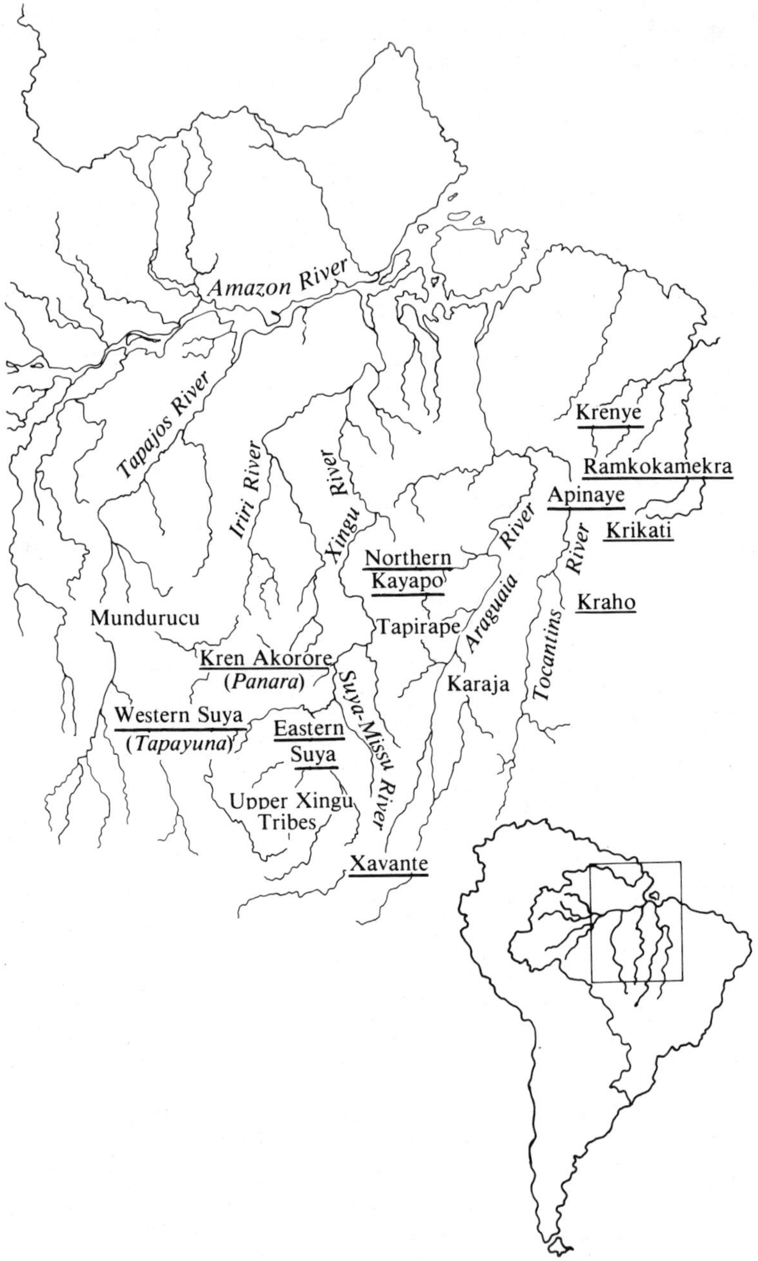

Figure 2.3 *Central Brazil, showing location of Gê-speaking groups (underlined)*

their preference for villages in the savannah, a mode of livelihood that is often called seminomadic and involves extensive trekking during parts of the year, as well as a tendency to concentrate in large multihouse villages for much of the year. They usually construct their villages in the savannah, the population is larger than tropical forest villages, the residence is uxorilocal (a man lives with his wife's family), and there are usually a number of important ceremonial groups and elaborate ceremonies, often involving rites of passage. These traits are shared by some other groups, such as the Bororo, Tapirapé, and Mundurucu, and it is often more convenient to talk about central Brazilian societies than the Gê language family. The Suya's most frequent peaceful contacts with Indians have been with the Upper Xingu tribes, which resemble tropical forest groups.

Prior to 1970 there were two widely separated groups of Indians speaking the same language, which I have called Suya since this was the name given to the first of the two groups to be contacted by Brazilians. That group, encountered by Karl von den Steinen on the Xingu in 1884, has lived on that river and an affluent known as the Suya-Missu for over 150 years. The other group, known as the Tapayuna or Beiço de Pau, lived some three hundred miles to the west, between the Arinos and Sangue rivers in Mato Grosso. Between 1960 and 1970 they suffered extreme depopulation. In 1970 the survivors of the western group were taken to live with the eastern group in a single village. There are some differences between those who lived on the Xingu River, the Eastern Suya, and those who lived on the Arinos, the Western Suya.

During my fieldwork the two groups were living in a single village on the right bank of the Suya-Missu some five kilometers from the confluence of that river with the Xingu. The village was located at approximately 11 degrees south latitude and 52 degrees west longitude within the boundaries of the Xingu National Park, an Indian reservation whose rough dimensions were forty kilometers on either side of the Xingu River from BR-080 to the headwaters of the Xingu, a total land area of some thirty thousand square kilometers (Villas Boas and Villas Boas 1973; E. Basso 1973, p. 2).

Both Eastern and Western Suya groups recall a similar legendary past. They believe that they originated far in the east and then moved to the west, crossing the Xingu and continuing to the Tapajós River. From there they apparently moved south and separated. One group, the Eastern Suya, traveled east to the Ronuro River and down that into the Xingu River system. The other, the Western Suya, continued south to the vicinity of the Arinos River where they were finally contacted and peace was established with them.[1] Both groups remember living on a river said to be an affluent of the Xingu called the "big black water" (*ngo-chindò tugu*). One Suya maintained that this was the Rio Fresco. They both also remembered a *ngo ndepti*, or "red river."

Eastern Suya oral history is one of constant conflict with other tribes. After they reached the region near the Tapajós, they fought with the white Indians (*kupen saka*) who never used *urucum* body paints (*Bixa orellana L.*) and who ate people. The Suya say that these are the Mundurucu. Later a witch (*wayanga*) caused another tribe to attack them, now said to be the Kren Akorore. Oral history has its imponderables, however. The Suya tell of a group called the *kupen tu-pã* (*kupen,* non-Suya; *tu-pã*, to smell) who had long noses like dogs. When an enemy approached, these Indians would run after him, track him by smell, and kill him with bows and arrows when they caught him! The Suya continued to fight, moving slowly southward until they were west of the affluents of the Xingu. Under pressure of repeated attacks they traveled east to the Xingu River system.

With the arrival of the Suya on the Xingu, oral history becomes more specific. This is because it was not very long ago and because the river provides a mnemonic device. When they arrived at their first village, they made contact with the Upper Xingu tribes. They were informed that there were more people just like them already on the Ronuro River. The two groups got together in a single large village (village 1, figure 2.4). That large village had two men's houses. Many people died there because of "Upper Xingu witchcraft" (possibly an epidemic). For that reason the village is called "the place where many of us died" (*mẽ tuk chi tà*). They moved from there to village 2 and village 3 but were harassed by Trumai attacks. To avoid Trumai harassment they moved to Diauarum (village 4).

It was while the Suya were living at the village at Diauarum that they were visited by the German explorer Karl von den Steinen on September 3-6, 1884. He was the first known white man to visit them and, until 1959, the last to do so and survive. He reports that he was invited to visit their village of nine closed houses around a plaza in which there was a wall-less house or shed.[2] People evidently slept there as well as met there. He describes the Suya as strong and relatively tall, possessing pots and hammocks but mostly sleeping on platform beds. He describes the men as having heavily scarred bodies that were painted black and red "without art" (Steinen 1942, p. 239). He estimates the total population at about 150 men, women, and children and notes that the Suya had flutes but that they were poorly made. The Suya were apparently quite conversant with the location and number of villages of the tribes upstream and for a distance downstream. They did not mention either the Juruna or the Northern Kayapo who attacked them while they were living at Diauarum, and had probably not made contact with them at the time. Von den Steinen's rather romantic account devotes more space to wondering about the grotesqueness of the Suya lip disks and about what they must think of him than to describing what he saw. Yet his account is virtually the only historical documentation for the Eastern Suya.

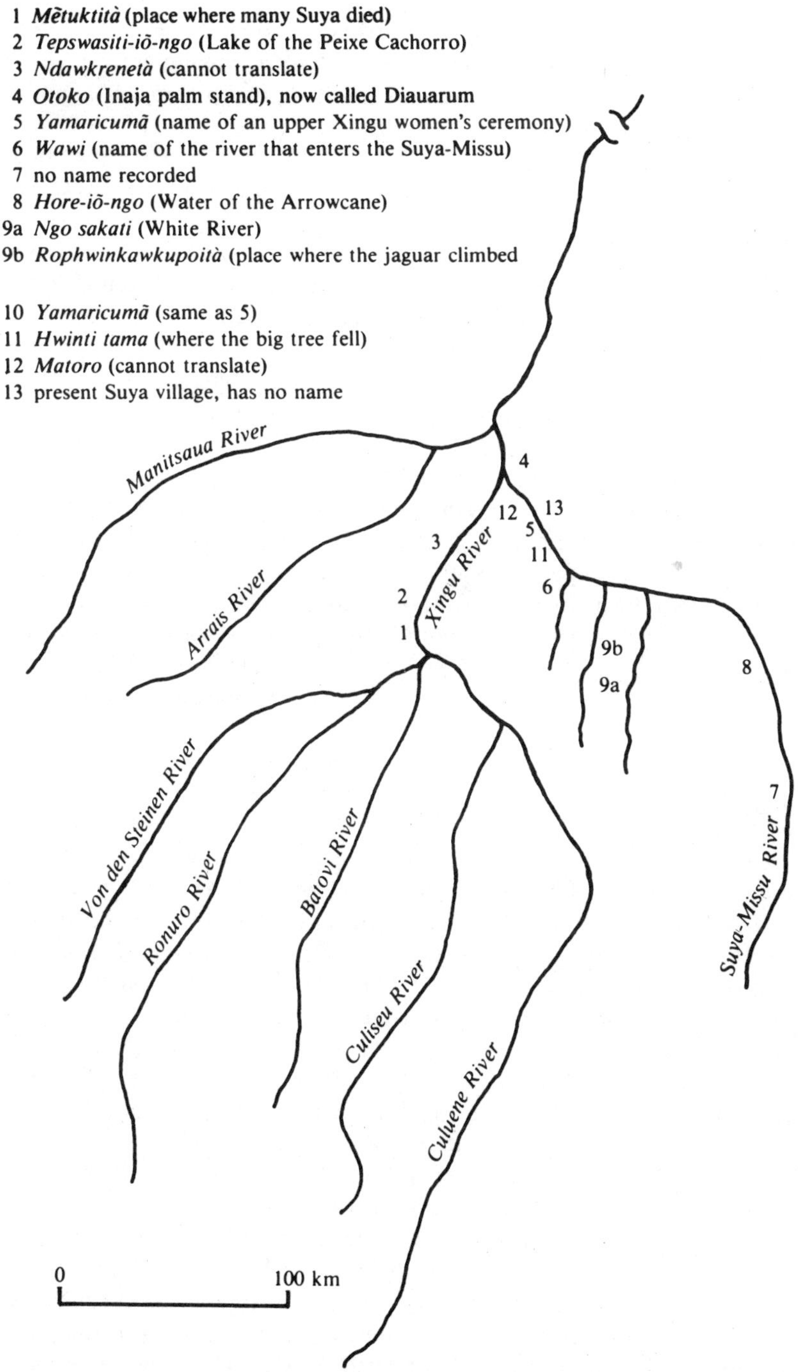

Figure 2.4 *Historical Eastern Suya village sites*

When they were still residing in Diauarum, the Suya were attacked by a number of enemies: by Juruna and Txukahamae moving upriver, probably as the result of Brazilian pressure on them, and by Upper Xingu Indians as well. They fought and later absorbed the survivors of the Manitsaua and Iaruma tribes. According to Cláudio and Orlando Villas Boas (1973, p. 35), the Suya lost nearly half of their population as the result of attacks on them at Diauarum. To escape persecution there they moved to a village called Yamuricuma (village 5), not more than a few hours' paddle up the Suya-Missu from Diauarum. While they were at Yamuricuma, they were trading with the Waura Indians for pots. They took offense at some bad pots that the Waura gave them, killed a number of Waura men, and stole a number of women and children. Partly to avoid reprisals the Suya moved their village again, this time to the Wawi River (village 6).

The village at the junction of the Wawi and the Suya-Missu rivers was a large one. Once more there were two men's houses in the plaza, one for the initiates of each ceremonial moiety—an indication of a large population. There were some factional disputes. A group of men moved their families from the main village to form a small settlement a few kilometers away, close enough to share manioc drink and sing with their relatives, but not part of the group. One man suggested that the main village was too big and proposed that they build a second village some distance away.[3] The initiates (*sikwenduyi*) of both men's houses began to cut new gardens for the second village. But then disaster stuck—two disasters in fact, both originating downstream—from which the Suya never recovered.

The first disaster was a retaliatory attack by the Juruna Indians sometime around 1915. They enlisted the help of some rubber tappers who owned Winchester .44 rifles. Juruna and rubber tappers surrounded the Suya village on the Wawi one morning before dawn. As the Suya began a morning ceremony they attacked. They killed a number of adult men, took some women and children captive, and burned the village—said to number fifteen houses—to the ground (Nimuendaju 1952, p. 433). The Juruna followed this raid with other raids, killing and capturing more Suya. As a result of the raid, the Suya divided. Some of them moved far upriver to found small villages (7 and 8), while others who had relatives among the Upper Xingu tribes moved in with them for a few years. The Suya finally regrouped at village 8.

The second disaster for the Suya occurred when a number of families were on an expedition to gather *piqui* fruit near Diauarum. They were attacked by a band of Northern Kayapo who killed some adult men and took a large number of women and children. Only a few young men were able to escape. The genealogy in appendix A clearly shows how many women and children were lost to the Northern Kayapo.

The second raid left the Suya with a shortage of women. The chiefs decided to raid the Waura again for captives and managed to abduct four women and a young boy at the cost of only one warrior. By raiding the Waura, rather than another Upper Xingu tribe, they obtained women who could make clay pots. They thus freed themselves from the obligation of trading for pots. On another occasion the Suya captured a number of Northern Kayapo women and children. Fearing retaliatory raids, they constructed a new village in a maze of small rivers and *buriti*-palm swamps off the Suya-Missu. There they escaped detection until a reconnaissance plane flew over their village. In the two or three years between the time the plane flew over the Suya and their encounter with the Villas Boas brothers, the village split and some families moved to village 9b.

Suya history before their peaceful contact with an expedition led by the Villas Boas in 1959 was one of considerable conflict. Fighting was not continuous; there were long periods of relative peace. Yet during the century following Von den Steinen's visit a number of tribes disappeared completely. The Suya barely survived, and only at the expense of their enemies. They were the scourge of the Upper Xingu tribes, especially the Trumai (Murphy and Quain 1955), and they incorporated survivors and captives from a number of other tribes into their population. Captives introduced new ideas, new songs, and new technology. From the Indians of the Upper Xingu the Suya learned to sleep in hammocks, to prepare their manioc in the style of the Upper Xingu, and to perform new ceremonies.

Although the Suya continued to initiate men after the Juruna and Northern Kayapo raids, there were few left to initiate. Several ceremonies were never performed after the Juruna and their rubber tapper allies raided the village on the Wawi. When the Suya lived on the Wawi River they controlled the earth, at least all that they needed. Now, especially with the specter of Brazilian encroachment, the Suya feel defeated, demoralized, and without much hope for the future.

The Suya were discovered by aerial reconnaissance. The actual work of pacification was accomplished by their traditional enemies, the Juruna, who took one of their Suya captives to the village in the swamp (9b) to explain the new situation in the Xingu. The captive told the Suya of the wonderful gifts of the Villas Boas and of how they were good to Indians, not like rubber tappers. She said the Villas Boas would soon visit the Suya and bring them presents. The Suya at that time were living in two villages. The farther village could not be reached by motorboat, so the families living in it agreed to stay at the first village to await the Villas Boas. Finally they heard the motorboat laboring up the twisting rivers. From the outset contact was peacful. After a few days, during which the

Suya sang for the Villas Boas party and gifts were exchanged, the expedition returned to Diauarum. At the request of the Villas Boas, the Suya agreed to move closer to Diauarum and to live in a single village. They resolved to move to their old village site of Yamuricuma.

While they were still living in a temporary shelter at Yamuricuma, the late ethnographer Harald Schultz visited them and published what he saw in two articles (Schultz 1960-61, 1962). In Schultz's census the tribe numbered sixty-five persons. The Suya were living in temporary shelters, making long trips to get food from their old gardens. Schultz was there only during the dry season; as a result his information is very sketchy. Amadeu Lanna, now professor of anthropology at the University of São Paulo, did some fieldwork among the Suya in 1962 and 1963. The Suya were only then consolidating into a single permanent village, a small one of only three houses. Like Schultz, and like myself on my first visit, Lanna stayed with the Suya only during the dry season, when their ceremonial life is at a minimum and they spend most of their time hunting, fishing, and gathering. He had no opportunity to observe the functioning of the moieties, plaza groups, name groups, and formal ceremonial relationships. This resulted in a number of inaccuracies in his reports on the Suya (Lanna 1967).

Within six years after they moved to Yamuricuma, all the older Suya men died of disease (243, 233, 204, 201). The Suya moved farther from Diauarum, to Hwin-ji-tama (village 11). There they constructed a small, four-house village with a men's house in the center. They remained there only a year or two. It was difficult to vaccinate and treat them at that distance from Diauarum. Fearing encroachments by Brazilian ranchers on their village, which was close to the margins of the reserve, and feeling the necessity of having the Suya closer to Diauarum, Cláudio Villas Boas convinced the Suya to move again. This they did, first building a village on the left bank of the Suya-Missu (village 12). That village was built on sloping, sandy soil and proved unsuitable. When the survivors of the Western Suya joined the Suya in the reserve, the united groups constructed a new, large village only slightly upstream of the unsuitable one, a move that required no new gardens (village 13).

There is little information about the Western Suya prior to their tragic contact with Brazilians. For decades they fought encroaching Brazilians and were repeatedly attacked in retaliation, their villages burned, their children killed. When the weakened tribe began to make peaceful contact with some local Brazilians, they were fed poisoned tapir meat and many members of one band died. Around 1968 they were contacted by a government pacification team. Tragically, a reporter infected some of the still suspicious Indians with a flu virus. They returned to their villages and died in large numbers. The survivors of this once powerful tribe were completely demoralized. They were taken to join the Eastern Suya in the

Xingu reserve where their health and well-being are protected. The elderly continue to succumb to pneumonia and the complications of malaria and flu, but the birth rate and low infant mortality rate are allowing them to increase under the present administration of the Xingu reservation.

The National Indian Agency (FUNAI) estimates of the Western Suya population in the 1960s were as high as 1200. My genealogies indicate that an estimate of about 400 would have been more reasonable. Of the estimated 400 living at the time of their poisoning, only 41 lived to arrive in the Xingu reserve. A few ran away from the men bringing them to the Xingu reserve and died before any expedition went to look for them. It is impossible to listen to the Western Suya tales of killing and being killed without attributing the horror of their decimation to a combination of inadequate protection by the Indian bureau, the rapacity of local settlers, and the weakness of the pacification team. Within a few years more than 90 percent of the population died or was killed.

Social Environment of the Xingu Reservation

When the Suya moved into the Xingu reservation (figure 2.5), they entered into a fairly complex set of relationships with the administration of the reserve and also with the other tribes who live within it in closer proximity to each other than they traditionally would have tolerated.

The administration of the reservation supplies the Suya with trade goods on an irregular basis. These are purchased with funds from the Brazilian government. It also provides some medical treatment. Very sick Indians can be taken to São Paulo hospitals for treatment, and during epidemics planeloads of medicines and teams of doctors are flown in to assist the regular nurses. In addition, the administration provides intangibles: approval and support for certain leaders, visits from people staying at the posts which usually involves some trading, and even such minor but enjoyable benefits as a ride in the post motorboat when there is a shortage of canoes.

In return the administration expects the tribes to be peaceful, remain within the boundaries of the reserve, help with jobs around the posts, and man pacification expeditions to contact still uncontacted Indians. For more than a year during my stay, various groups of Suya men were on an expedition to pacify the Kren Akorore. Every man younger than thirty-five and over fifteen had been on an earlier expedition to contact the same tribe. These expeditions were one of the main vehicles through which the Suya learned Portuguese and learned about the ways of Brazilians and began to emulate them.

The administration of the Xingu reservation espouses a policy of noninterference in tribal affairs. Noninterference has real meaning

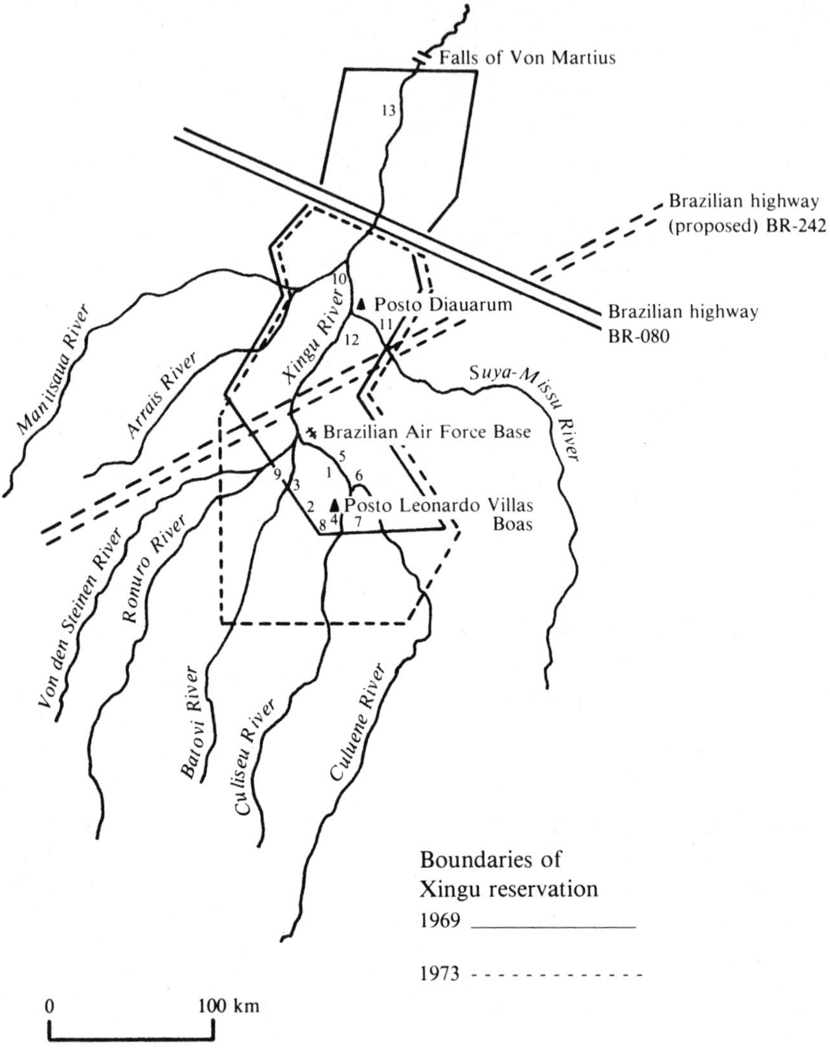

Figure 2.5 *Xingu reservation, showing tribes in region. (1) Txikao. (2) Yawalipiti. (3) Kamayura. (4) Mehinacu. (5) Matipu. (6) Kalapalo. (7) Kuikuru. (8) Aweti. (9) Waura. (10) Juruna. (11) Suya. (12) Kayabi. (13) Txukahamai (Northern Kayapo). From Junqueira (1973, p. 11).*

primarily in a comparative sense. Most administration posts in Brazil, run by missionaries or FUNAI bureaucrats, impose new forms, new ideas, and alien work styles on the natives. This is not true in the Xingu reservation except in a fairly mild form. Missionaries are not allowed to proselytize. There are no schools, no prisons, and no Indian guards (described vividly in Hanbury-Tenison 1973, p. 104). This is not to say that there is no intervention in the lives of the Indians. There is. The administrators' ideas about witchcraft and infanticide are supposed to be respected. Still, the tribes are not entirely peaceful, and they kill their witches and bury their undesirable children. The Suya were urged to discontinue their custom of piercing boys' lips in the interests of their eventual integration into Brazilian society. Non-Suya as a rule find lip disks ugly and disgusting. The administration also groomed the son of the strongest chief as a leader of the village and communicated with the tribe through him.[4]

The administration, until very recently the exclusive supplier of trade goods, controls the entry of outsiders into the reservation. Only in the past several years have other representatives of Brazilian society entered the region. Cláudio Villas Boas, who commands great respect among the Suya, led the expedition that first contacted them. As codirector of the reservation, he gave the Suya presents and nursed them when they were sick. The old men of the tribe called him brother and all the Suya now call him father. He acted much as a Suya chief is supposed to behave: he talked, exhorted, and chastised. He also mediated between tribes and between the Indians and the Brazilians. Prior to 1975, when the Suya were in Diauarum they often gathered in Cláudio Villas Boas's house at night. There, by the light of a flickering kerosene wick, he read and talked with them for hours. He advised them how to handle the influx of Brazilians, how to maintain corporate identity, and how to continue peaceful relations with other Indian groups. The Suya admire Cláudio because he stayed to help them while others came and went. They feared his anger because they feared the loss of the privileges and presents that they enjoyed. And they ultimately feared his departure from the Xingu and loss of their lands and their rights.

The Suya had some grievances against the administration. While they willingly did odd jobs around Diauarum, they were not always eager to join the Villas Boas brothers on the second Kren Akorore expedition. They did so only when Cláudio sent a radio request with the names of individual men whom he invited (he did not order them) to join him. The administration has also been behind the Suya move to the present village near Diauarum where the land is not very good. During my visit the supply of trade goods at Diauarum was faltering. Since the tribes were no longer a threat to Brazilians in the interior, it was increasingly hard for the Villas Boas to obtain money to keep up with the Suya's growing taste for trade goods. Cláudio knew the Suya made occasional forbidden trading expeditions to the ranches being cleared outside the reservation. The visits were clandestine, all male, and brief.

The Villas Boas brothers retired from active control over the Xingu reservation in 1974, and until 1979 Olympio Serra was in charge of the region. He was capable and imaginative, but he lacked the long familiarity of the Villas Boas. The Suya, on my last visit, were still waiting to see what they thought of his efforts. Olympio had plans to introduce rice production and elementary education in the region, and the Suya were interested but cautious. They have recently suffered some minor conflicts with the ranchers who occupy their former territory, beyond the reservation boundaries. Because of the strong economic interests that threaten any Indian land the future of the Xingu reservation is always in question, and the Suya have some reason to be concerned for their future.

In 1975 the Suya were given the additional task of hosting the survivors of the Kren Akorore tribe which had been transferred to the Xingu reservation. How the Suya ended up with this is a case study in itself, and I shall merely add it as one of the responsibilities they have had within the Xingu reservation. Although the Kren Akorore were something of an economic burden, they were also interesting—especially to the Suya men, who, much to the disgust of their wives and lovers, found Kren Akorore women irresistible. In 1977 the Kren Akorore planted their own gardens some distance from the Suya and constructed a new village of their own, on the Xingu River, and that brief period of intense interaction and responsibility has ceased.

Each of the five tribes that live in the northern part of the Xingu reservation has a territory of its own. The Suya live on, and consider their territory to be, the Suya-Missu River with the exception of a couple of kilometers near the mouth which are utilized by people at Diauarum for fishing. Although the territories are largely respected, the relations of the Suya with their neighbors are marked by caution. Two of the groups, the Txukahamae group of the Northern Kayapo and the Juruna, are most numerous and have threatened the Suya in the past. The fourth group, the Kren Akorore, is a recent arrival.

Diauarum is an important arena for interethnic relations. To Diauarum come visitors to the Xingu reservation: doctors, scientists, industrialists, and journalists. In their contact with non-Indians the Suya have always been the recipients of gifts. They visit Diauarum to look at the strangers and to obtain trade goods. When Cláudio Villas Boas was away from Diauarum there were fewer visitors, thus fewer outsiders with whom to trade. In general, I suspect that outsiders visited the Suya less frequently once the Suya gained a taste for clothing and wore clothes instead of going naked and painted as they had in the past. The tribes also meet in Diauarum and trade with each other. Far more rarely do they visit each other's villages. The Suya go to Diauarum to use the Kayabi curers when they are sick; the Juruna like to use Suya curing chants. Diauarum provides a neutral ground on which the different tribes feel fairly secure.

Since 1975 the Indian societies in the northern part of the Xingu reservation have increasingly developed a feeling of solidarity in opposition to the threat posed by the whites, be these ranchers invading their lands or new and unwanted FUNAI administrators. This is part of a growing Indian movement, as yet new and fragile, which seeks to find a way to ensure self-determination for the groups without loss of their collective rights to land and assistance from the federal government. This, in itself, is an interesting and important development, but one too new and too threatened to say much about.

The Suya's experience with non-Indians has been marked by traumatic population loss. They live today largely due to the protection they have received in the Xingu reservation; it is very likely that without it they would have become extinct as have so many Brazilian native societies in the past century.

At the moment the Suya are neither wholly isolated from Brazilian society nor much integrated into it. They are presented here at a specific historical moment, the time in which I had the privilege of knowing them. If I have not dwelt on the impact of Western society in my analysis, it is a theoretical option, made with the approval of the Suya: they too think their society is important and interesting in itself, not merely in relation to our own.

My analysis of Suya cosmology is not a reconstruction of a vanished society. Although Suya society may appear to be a haphazard collection of individuals, it is thought of by the Suya, and organized by them, in much the same way as it was when their population was larger and they ruled their part of the earth. Men are still talked about as members of age grades, even though there are few of them in certain grades; ceremonial organization is still important although some ceremonies have fallen into abeyance. The relations between nature and society are fundamentally the same as before; they are organizing principles used to construct and interpret the world.

3

The Domains of Time and Space

THE SUYA DIVIDE what members of Western societies usually consider a flat grid of space and a steady forward movement of time into discrete units. These units are not of equal size or duration, and they have important symbolic meanings. Since all events, both mythical and actual, occur in the contexts of time and space, all aspects of social organization and behavior are embedded in the meaning-laden categories of time and space. The meaning of an action depends partly on its context within these categories.

Time

The Suya have two ways of reckoning time. One is the cyclical pattern of natural phenomena and the other is the relationship of certain events to other noncyclical, historical events or the historical individual life cycle. David Pocock (1964) is correct in stressing the importance of events in time reckoning, as well as the cosmological notions advanced by Edmund Leach (1966). Neither way of reckoning time is itself an adequate representation of Suya concepts.

The Suya have no abstract notion of time as a continuous procession, but associate it with the periodicities of sun, moon, season, and life cycle as well as discrete historical events. Their concepts of space are similarly concrete and cannot be readily separated from the village plan. This correlation of time with specific periodic events and space within the village is due not to vagueness or lack of precision but to a concreteness in the way the Suya talk about space and time (Lévi-Strauss 1966c, chap. 1).

Time past and time future are of relatively shallow depth when contrasted with some African tribal societies, for example the Tiv (Bohannon 1952). Only one man could name his third ascending generation kinsman (his great-grandfather) without hesitation, and he had good political reasons for remembering since some of the legitimacy of his chieftainship depended on the relationship. Everyone else who could grasp what I meant when I asked about third ascending generation relatives said, "I do not know," and often added, "I never saw them." The past quickly becomes generalized; specific figures are not very important.

Suya speech about the past is contextual. The word *tarama* means "in the past" anywhere between yesterday and the beginning of social life as it is known. A stronger emphasis may be given to the second syllable (*taráááma*) instead of *tarama*) but the emphasis on the middle syllable may be used to distinguish the beginning of the world from the recent past as well as to distinguish a month ago from a week ago. Some confusion is avoided by reference to historic events.

The historic events used by the Suya to date other events include village sites (where the Suya were living when a certain event occurred), the massacre of the Suya by the Juruna and their rubber tapper allies, and the peaceful contact made by the Villas Boas brothers, which marked the start of their association with non-Indians. In addition they often refer to an eclipse of the sun, which no living Eastern Suya saw but the oldest Western Suya witnessed, to place events in time.

The Suya have no creation myth in which the world or mankind is created. The natural or physical world was always substantially the way it is now. The most distant past is therefore a mythical time in which men and animals were more like each other than they are today. The cultural world was unformed. Men ate raw or sun-dried meat, had no gardens, and were without names. They could transform themselves easily into animals, and they did not die.

The establishment of society as it is today is told in a group of separate myths. Fire is obtained from the jaguar, maize from the mouse, gardens are planted, an old woman instructs men about eating fruit, a captive enemy from under the earth teaches them about names, and death becomes permanent because the relatives of a man burn his belongings. These actions constitute the establishment of Suya society as it is now. It was a process of transformation. As soon as men had fire, gardens, maize, names, and funeral customs, they ceased to be so much like animals, and the distinction between men and animals is now rigidly maintained.

While Suya discussions of the past are couched in a vague, contextual *tarama,* the Suya are far more exact when discussing the future. They count, albeit laboriously, a number of days on their fingers saying "tomorrow, another tomorrow, another tomorrow, another tomorrow, this many [indicating fingers] tomorrows." Although there are words for one, two, three, four, and possibly six, everything above three is "many."

Even on their fingers the Suya get lost over seven days. Instead they indicate the future by the stages of the moon, by a number of moons, the movement of the constellations, the number of rainy seasons, or by stages in the life cycle. They frequently use these measures of time for discussing future trips, ceremonies, and the arrival of visitors.

Times of day are important in myths and ceremonies. There are many words that refer to periods during the day. The more important periods have more elaborate terminology. However precise the definitions may be in theory, the Suya are not overly rigid in their use of them. A hunt arranged for "before day" may leave after the sun has risen. When a ceremony should begin with the sun at a certain position in the sky, they may just think about beginning it at that time and actually start considerably later. The precision of Western units of time and wristwatches was a source of constant interest, although no one ever did learn to use them.

Figure 3.1 shows the important divisions of the day. Rather than use our division of the day into hours, I divide the twenty-four hour period into day and night. Since the time that the sun rises and sets varies in dif-

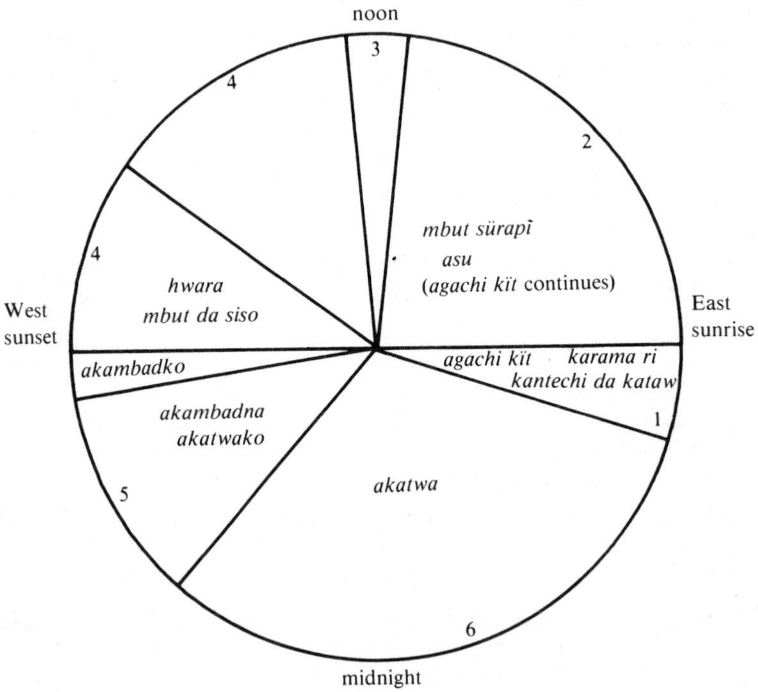

Figure 3.1 *Times of day*

ferent seasons, this is both more accurate and more convenient. Each of the time divisions is marked with a number corresponding to the following comments.

1. The first time division is the most important time of day, both in terms of ritual importance and the elaboration of terms for it. It roughly includes the time from the first light of the morning star in the east to full light just before sunrise. Terms commonly given for this period are "still dark" (*karama ri*), "not yet day" (*agachi kït*), "going toward dawn" (*asu sülü*) and less often used but given by informants "not yet daylight" (*asu karama kïtïli*).

2. During the day, time is usually marked by the position of the sun. Instead of naming the positions, the Suya usually indicate a time with a gesture and say "the sun there" (*mbut ta one*), but there are ways to refer to times of day: "the sun is recently risen," "the sun is rising in the sky," and "the sun is really high," which is used to emphasize that it is late. These three divisions of the morning are not often used in conversation or myth.

3. When the sun is roughly overhead it is said to be in the "center of the sky" (*kaikwa ihogri*). This is also a ceremonially important time.

4. The afternoon is marked by the descending movement of the sun. I could elicit a number of terms for the degrees of afternoon, but there was only one important one, *hwara*. Depending on the context this could be between 3:30, when the shadows were long, until sunset. In addition to that often used form were precise ways about talking about afternoon: "the sun is descending" (*mbut ta sisò*), "the sun is really descending" (*mbut ta sisò-kumeni*), "the sun is about to come down to earth" (*mbut ta rü sülü*), "the sun has reached earth" (*hen mbut ta rü*), and "sunset" (*hwara mbedili*).

5. As soon as the sun sets, the light diminishes noticeably. Evening is called *akambadna*. This is an important time of day, and there are several terms for it.

6. *Akatwa* means "very late at night." It is an undifferentiated period and continues until the light in the east which precedes the rise of the morning star. Nights are less differentiated than the day unless there is a moon, when the times are measured by the moon's position. When the moon is new, its position at dusk and the time of its setting are used to mark time. When it is full, it is used much as the sun. When it is waning, the time of its rising is most often used. An important indication of time since contact and the subsequent adaption of chickens as domestic animals are the first crows of the few chickens that the Suya were raising. An early hunt could be agreed on for "the crow of the rooster" (*kara-kara-ko kà*).

The points of transition from night to day and morning to afternoon are the ritually important periods. The importance of transitional periods is also notable in the seasons. The period before dawn, the late afternoon, and the time when the sun is overhead are all important. The Suya say that no rituals begin in the morning hours after sunrise. Rituals must start either before dawn or in the afternoon.

These transitional times are ordered in importance. If a rite is performed at all it is usually performed before dawn (1). If it is repeated at all during the day, it is in the afternoon or evening (4 or 5). If it is performed three times, the third time is when the sun is overhead (3). Young men living in the men's house were supposed to sing at each of those times. Keening occurs at the same times, as do various purification rites, though they are most common at dawn and optional at the other two times.

Finally, the other periodic events used to reckon time are the position of the Pleiades, the rainy and dry seasons, and the human life cycle. Phases of the moon are used to mark time, such as the return of a hunting or fishing expedition. Although lunar cycles are sometimes used to make observations about the annual cycle (as in "two moons and the rain will fall"), more frequently seasons are predicted by the position of the Pleiades.

The Pleiades are said to be the circular design on the underside of the lip disk of a young Suya man (of the *sikwenduyi* age grade) in the sky. The word for the design on the underside of Suya lip disks is the same as that for the Pleiades (*ngroro*). As the Pleiades appear farther and farther toward the western horizon in the evening, the Suya frequently comment on how soon it will be the dry season. They say, "When the Pleiades are far over there, it is already the dry season." When the Pleiades begin to rise just before dawn, it is time to finish cutting the gardens. When they are fairly high in the sky at dawn, it is time to burn the gardens and plant. When they are setting just before dawn, the rains begin and the rainy season rituals commence.

The annual cycle of rainy and dry seasons is paralleled by a cycle of available foods. This combined cycle is important, and any Suya can describe the year in terms of the rains and the flooding, the foods that he eats, the rituals that should be performed, and the position of the Pleiades. This interrelationship is shown in table 3.1.

During the year, the ritually stressed periods are the beginning of the dry season and the beginning of the rainy season, as well as the ripening of the corn. Ritual activity falls to a minimum during the dry season.

The life cycle is important in discussing time. It is marked by a series of discrete stages. The beginning of each stage is marked by a rite of passage: birth, the start of sexual activity, the first child, the first man killed, old age, and death. One informant stressed the cyclical nature of these periods. He said that young men would enter the men's house, then they would father several children, and as younger men left the men's

Table 3.1. Annual cycle of seasons, subsistence, and ceremonies

	Jan	Feb	March	April	May	June	July	Aug	Sept	Oct	Nov	Dec
Rains									—variable, stormy—			
	—heavy rains—		—light rains—				—(only occasional thunderstorms)—			—light rains—	—heavy rains—	
Hunting, gathering		—turtles—						—turtle eggs—				
		—matrinchã—					timbo—			—piqui—		
							—tukunaré with arrows—					
	—fish scarce—		—hunting—		—fish scarce—					—fish scarce—		
Garden crops	—green corn—							—new manioc—				
					—sweet potatoes—							
Position of Pleiades			setting in West at night			rising in East at dawn			high in sky at dawn		setting in West at dawn	
Ceremonies	amto ngere			huru iaren mben ngere	pebji tugu			Upper Xingu ceremonies			end pebji tugu log races	
		—rainy season songs—					—tep-kradi (dry season songs)—				—rainy season songs—	
Season names	ndawiti		hen ndarare							hennda tama		ndawiti
			—nda—				—ambedi—				—nda—	
Degree of flooding			high water						low water			

house these children would enter it, as a kind of exchange for the people leaving. The image is of an endless stream of people who grow old and whose children enter the men's house and father children who themselves enter the men's house. This ideal no longer represents Suya society, but it is still held. The stages of the life cycle are used to mark certain events, as "when my father was a *sikwenduyi.*"

In sum, the Suya divide the day into several discrete periods, as they do the moon cycle, the yearly cycle, and the life cycle. Certain parts of these cycles are more meaning-laden than others. Thus dawn and dusk, the beginning of the rainy and the dry seasons, and the new moon are more often the times when rituals take place. The Suya often discuss time among themselves in the evening when they plan their activities, which are quite regular over the years and yet take considerable planning for their accomplishment. Furthermore, periods of time have multiple meanings in terms of ritual, food, weather, and astronomical events. Space has a similar multivocal quality.

Space

Gê villages impressed early visitors, and the importance given to spatial representations has a long history. Village diagrams are displayed and discussed in Nimuendaju (1939, 1941), T. Turner (1966), Maybury-Lewis (1967), Bamberger (1967), Lave (1967), Melatti (1970), and Da Matta (1976). Da Matta has also drawn an intriguing parallel between the central Brazilian societies and an imagined society in a short story by Edgar Allan Poe (Da Matta 1973).

The Suya and other Gê are especially accessible through their concepts of space because they are what might be called "this-world oriented." Their cosmological and social concepts are concretely expressed on the spatial plane; each village is the center of its own universe, relatively independent of extra-village or religious centers. In this the Gê contrast strongly with the groups of the Northwest Amazon such as the Desana, or with the Jivaro, who through their use of fermented drinks and hallucinogenic drugs make inner journeys into another reality. The Gê do not make much in the way of drinks, use hallucinogens, or even usually have tobacco before contact. Those that go to another world (in the case of certain ritual specialists) report that it is structured in the same way as the one on earth.

Lévi-Strauss, in his insightful analysis of space and social organization "Do Dual Organizations Exist?" (1963, chap. 8), draws much of his evidence from central Brazil. He departs from an observation by Paul Radin that the Winnebago Indians drew diagrams of their villages in two different ways, which Lévi-Strauss calls concentric and diametric. The Suya also have both a concentric and diametric aspect of space.

The most important spatial referent is the Suya village. It is the realm of the social, of humans, and is opposed to the surrounding forest, which is the realm of nature. A series of concentric rings, spatial categories based on the opposition of village and forest, mediate the two opposed poles. This is the concentric model of space. It is complicated by the opposition of east and west at a number of different levels. Among the Suya, diametrical space usually contrasts two relatively equal aspects of human society instead of nature and society.

The Eastern Suya refer to themselves as *mẽ kin seji*, which best translates as "people of the large round village places." One informant said that they gave themselves this name because they made large villages and cut all the trees around the village as well.

In terms of concentric space, six separable categories may be distinguished, as shown in the schematic diagram in figure 3.2.

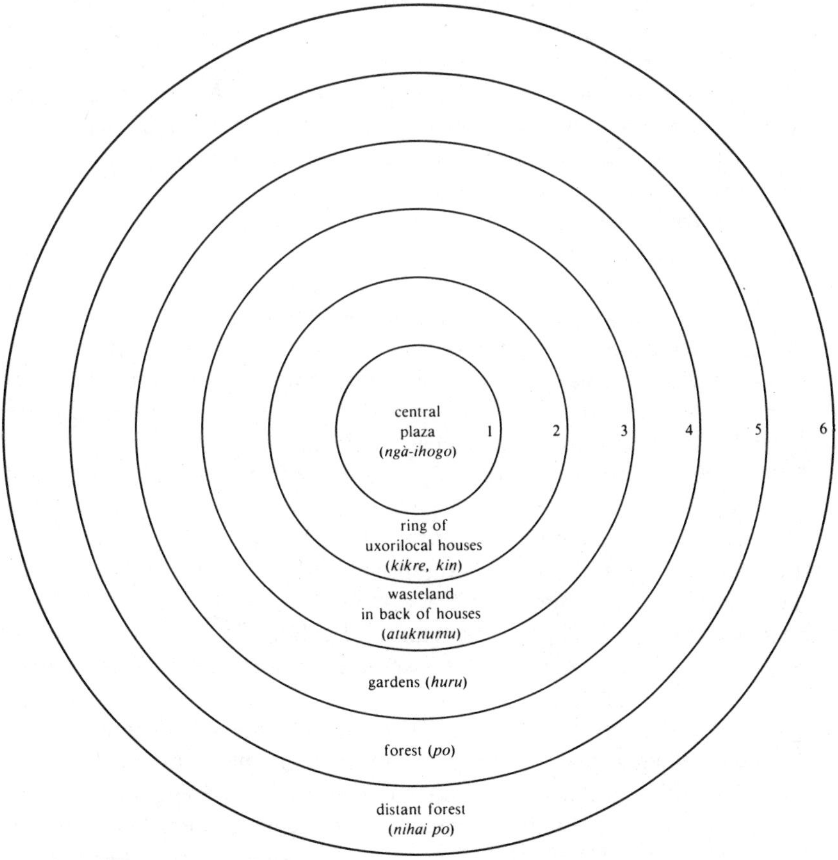

Figure 3.2 *Concentric categories of space*

The center of the village (1) is called the *ngà-ihogo*, or "center of the plaza" (*ngà*). Depending on the context, *ngà-ihogo* refers either to the whole plaza inside the peripheral paths connecting adjacent houses or to just the very center of it. The *ngà-ihogo* is an important ritual space and is usually kept clear of all vegetation, special care being taken to clear it in ceremonial periods. The center of the plaza is the location of the nightly men's council, which is often carefully located at the point of confluence of lines drawn from the doors of opposing pairs of houses. Children and women may be chased from the men's council area, and women usually meet at night in houses. The *ngà-ihogo* in the larger sense of the entire plaza always contains one or two men's houses, called *ngàwe*. The Western Suya always had a single men's house located in the center of the plaza. The Eastern Suya constructed two when the village had a large population, and they always had at least one, located to one side of the center of the plaza in symbolic opposition to the (absent) second men's house, as in figure 2.2. The men's house possesses most of the attributes of the center of the plaza. It is a male domain. Girls and women and children may be chased away from it. A part of all major ceremonies occurs in the *ngàwe* where, until a few years ago, young men lived after their lips had been pierced and before they fathered a child and moved to their wives' houses.

Chiefs (*mẽropakande*), their wives, their sons, and their daughters may be buried in the plaza (*ngà-ihogo*). This distinguishes them from the rest, who are buried in their houses. The burial site of chiefs is congruent with the importance of the plaza as a political arena as well as a region that transcends the kinship ties of the houses. *Mẽropakande,* their wives, and their children play a role in the village above and beyond their kinship ties. A chief's kinship ties are extremely important, however, and are an ambivalent feature in the concept of leadership.

The second important zone (2) is the *kin,* the circle of uxorilocal residential houses which are arranged lengthwise around the plaza with their major entrance onto the plaza. This zone includes the area inside the circle of houses but outside the peripheral paths linking the doors of the houses. The area immediately in front and in back of the houses is kept clear by the members of each house. Each house is a named, extended family residence in which (ideally) live an old couple, their married daughters and their husbands and children. The ring of houses and the spaces immediately in front and in back of them are a domestic and female-dominated area. Women spend most of their time in this area, preparing manioc, spinning cotton, caring for the children, and performing other tasks. At night women and children sit and talk, watch ceremonies, and sing Upper Xingu songs in front of the houses.

The houses figure in certain ceremonies when some singing is done inside each one. There is, however, a clear opposition of the residential circle and the men's house and plaza.

The *atuknumu* (3) is rarely referred to, though it appears in one of the Suya myths. It is the zone of wasteland in back of the houses. The area behind each house is a more private domain than the area in front of it. Private rituals and activities the Suya do not want everyone to know about occur behind the houses: ritual baths and leg scraping of people formally in seclusion as well as some cooking and eating of food. Beyond the cleared place and a few planted trees lies a scrubby area where refuse is dumped, people defecate, and some lovemaking occurs at night. That zone is the *atuknumu* proper. The particle *tuk* when it appears separately has meanings including "death" and "black." One informant said that the wasteland is called the *atuknumu* because "there are no people out there." It is an area of human waste and often illicit affairs. It ends where the gardens (*huru*) begin. In 1972 some of the houses had gardens directly behind them and their *atuknumu* was off to one side rather than directly in back.

Gardens, *huru* (4), surround the Suya village on three sides; the river flows on the fourth. Without the river, the gardens would form another concentric ring. Gardens, like the houses, "belong" to women. Sexual relations, both licit and illicit, usually occur in the more distant gardens during the day and the nearer ones in the darkness. Women consider the gardens frightening, and a woman does not go there alone for fear of spirits (*mẽgaron*), but group excursions are common. In 1972 some gardens lay more than a thirty minutes' walk from the village. In 1976 some were far more distant. The Suya say that when the gardens get too far away, they move their village.

Beyond the gardens lies the forest (*pò*) (5). In some past villages there was also open savannah (*sika*). These are the domains of wild animals that are hunted and wild products that are gathered. The Suya usually clear narrow trails through their thorny jungle for ease of hunting. The vicinity of the village is hunted especially for birds and for animals that raid the gardens. Collective hunts go farther afield, usually by paddling to some location away from the village before beginning the hunt. Longer excursions of a week or several weeks go to yet greater distances. The jungle is considered a decidedly antisocial zone in which men may be transformed into animals, kill their affines, and do other antisocial things. The Suya frequently report signs of enemies lurking, and a number of monsters are said to intrude into the nearby forests as well. The Suya name many of the features of the river and many parts of the jungle itself. Space is named beyond the gardens, and naming is one of the things that distinguishes the "near forest" from the "distant forest" (*nihai pò*), which has no place names.

The distant forest, *nihai pò* (6), is the dwelling place of various types of monsters that the Suya talk about and tell tales about. These include cannibal monsters, monkey-like humans who live in trees but turn into butterflies when shot, and bad women with penises on their thighs who live far to the east. Now that the Brazilians are known to have moved into much of the distant land, the Suya say that most of the mythical beasts have been killed by the intruders.

This distant realm of monsters is the last in the Suya concentric concept of space on the two-dimensional plane. They also have some ideas about vertical space. The sky, shaped like a bowl, comes down to earth at the sides. Directly above the village is the village of the dead, reached by going east, climbing a tree, and returning to the middle of the sky. Underneath the earth is another world similar to the Suya world. The Suya were once attacked by members of a tribe living under the earth, but they retaliated and killed all except a young boy who taught them about naming and naming ceremonies. These are the only important vertical dimensions. The Suya thus may be contrasted with other groups in Brazil which have more elaborate cosmologies.

The house itself has several important spatial domains. Every house opens onto the public side (the plaza) and onto the private side (in back). There is a contrast between inside (*kre kàmà*) and outside (*sika kàmà*). There is another contrast between front and back. The front, or plaza side, is called the *ngá-ihogri numu* (A in figure 3.3). The back side is called the *atuknumu* (B). Suya houses have two major roof posts in the middle of the house (C). The space between them (D), inside the en-

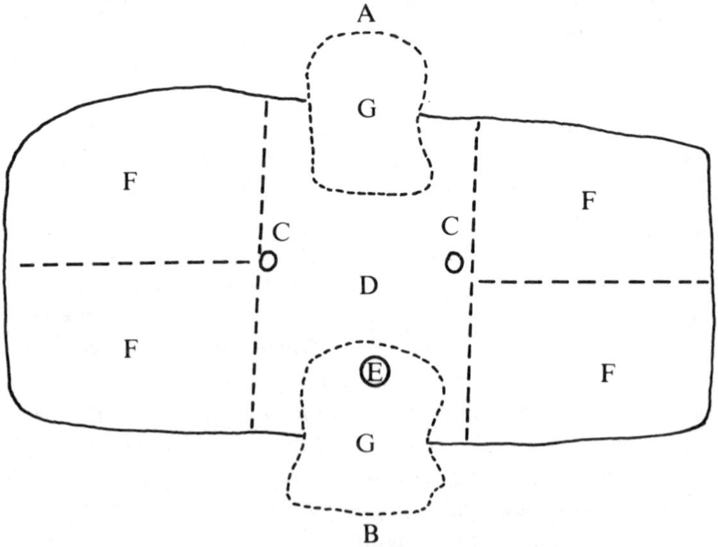

Figure 3.3 *Schematic house plan*

trance, is a public area. It is called "the center of the house" (*kikre kre ihogri*). It is the best-lit part of the house. Most formal visiting and ceremonial activity takes place there. When people are buried inside the house, they are buried inside the doorway into the back (E). The entrances themselves, "mouths" of the house (*saikwa*), include the space just inside and just outside of the entrances (G). The sleeping areas of the house are called the *tchï* (F). They are located on both ends of the house, toward walls from the center. There are two, but they may be divided so that there are four separate living spaces. They are divided in terms of use; there are no internal divisions inside a Suya house. Cooking is usually done on one hearth in each large house, the hearth being located in one of the *tchï*. This house space becomes important in discussions of kinship and figures in myths and ceremonies as well.

The diametric conception of space is dominated by the division of space into only two named directions and by the presence of spatially oriented ceremonial moieties. The two name directions are east (*kaikwa kradi*) and west (*kaikwa indaw*). North and south are referred to by a single term meaning "the edge of the sky by" (*kaikwa iaküt kodo*). East and west are not cardinal points, as on a compass, but arcs, varying according to where the sun is rising or may rise. Alternative names for the two directions are "the place where the sun rises" and "the place where the sun goes in".

The two directions are important in defining and localizing the ceremonial moieties, orienting the bodies of the dead, and in other ceremonial and life passage events. Every Suya man belongs to a ceremonial moiety by virtue of the name set that he receives shortly after birth. These are the *Ambànyi* and the *Krenyi.* The *Ambànyi* sit on the eastern side of the men's house, or if there are two men's houses they sit in the one on the eastern half of the village plaza. They are associated with the *kradi*, or beginning, not only of the sky (east) but also of the racing logs (they carry the lower part of the trunk). The *Krenyi* carry the upper part of the log (*ngwaindò*) and are associated with the "end" of the sky (*kaikwaindo*). In general, the ways in which the moieties are distinguished imply not hierarchy but rather complementary opposition. The *Ambànyi* walk counterclockwise when they sing individually in the plaza, while the *Krenyi* walk clockwise. Each moiety is the controller of a few ceremonies which the other must initiate by asking the controlling moiety for permission to perform them. They act in fairly symmetrical opposition.

The village plaza is conceptually divided into an eastern and a western half, each a domain of one of the moieties. This radical division of space within the plaza is most important in those ceremonies in which the Krenyi-Ambànyi moiety pair figures prominently: log races and a "small bow" ceremony. Other ceremonies involve other groups and do not emphasize the opposition of east and west to such a degree. The division of the plaza into east and west on moiety lines does not affect the residential arc because the moieties are exclusively ceremonial. They do not regulate marriage or regulate relations among persons at other than ceremonial times. Pairs of brothers usually belong to opposite moieties, and women either have no moiety affiliation or have one only because they bear male names. Women are not usually active in moiety affairs.

The residential arc also has a dyadic orientation. When the Suya construct a new village, care is taken to construct it so that pairs of houses face each other across the plaza. The doors of opposite houses should be positioned so that a line from door to door would pass through the center of the plaza where the men meet at night. There is also a diametric feature to the positioning of the houses. All Suya houses are named, and one house, "the house in which animal ceremonies are danced" (*kikre mbru kin tà*), should be in the easternmost part of the village circle. Opposite it should stand *kikre ngròye* (no meaning could be elicited for this name). In ceremonies having to do with animals, which are most of those which have not been adopted from the Upper Xingu, the men dance and sing first in "the house in which animal ceremonies are danced" and second in *kikre ngròye*. After that, they sing counterclockwise around to the other houses. In the present village *kikre ngròye* is located in the east instead of in the west because the main entrance to the village is now in the west (the river) rather than on a log-racing path entering in the east. The Suya recognize the present situation as inconsistent with the ideal but stress the importance of the spatial opposition of the houses in relation to each other, which is being practiced. Of seven former village sites that I visited, "the house where the animal ceremonies are danced" was located in the easternmost part of the circle in four, in the southernmost part in two, and in the western part only in the most recent village.

Aside from the location of certain monsters in the east and the west, I could find no larger diametrical aspects to the universe. The relation between diametric and concentric is that of the superimposition of the diametric on top of the concentric in ceremonial periods. The diametric divisions of space are associated primarily with the division of the world into two directions and of the men into moieties. The concentric model of space is based on the opposition of human society (especially masculine society) and nature (especially animals) as these domains are defined by the Suya. There is almost certainly no association of one of the men's moieties with the periphery as among some Timbira groups. Suya moieties are "of the plaza" and in concentric opposition to the women who have no moiety affiliations and to the circle of female-controlled houses.

Dyadic and concentric zones of space are carefully demarcated in ceremonies. The village plaza and entrances to the village are cleared. Greater attention is paid to keeping women and children out of men's areas. The ceremonies themselves make important use of space—camps in the forest, processions through the marginal zones and entrances through the back doors of houses, singing in the plaza and on the plaza paths, and ceremonial events in the men's house. All the spatial zones except (6) are used in most Suya ceremonies, and the spatial location of a certain part of a ceremony is important for its interpretation. The concentric and dyadic forms of space are heightened in ceremonies that deny differentiation within the spatial zones and among members of the ceremonial groups.

In nonceremonial times the concentric and dyadic divisions of space exercise a less rigid control over individual activities. There are always several possibilities for an individual actor. Through his choice of the use of space he may express individual attitudes and character. An action that is normal and evokes no comment in one domain may reveal daring, humor, originality, or other traits in another spatial domain. Sexual relations provide a good example. Having sexual relations in the gardens is normal and generally not commented on. A couple may use the house, where their activities are a subject for amusement if the walls shake or if they are seen. A "daring" or "shameless" couple may choose the edge of the plaza at night, where marks in the dust are commented on in the morning by the entire village. Under certain ceremonial circumstances sexual relations may take place in the men's house. It is precisely because of the coherence of the Suya domains of space, and the way in which they modify the significance of actions, that the anlysis of concentric and dyadic space is an important approach to these societies.

Another aspect of space reveals the operation of time and process and appears especially in the residential circle (2) and in the forest (5) or terrain surrounding the village. Far from being undifferentiated domains of space, the flexible and changing divisions of the concentric spatial domains reveal important aspects of Suya social organization. The spatial relations of houses, of residential clusters, and of gardens, and the names of places all reveal the importance of process, be it political, economic, or cosmological.

All Suya houses, not only the ones on the eastern and westernmost parts of the village arc, have names. (Figure 2.2 gives the names of the houses now appearing in the Suya village.) Two houses have alternative names due to complications arising from the widespread marriage of captives and an ensuing virilocal residence. In principle, however, a house name is matrilineal. In the village diagrams that I collected from the Western Suya, every village had groups of houses with the same name, often located in the same part of the village circle.

Named houses, or groups of houses, are exogamous. Men should only marry women of other house name groups. Members of houses with the same name also tend to share food among themselves and freely enter each others' houses. Food sharing and free entry are not characteristic of houses relatively distant from one another on the village arc. Houses, and residential clusters, are also important features in the formation of political factions. The core of most factions is, depending on the age of the leader, either a group of brothers or a father and his sons.

The Eastern and Western Suya, although at one time apparently the same group, at present have only two house names in common. There is no attempt to preserve the house name when its members seem to be on the verge of dying out, nor is there any grouping of them into larger units such as phratries or moieties. They are flexible in size—expanding over time when members have many children, disappearing when members die out. The Western Suya explained that when a house was crowded, some of its members would build a new house near it which would have the same name.

The sociological nature of these houses and residential clusters is important. Just as the concentric and dual aspects of space are associated with sex, age, and ceremonial groups, so the differentiation of residential units rests on kinship-based groups. These kinship-based groups cannot well be expressed in terms of lineage theory, nor is it really useful to think of named and house clusters as clans, since the Suya completely ignore ancestors above the third ascending generation and they do not act together as corporate groups.

Kinship relations are the key to relationships in the named houses and groups of houses, while ceremonial (naming) relationships are central to activities in the plaza. In ceremonies the particularization of residential segments is clearly denied. All the houses are entered and sung in by all the men. Food is communally distributed and eaten. Thus in ceremonial periods the concentric units of space, including that of the houses, are homogeneous. Correspondingly, the named houses and groups of houses play very little role in ceremonies. There is no painting style appropriate to them, nor do they dance as groups. Kinship, physical identity, politics, and economic relations of nonceremonial periods are deemphasized in ceremonies where groups are based on other forms of recruitment (names), presided over by ceremonial leaders, utilizing different types of exchange for food.

Residential clusters have been described for the Kraho and Krikati. Although they are neither necessarily corporate nor permanent, the residential segments of the Suya, Kraho, and Krikati villages are important social units. They are not timeless features of the Northern Gê as are the name sets. Instead these are relatively transient groups operating in the social and political (but not ceremonial) life of the village.

Just as houses are individualized, so are the gardens. Each nuclear family plants its own gardens, whose produce is distributed through elaborate networks to various social groups, depending on the product. The men, when asked about the identity of a garden, usually give the name of the man who cut it. The women give the name of the woman who has primary rights over its products. A person can be criticized for his appearance in the wrong garden. Although they are used for only two or three years, present and past gardens belonging to different families are clearly defined locations in the area surrounding the village.

For the Suya who have lived on the Xingu and Suya-Missu rivers during the last 130 years or so, the rivers and surrounding forests are familiar and named. To take a long hunting-fishing-gathering trip with some Suya is to be introduced to their history, their geography, and their perception of space outside the village. Place names are considered an important part of a person's knowledge, and children are taken on long trips by their relatives (fathers or mother's brothers) so that they will learn to identify the locations and learn the oral history attached to particular spots. On several such journeys I was given the names of these locations and later required to recite them in the men's circle and was quizzed about them: "What was the name of the place where we ate fish?" or "What was the name of the place we caught piranha and slept?" Part of my education as a "person who did not know anything" was to learn the names of the places I visited.

Table 3.2 gives the names of a stretch of river lying between the present village and former villages of the Suya, told to me on a two-week hunting-fishing and gathering trip in 1972. I was given forty-six place names. Twelve of them refer to places where a certain kind of game is found in abundance: "the water (river or lake) of the turtle" or "place where the *tukunaré* gather." Roughly seventeen (there is some overlap with the previous group) memorialize certain actions of "old Suya" ancestors. These include places such as the one "where the honey was robbed," which refers to an expedition of belligerent Suya who paddled all night and left the river at the place to go far inland to rob honey after which they returned and continued paddling. Others refer to places where logs were cut for log races, and so on. Another type of name refers to geographical peculiarities: "place where the water turns" refers to a very sharp bend in the river with strong eddies. There are ten of this type. A residual category consists of place names that I wrote down without noting their significance. I was not interested in these names at the time and did not pay as much attention to them as I have since. I am therefore not sure of the referents for nine named places.

Place names are constantly being generated. New ones are being given, and old ones may be forgotten. Certainly older men know more place names than younger men. Number 3, "place where the coati was killed," refers to a part of the river that had previously not been named or whose name had been forgotten. The year before we paddled by it, the strongest political leader had killed a coati there. The man we were with told me that he now called it "the place where the coati died."

Table 3.2 Suya place names

1 *Ngwa kuhu tà*: "log-wrapping place"; where Suya cut logs for a log race several decades ago
2 *Ambe tukti iõ ngo*: "water of the sarapo"; where there are many sarapo fish
3 *Komduho iõ ngo*: "water [lake or part of river] of the stringray"; where there are many stingrays
4 *ngwa ro hwin hrechi tà*: "log-wrapping place"; where Suya raced with logs several decades ago
5 *likso katòrochi tà*: "place where inajá palms grow"
6 *ngwachi tà krã sülü tà*: "log-racing path head"; the starting point of a Suya log race several decades ago. Names a small river
7 *tawm mbed niaho*: (?)
8 *kwàrãchi kachi tà*: "place where there are many *peixe pintado* fish"
9 *ngo kika hone*: (?)
10 *rum swa ku*: "eat *sauva*"; place where Suya once ate many *sauva* ants
11 *krã grã mbedi*: (?)
12 *rop hwinkò kupoi tà*: "place where the jaguar climbed into the canoe"; also names a village site at this location
13 *sàg santoretà*: "place where birds were shot" (by Suya ancestors)
14 *kahranti kre*: "The turtles' deep"; where there are many water turtles
15 *haw kro*: (?)
16 *ngrõch iõ ngo*: "water of the *piau* fish"
17 *po iõ ngo*: "the river of the forest"
18 *hwinkò kambrikchi iõ ngo hwa kradi*: "beginning of the lake of the red canoe"
19 *kupen wumba mẽ krĩ tà*: "where the Suya camped when they were afraid of their enemies"; names a specific lake
20 *ngo taküti*: "strong-smelling water" (?)
21 *ngo twa si*: "water of the small tooth" (?)
22 *amtüia sàk tà*: place where wasps stung Suya ancestors, several decades before
23 *hore ho sin krowe*: "small arrowcane grows"; lake where small arrowcane is gathered
24 *kukwoiti iõ ngo*: "water of the monkeys"
25 *kambere ko*: "stand of bacaba palms"
26 *wausü da krãta*: "corn is cut down"; a place where the now extinct Iaruma planted corn but the corn burned before harvest
27 *tep si kambrikchi iõ ngo*: "water of the *matrichan* fish"
28 *kupen tük huru*: "black Indians' garden"; a place where the now extinct Iaruma had cut gardens.
29 *ngo sàgna*: "falling water" (a small rapids)
30 *hware kasàgnà*: "bad stream"; a stream that a witch spat into and the water became "bad"
31 *kahran kukrechi iõ ngo*: "water of the turtle"
32 *huru kaikawchidà*: "poor garden"; a place where old Suya planted gardens but nothing grew
33 *karaí sülükwẽ*: "Whiteman's sleeping place"; site of an abandoned ranch
34 *mben iahok tà*: "place where honey was robbed" by "old Suya"

Table 3.2 (continued)

35 *Mbüdlü piri tà*: "where a man called Moon was killed" by the Juruna Indians early in this century
36 *mben iahok tà hware*: "river near place where honey was robbed"
37 *hwinti tàma*: "Where the big tree fell"
38 *wunditi ñiwhedi*: "fly larva made it"; refers to a small lake shaped like a donut
39 *hw̥àt krã to niuru*: (?)
40 *ngo ru*: "long lake"; a long thin lake
41 *hwinkrã poro ñiwhedi*: "where we made arrow whistles"; refers to a time when Suya ancestors made whistles for arrows in this place
42 *Kwarakwara*: stream with sweet cold water (?)
43 *nga kaikepti*: "turning water" (sharp bend in river)
44 *swakõ pĩrità*: "where the coati died"; where a man recently killed a coati
45 *samdawti kusei*: "the *tukunare* fish gather"
46 *kràt-ti iõ ngo tà piri*: "place where you leave river to get to lake of the *traira* fish"

Inland regions were also named. Since most of my longer journeys with the Suya were made in canoes, I do not know the inland names as well as those of the rivers.

Through naming of places, a large geographical area is in a sense socialized. The names do not represent merely an individual's becoming acquainted with a new terrain; they also form a cultural map complete with significance. In learning to identify places and their names, a Suya learns history and the practical art of where to obtain food and other objects of collecting trips. Since the history of the Suya has involved large-scale migrations under pressure of enemy attack, probably from the Tocantins to the Tapajos and back to the Xingu, they have repeatedly had to orient themselves in new areas and name new places. Unlike Australians, whose ancestors of the "dream time" accounted for and named many of the features of the terrain, the Suya continue to name them or their ancestors named them in the fairly recent historical past.

The Suya concepts of time and space are important for understanding the rest of Suya society. In both time and space there is an opposition between human and animal, between Suya society and animal domains. Temporally this is expressed in the difference between the mythical time—when men ate rotten wood and had no names and no gardens, while animals planted or cooked food and enemy Indians had names—and the present—when men have gardens and fire and the enemy Indians with names are all dead. Spatially the opposition is expressed in the concentric model of space, the plaza being opposed to the distant jungle.

The plaza, cleared of all vegetation and the location of the men's house and men's meeting place, is the most socialized of the domains. The distant jungle, by contrast, is untouched by clearing and has no Suya in residence. It is the realm not only of animals but of monsters as well. There are no place names in it; it is completely unsocialized. Diametrical space is less an opposition between nature and society than between two fairly equal but different parts of society. The Suya differ from other Gê groups in that they do not dichotomize the whole universe but rather only a fairly small part of it (Da Matta 1976, p. 66).

The concentric opposition between society and nature is not a single one. Several intermediary domains are considered either natural or social depending on the context. These are zones in which transformation may take place—they may be socialized. The opposition is thus not simply one of center and periphery. It is precisely the importance of intermediary zones that needs to be stressed. Most analyses of the opposition of nature and culture, and most analyses of space and time, present the categories as static oppositions. There are indeed clear categories of time and space, but there is also a process in which the natural is "socialized" and in which the social is threatened by natural forces. In myth this takes the form of the process of the origin of society as it is today. In space it consists of the naming of space beyond the village which distinguishes known terrain from that which is categorically the domain of cannibal monsters and evil women.

These spatial categories are active ones. The very construction of a new village, which occurs at least once every ten years, is the transformation of a natural area into a social one. Furthermore, in the nonceremonial seasons grass grows in the plaza, the racing paths become narrowed, and nature invades social spaces. These are recreated and redefined every time a major ceremony is performed, by clearing the social spaces and observing more carefully than usual the appropriate behavior in appropriate times and places. Spatial categories do not have a static existence; they are continually imposed and recreated.

The use of concentric and dyadic models of space has often been associated with a vision of the central Brazilian societies as societies that deny time and are not interested in history. There is a way in which they do this, both in terms of their concepts of space and time and in their social organization. But there is another side to these societies, one not perceived by earlier anthropologists such as Nimuendaju (1939, 1941, 1946)—that of flexibility and process. New villages are constructed and the natural domain is named. Named houses may grow to control whole arcs of a village circle and then disappear. Naming not only identifies places but establishes a history beyond the memory of any living person. The Suya do not have lineages, nor do they have interest in the past that inherited status usually involves. But they have a spatial history. The

Eastern and Western Suya both remember place names of rivers that they encountered before they were separated over two hundred years ago. The historical, temporal dimensions of Suya society are to be discovered in the socialization of the natural domains *beyond* their circular villages. History (time) is remembered through space. The two domains are intimately related.

Suya concepts of time and space clearly illustrate both the opposition of nature and society and the existence of levels of contrast and processes of transformation.

4

The Human Body and Modes of Perception and Expression

JUST AS TIME AND SPACE are not perceived by the vast majority of human societies as a regular continuum and grid, so the human body is rarely thought of in strictly biological terms. Parts of the body are endowed with special meaning, and the body itself is altered and ornamented. Infants do not long stay naked; they may be covered by clothing or decorated with bracelets, necklaces, waist belts, and knee, ankle, or other ornaments. In many societies the body itself is altered through circumcision, subincision, ear piercing, nose piercing, scarring, tattooing, stretching, branding, and other operations.

Alterations and ornamentations have usually been treated by anthropologists as incidental or cosmetic, bits of folklore to be collected and compared in terms of distribution instead of in terms of their meaning in a society (for example, Colette 1934; Charlin 1950; Labouret 1952; see Ucko 1969 for an evaluation). Such a perspective is fundamentally incorrect.

The perception of, alteration of, and ornamentation of the body is especially important in lowland South American societies where clothing is little used. Ornaments do not simply contrast one society with another; they contrast members of societies among themselves, usually according to differences of age and sex and sometimes other status considerations. The Suya define themselves as a group in part by their body ornaments.

The Caduveo did so by their tattooing (Lévi-Strauss 1955).

At the very simplest level there are differences in ideas about the composition of the body. The Suya say that the body is the accumulated semen of the father. Other societies say that it is the coagulated blood of the mother. Western societies believe that it is the result of the splitting of DNA. At a more complex level, parts of the body are given different meanings in different societies. In some societies the head is the center of knowledge; in others it is the liver. Different faculties are thought to convey different information. "Seeing is believing" may be true in some cases; for others hearing and smelling are surer means of verification. When English speakers wish to avoid involvement in something, they "hear no evil, speak no evil, and see no evil." Who has not seen statues of three monkeys covering ears, mouth, and eyes? But why is the nose ignored? Isn't something "rotten in the state of Denmark"? Noninvolvement might involve different parts of the body, such as the nose and the genitalia. The meaning given to parts of the body varies with the society and is expressed in many ways, among them body ornamentation.

The five senses are given different emphases and different meanings in different societies. A certain sense may be privileged as a sensory mode. It is important to analyze how people think they perceive. Suya body ornamentation is closely related to their ideas about perception, and the differences in ornamentation emphasize important differences between men and women, between children and adults, as well between "good" Suya and witches. The basic conceptual principles that the Suya use to talk about human beings and animals are hearing, speaking, vision, and odor.

The permanent body ornaments of the Suya are ear disks, lip disks, and body scarring. Both men and women wear ear disks, made of rolled palm leaf or wood, which may reach a diameter of eight centimeters. Eastern Suya women no longer wear these ornaments, which were observed by von den Steinen in 1884, because of the intense contact and extensive capture of Upper Xingu women, who do not wear ear disks. Western Suya women continue to wear such disks. The ear ornament is painted with white clay on the side worn outward. It is slightly concave on that side, resembling a shallow cone, or hi-fi speaker.[1] Adult men wear an elliptical wooden lip disk which may reach the dimensions of eight by seven centimeters and a thickness of one centimenter at the edges. The disk is worn in a hole in the lip which is made during initiation and gradually enlarged to hold larger and larger disks. The top of the lip disk is almost flat and is painted red with *urucum* (*Bixa orellana L.*). The underside is left the color of the wood with the exception of a fine circular design painted in dark stain (*Genipapa Americana L.*) around the bottom of a slight cone rising from the center. The lip disk rests directly against the lower teeth and gums and is held in place by the stretched lip around the outside. It is usually worn horizontally (see Schultz 1962 for photographs).

Men never appear in public without their lip disks, and they sleep with them in place. Men and women often do not wear their ear disks during the day, preferring to wrap the loop of earlobe around the ear itself to protect the thin loop from getting caught on things in the forest. When there is some important social event, men rub their ear disks with fresh white clay, spread more *urucum* paint on their lip disks, and congregate in the village plaza. Preparations for a ceremony usually include making and inserting new lip disks and ear disks which are strikingly colorful and distinctive compared with those that have been worn for a few weeks. Lip and ear disks may be further decorated with tassels, strings, and other additions on ceremonial occasions.

The Suya define themselves as a tribe in terms of their lip disks, their ear disks, and their individually shouted songs called *akia*. Comparisons with other tribes are derogatory: certain ones do not have ear disks, the Northern Kayapo (Txukahamae) have lip disks, but they are ugly, unpainted, dark red ones. No group seems to have songs like the Suya *akia* except for one group which appears in myths—a group exactly like the Suya except that they were cannibals.

The importance of a cultural trait in the ideology of a culture may well be reflected in the use of that feature as a standard of comparison. Western anthropology has frequently used means of subsistence and technology to distinguish groups. The Suya have chosen body ornaments and song as a mode of comparison, and this choice is important. It reflects the qualities that they believe are necessary for being fully human. One could probably generalize and say that any society uses itself as a measure of others and is interested more in what another society lacks that they themselves have (as in ear disks and painted lip disks) than in what the other society has that they lack.

Suya body ornaments are also important within the society because they mark entrance into certain social groups. Children, who are not expected to be good listeners or speakers, wear neither ear nor lip disks. Women following puberty and young men following puberty but before entering the men's house are expected to listen a lot, but they do not engage in oratory or much singing. Following their initiation and the piercing of their lips, young men are supposed to sing all the time. When they have children, they begin to orate. As they age, the design of their ornaments changes and they assume different roles. The degrees of socialization in the life process are marked by the socialization of certain parts of the body through operation and ornamentation.

In addition to the piercing of the earlobes and lower lips for the insertion of ornaments, the Suya practice two other mutilations of the body. One is the scarring of the bodies of adult men who kill enemies. Numerous parallel, horizontal scars are made on the chest, legs, arms, back, and shoulders, and a few vertical scars are made on the buttocks and the lower back. Killing an enemy and passing through a scarring ceremony confers membership in a special status group with its own ritual rights and duties. This has fallen into abeyance since pacification. The second form of mutilation is the stretching of the lips of the vulva. The Suya men say that a good vagina is made, not born. To this end they pull and stretch the lips of the vaginas of women to make them especially large. They maintain that in the "good old days" women's vaginas hung down several inches. While there is no reason to believe that the good old days are much different from the present, sexual foreplay does involve considerable pulling and stretching, and certain men are known as good "vagina makers." This alteration, in contrast to all the others, is private rather than public and is considered to be of a different order.

The Suya emphasize hearing and speaking as eminently social faculties and vision and smell as eminently natural, or antisocial, faculties. The Suya word *ku-mba,* alternatively *mbai,* has several meanings in English, one of which is "to hear." The Suya words *kaperni* and *saren* each have one meaning, roughly equivalent to "to speak" for *kaperni* and "to tell" for *saren,* but they have a much larger universe of meaning than their English equivalents. To understand the Suya, or realize the importance of hearing and speech, analysis of Suya concepts, beginning with their linguistic meaning, is essential. The linguistic level of meaning is not necessarily prior or controlling. It is merely a concrete example of the pervasiveness of these faculties in Suya concepts. Words always have more than a single referent, and these are important though not unique referents.

Vision is a potentially antisocial mode and involves a consideration of witchcraft beliefs. Keen sense of smell and odor are particularly animal-like attributes and are used to classify both animals and some humans.

Hearing

The Suya word *ku-mba* (variant *mbai*) has referents in addition to that of the English word "to hear." When a Suya says, "*Hen ga ku-mba?*" (*hen,* past marker; *ga,* second person singlar; *ku-mba,* to hear), he is asking, "Did you hear?" and "Did you understand?" and "Do you know?" To English speakers this is confusing. A Suya cannot say "I hear but I do not understand." Nor can a person say "I understand but I do not know." A Suya can say only "I do not hear-understand-know" (*mbai kïtïli: mbai,* to hear-understand-know; *kïtïli,* negative) or "I hear-understand-know badly, or poorly" (*mbai kasàgà: kasàgà,* bad, ugly). It is high praise to be told that one hears-understands-knows well (*mbai mbechi: mbechi, good, beautiful).*

The Suya word *ku-mba* has more referents. They include the Suya morality, moral sense, acceptable behavior, and judgment of other people.

The crucial phrase in Suya morality is *añi mbai kïdi* and its opposition *añi mbai mbechi. Añi mbai kïdi* translates as "to not hear-understand-know" (*añi mba,* a reflexive roughly equivalent to *ku-mba,* to hear-understand-know;[2] *kïdi,* negative, a shortened form of *kïtïli*). Its opposite means that one "hears-understands-knows well" (*mbechi,* good). A child who does something that he has been told not do do is *añi mbai kïdi.* An adult who does not share his belongings and food but hoards them in opposition to Suya norms on sharing is referred to as *añi mbai kïdi.* People who engage in sexual relations with certain relatives with whom sexual relations are not socially acceptable are *añi mbai kïdi.* Finally, people who do not obey restrictions on activity, especially sexual activity, and diet after the birth of a child, the injury of a relative, or the killing of an enemy (to name just three of the Suya periods of restriction) are *añi mbai kïdi.*

All the cases in which a person is *añi mbai kïdi* occur when the individual is not behaving according to the social norms of the tribe. The person is in some respect wanton. Immoral people do not hear-understand-know. A person who fully observes custom and etiquette hears-understands-knows well (*añi mbai mbechi*).

The ear, then, is the receiver and holder of social codes. A fully social person hears, understands, and knows clearly. And he acts according to what he knows. A person who hears, understands, and knows badly, of course, acts badly. When someone is about to do something that he should not, such as throw feces, one shouts "*añi-mba!*" or "Behave correctly!"

Speaking

Speaking and hearing are complementary. While listening is largely passive, speaking is active. Among the Suya speaking is often used aggressively. The Suya place great emphasis on speaking. Speaking and not speaking are important social acts. One does not speak to people toward whom one has shame. On the other hand, to stop speaking to people with whom one usually converses is a sign of anger. In addition to the important social acts of speaking and not speaking, the Suya define several kinds of speech.

The Suya word *kaperni* translates as "language," "speech," "to speak," and "to exhort." Animals as well as human beings have languages (*kaperni*), and only certain people can understand the speech of other species. Suya speech is divided roughly into common, everyday speech (*kaperni*) and heightened oratory, literally "plaza speech" (*ngà-ihogo kaperni: ngà-*

ihogo, center of the village plaza; *kaperni*, speech). While common speech is used in everyday discourse by males and females of all ages, plaza speech has a special rhythm, sets of formulas, place of delivery, and style of delivery. It is spoken only by fully adult men, and one of its forms is spoken exclusively by chiefs and ritual specialists.

The form of plaza speech that is restricted primarily to chiefs and ritual specialists is "everybody listens speech" (*mẽ mbai wha kaperni: mẽ,* Suya; *mbai,* to hear; *wha,* everyone, completely). The Suya say that the primary function of a chief is to coordinate group effort. The ritual specialist coordinates group effort for the performance of ceremonies. Chiefs and ritual specialists traditionally orate at dawn and in the evening when the men gather in the center of the plaza. Chiefs and ritual specialisits have few direct sanctions. Their main coercion is through the appeal to custom and proper conduct made in their plaza speech. When they have spoken, everyone else in the village is supposed to have "heard it all" (*mbai wha*). If people do not act in accordance with what has been spoken, they are *añi mbai kïdi.* If they act according to the ideal, they are *añi mbai mbechi.*

Another important Suya speaking concept is *saren,* best translated as "to tell" or "to instruct." A person who agrees strongly with a statement made by another person may say, *Ga wi saren,* which translates well as "You tell it like it is." *Saren* also means to instruct. One of the important responsibilities of a man to his son and of a woman to her daughter is to instruct them. A father may speak (*kaperni*) to his son in an exhortatory sense, or he may instruct (*saren*).

Exhortation and instruction are two important mechanisms of socialization. Speech is also an important part of being a fully adult man. A father must instruct (*saren*) his children, and only adult men can use plaza speech. A Suya man does not marry until he has had his lip pierced, between sixteen and twenty, lived in the men's house for a couple of years, and fathered a child. The lip disk is associated with the coming of adulthood and the necessity of speaking.[3] Its association with adulthood is also obvious in music, for the newly initated man does little more than sing and make new, gradually larger lip disks while he is in the men's house.

The Suya have elaborated the modalities of speaking and hearing to cover all types of instruction, even visual. An English-speaking person who wants to learn how to do something says, "Show me how to do that." The word "show" has a visual component. A Suya says, "Tell (*saren*) me how to do that, I would like to hear-understand-know (*kumba*)." An English speaker who has learned something says, "I see," and "I know it by heart." The Suya say, "It is in my ear." Even Suya medicine stresses orality. Although they use some medicinal plants, incantations are thought to be more effective, and curers who blow on their patients are believed to be the most effective.

The height of oral expression, both individual and collective, is song. A completely social man must hear-understand-know (*ku-mba*) songs well. Especially as young men, Suya are expected to learn quickly and sing frequently. Young men in the men's house do not clear gardens, hunt frequently, or even fish much. Instead they are supposed to sing a lot: before dawn, when the sun is overhead, in the early evening, and at night—this quite apart from ceremonies.

With the exception of certain flutes that the Suya learned of from some neighboring tribes, Suya music is exclusively oral. The only traditional instruments are two kinds of rattle. Oral music can be divided into two main types: *akia,* which are individual songs, sung in a high register, and *ngere,* which are sung in unison in a low register.

Akia are a highly structured form of individual oral expression. They are composed by certain older men who can hear (*ku-mba*) the singing of various animals, fish, birds, bees, and plants and who teach (*saren*) these songs to their fellow humans. Every man has his own *akia* for every festival, and every man has a new *akia* each time a festival occurs.[4] At the beginning of every ceremony, the women, whose role is primarily that of audience, listen excitedly to the new *akia* sung by the men. Importance is placed on the originality (within defined limits of the genre) of the song and on its being heard individually over the rest. In many ceremonies the men all sing their *akia* at the same time, with cacophonous effect. A single man knows many *akia;* he knows those from many ceremonies, the most memorable ones sung by his father, grandfather, and sometimes name giver.

The other major genre of Suya song, *ngere,* is sung in unison, in a low register, and is less changeable than *akia.* The *ngere* in a given ceremony are the same from performance to performance. New *ngere* are introduced only occasionally.

All the major Suya ceremonies involve the singing of *ngere* and *akia* all night. Often a critical part of the ceremony begins at dusk, and the ceremony ends before sunrise the following morning. No large fires are kindled, and the position of the moon is not important. The singing and dancing are done in the dark, illuminated only by the night sky. Except for an Upper Xingu ceremony the women have no *ngere.* They only rarely have *akia.* I observed none during my stay. Women listen (*ku-mba*).

Vision

English speakers, when they understand, may say "I see." It is a commonplace in English to say, "The eye is the window of the soul." Women in Western society emphasize their eyes as one of their attractive features with paint, false eyelashes, and eyelid fluttering. People with new ideas are called visionaries. Suya speech and practice places no emphasis on vision as social or desirable.

Yet the eyes and exceptional vision do have a place in Suya thought. Hearing and speaking are important modalities of the social person; vision is the important modality of the antisocial person. The eyes are literally the seat of antisocial power. Vision has two aspects: seeing in the everyday world and having extraordinary vision.

Good everyday sight is apparently unrelated to hearing and speaking and is not symbolically important. Everyday vision is taken for granted and is not stressed as an important feature. The Suya prize a good hunter who can accurately shoot fish and game and spot honey; but it is the accuracy of his shooting, not his sight, that is stressed. Hunting medicines are applied not to the eyes but to the forearm, to make a man a good shot. There are no medicines or chants to make a person see well.

Extraordinary vision is related to Suya ideas of witchcraft. It is also used to refer to the tameness or wildness of animals and the power of strong, aggressive chiefs. Animals that are swift and difficult to kill are called strong eyed or hard eyed (*ndò tüt*), as are belligerent chiefs who are always on the lookout for enemy Indians. Animals that are easily killed and enemy Indians who are easily killed or captured are said to be weak eyed or tame (*ndò ntegrï*). Thus the attributes of vision, when used to refer to other persons, are applied to chiefs who have much power and to enemy Indians. Vision is an attribute ascribed to animals and especially to witches (*wayanga*).

Suya witches and curers are both referred to as *wayanga*. They are distinguished situationally. A curer is a *wayanga* who is not involved in a particular sickness and who uses his special powers to help a particular person recover. The curer is never wholly trusted and may easily turn to causing sickness himself. All *wayanga* are antisocial in terms of their recruitment, behavior, and powers. *Wayanga* are thought to be responsible for all deaths and most sicknesses. A *wayanga* who is believed to have been responsible for a person's death may be killed by the relatives of the deceased.

A person becomes a *wayanga* because a "witch-thing" (also called a *wayanga*) comes and lives in his eye and gives him extraordinary vision. Literally, he can "see everything" (*sòmo mbedïli: sòmo,* to see; *mbedïli,* completely). He can look up and see the village of the dead in the sky. He can look down and see the fires of the people who live under the earth. And he is able to see all the other tribes of Indians by looking around him.

The witch-thing comes into a person's eye because he is in some way *añi mbai kïdi.* A *wayanga* does not inherit the witch-thing in his eye from a relative, nor is he born with it. He gets the witch-thing only when he has behaved immorally, when he has failed to hear-understand-know and behave properly. People become witches because they do not share their food and belongings, because they do not observe restrictions on sex and diet during a critical period, or because they harbor grudges against people who do not give them food. An often cited way of becoming a witch is through killing one. The reciprocity that permeates Suya life is expressed here with respect to killing witches. When a man kills a witch, the relatives of the witch are not supposed to be angry. Instead they are supposed to say to themselves, "Wait until one of us dies; then we will kill him." In fact this retribution seldom occurs because the families of assassinated witches are usually very small and the families of the assassins are large, but the reciprocity is reflected in the ideology. To avoid becoming a witch after killing one, a man must observe diet and behavior restrictions scrupulously.

The other ways of becoming a witch, by stepping on a person's grave, touching a dead witch, or having sexual relations with a living one, operate only if a person is already *añi mbai kïdi.* They are necessary but not sufficient causes. One need not become a witch after killing one, or burying one, or sleeping with one if one obeys to the letter all the appropriate restrictions. It is when a person does not listen (*ku-mba*) to the exhortations (*kaperni*) of his father, his chiefs, and his ritual specialists or to the instructions (*saren*) of his elder relatives that he is *añi mbai kïdi* and in danger of becoming a *wayanga.*

Wayanga see things that normal men cannot see. They do not hear-understand-know as normal men should. Furthermore they have their own kind of speech, a kind of antispeech. The Suya witches are supposed to speak "bad, ugly speech" (*kaperni kasàgà: kaperni,* speech; *kasàgà,* bad, ugly). Bad speech is in various ways the opposite of plaza speech. It is not spoken in the center of the village, and it has no special oratory style. It appears to be particularly malicious gossip and selfish talk.

The Suya steadfastly refused to repeat any bad speech to me while I was there. It is something that witches do and good people do not even repeat. One form of bad speech is a misuse of the possessive form. A Suya should never say "It is my pot" (*i-ngoi: i,* my; *ngoi,* pot) but "It is our pot" (*aji-iõ-ngoi: aji,* third person plural; *iõ,* indication of ownership, control; *ngoi,* pot). I discovered this only after nine months of using the witch's form.

Smell and Odor

The Suya place great emphasis on odor. Animals are thought to have an especially keen sense of smell and are classified according to their odor; there are strong-smelling, pungent, and bland-smelling animals, each group having other attributes in common. People and substances are also classified according to odor. Strong-smelling things are considered animal-like and dangerous, while the most social things have little or no odor. There have been few discussions of odor other than Lévi-

Strauss's *Mythologiques,* but all the evidence suggests that odor is an important concept in many lowland South American societies (Viveiros de Castro 1977).

Taste (closely related to smell), touch, and other faculties are less important symbolically and are used to describe fewer semantic areas. The Suya relationships among the four most symbolically elaborated faculties are summarized in table 4.1. In a situation where one faculty is highly stressed, the others tend to be less important or negatively stressed. A good example of this is Suya ceremony. The major ceremonies end with all-night dancing and singing, which usually starts at dusk and ends at first light, before the actual sunrise. During the night, the men march around singing in the dark. The visibility of the dancers is not important, but a man must sing loudly enough to be heard by his sisters and the men should keep singing during the night. The women, who give food to relatives in the late afternoon and act as an audience but do not sing, usually retire to their hammocks during the night. They do not sleep much but listen to the men singing. They rise with the morning star to play important parts in the final minutes of the ceremony. In Suya ceremony, then, song is stressed, vision is unimportant, and the audience listens rather than watches during the night hours (Seeger 1979).

Both vision and speaking are unstressed in the relationship of "shame" (*whiasàm*), which obtains between a man and his wife's relatives, his ritual relations, and to a lesser degree his elders when he is not fully adult himself. People in a shame relationship do not look directly at one another, do not usually speak directly to one another, and are supposed to listen attentively.

Witches are an example of the stress on vision: they speak bad speech, do not hear well, and have extraordinary vision. Smell, being more

Table 4.1 Comparison of faculties, roles, and ornaments

Anti-social, animal-like	
Emphasized vision	*Emphasized smell*
characteristic of witches and certain birds	characteristic of animals and powerful, antisocial things
organ: eyes	organ: nose
ornament: none	ornament: none
Social, human-like	
Emphasized speech and song	*Emphasized hearing and morality*
characteristic of adult men	characteristic of "good" adults of both sexes
organ: mouth	organ: ears
ornament: male lip disk	ornament: male and female ear disks

associated with animals, does not figure in the system of relationships to the same degree. Hearing, speaking, and vision, however, form an interrelated system of faculties.

Each faculty is associated with an organ or part of an organ. Each is also associated with certain types of human being or animal and with certain types of behavior. The two faculties considered social by the Suya are elaborated with body ornaments. The eyes are not ornamented, tattooed, or specially painted. The nose is also without ornament.

Lip disks and ear disks are clearly associated with the cultural importance of hearing and speaking as they are defined by the Suya. This association is borne out by what the Suya themselves say. They maintain that the ear is pierced so that people will hear-understand-know. They say the lip disk is symbolic of, or associated with, belligerence and bellicosity, which are correlates of masculine self-assertion, oratory, and song. The color of the artifacts is also important. The lip disk is red on the top and sides, a color associated with heat and belligerence. The circular design on the underside represents the Pleiades constellation, which the Suya say is the design on the lip disk of a man in the sky. The ear disk is painted white, a color associated with coolness and passivity. When they are separately painted—as on hunts or in ceremonies in which men "become" animals—the eyes and nose are often painted black, the color associated with antisocial attributes and witches.

Suya body ornaments are installed in rites of passage and are marks of status. They also mark the social emphasis of certain faculties at particular times in the life cycle. The ears of both sexes are pierced at the first signs of sexual activity; men's lips are pierced when they are "big" (in their late teens) and old enough to be considered fully adult men. Children are not expected to hear-understand-know or behave particularly well. The Suya are very tolerant of their children. Around puberty, however, they are expected to listen to the instructions and exhortations of their elders and their chiefs and they are considered *añi mbai kïdi* if they do not observe the norms with respect to sexual activity, the distribution of food and property, and dietary and activity restrictions. When boys are big, their lips are pierced and they enter the men's house. While they are living in the men's house, prior to fathering a child and taking up uxorilocal residence, young men are supposed to sing constantly and devote their energies to making increasingly larger lip disks for themselves. Thus the use of body ornaments distinguishes important groups by sex and age. Children are not expected to behave morally, but adult men and women are, and their ears are pierced in order to achieve that. Only adult men engage in plaza speech, *akia* singing, and belligerent behavior; their lips are pierced so that they will behave that way.

The mouth and the ear are the most important organs for the Suya man; hearing and speaking are the most important social faculties. They are physical representations of the conceptual elaboration. Through the perforation of the mouth and the earlobe and the insertion of painted disks, the body itself is socialized. Ear disks and lip disks are related to fundamental concepts of person, morality, and the symbolism of body parts.

The eyes and the nose are not socially important. If the eyes receive any elaboration, it is the plucking of eyebrows and eyelashes. The nose is not elaborated.

A similar constellation of beliefs and ornamentation appears in the other Gê-speaking tribes (Seeger 1975a). There is some evidence that variation in the ornamentation of a body part reflects variation in the emphasis on the related faculty. In New Guinea the nose is often elaborately ornamented. But the nose itself becomes a socially important organ. Among the Wiru the nose is the seat of anger, which comes from the thought center located where the frown is on the forehead, while among the Mount Haganers ideas about the nose are synonymous with ideas of leadership, leaders "going in front of" others just as the nose "goes in front of" the rest of the face (Andrew Strathern, personal communication). See also Rappaport (1968, p. 119).

Widespread around the world, body ornaments make intangible concepts tangible and visible, and they readily separate groups of people on the basis of sex and age. The ear disks and lip disks of the Suya are symbols with a variety of referents, and they unite the organs and the senses with components of the moral and social order. The Suya could be said to internalize their values by literally embodying them through their symbolic manifestations, the body artifacts.

5

The Classification of Animals and Plants by Odor

THE SUYA CONSIDER strong odor a particularly animal or natural property. The perceived, or claimed, odors of animals, birds, and fish, as well as of herb medicines are used to classify them, but the classification of animals, plants, and humans by odor is more than a simple scheme by which these entities are divided into groups. It divides them into meaningful groups. The strongest-smelling animals are also the most powerful or dangerous. The least odorous are the least dangerous. People who are classified as strong smelling are also the most powerful or dangerous. Odor may be less a mode of "objective" olfactory classification than a way of expressing power, force, or dangerousness. The categorization of the world in terms of odor provides an important system for the interpretation of Suya actions and attitudes.

The importance of odor is generally ignored in anthropology, but it should not be unfamiliar to nonanthropologist Americans. For years U.S. television has shown nosy neighbors sniffing odors in a woman's house, forlorn lovers with bad breath, and unsuccessful businessmen with underarm odor. In fact, the odors of the human body are as animal-like and disagreeable to many Americans as they are to the Suya; the socially correct American should smell like a flower rather than a mammal.

With the exception of Lévi-Strauss's suggestive treatment (1964) and a few references to it in lowland South American ethnographies (Reichel-

Dolmatoff 1971; J. Dumont 1976), odor is omitted entirely from the anthropology of lowland South America. Recent researches have shown that odor is an important concept in the Upper Xingu though to a lesser degree than among the Suya (Viveiros de Castro 1977).

Problems of translation are accentuated in a discussion of odors. Describing odors from one culture to another is somewhat like describing color to a blind man, but at least with color it is possible to refer to a visible spectrum of colors. In the case of the Suya, describing odors is even more difficult since the Suya are not talking only about odor. Terms that refer to odor in the olfactory sense are used to classify animals, humans, and, to a lesser degree, plants. They have a variety of referents relating to qualities, states, and olfactory stimulation at the same time. In discussing the Suya classification scheme I have translated the terms in their olfactory sense, but other concepts are involved, such as powerfulness and dangerousness.

There are three main grades of odorousness. The strongest is *kü-kumeni,* which I have translated as "strong-smelling" although "gamy" might do as well. The word is also used to talk about sexual excretions and slightly tainted, but not rotten, food. The next most powerful smell is *kutü-kumeni,* translated as "pungent." It is less strong than strong smelling and is also used to describe sweat, perfume, and mosquito repellent. The third important word is *kutwã-kumeni.* I have translated it as "bland," although it is sometimes used in the sense of "without smell" (contrasted with strong smelling) and also of "delicious" smelling. In addition to this spectrum of smells, there is another which I have translated as "rotten" (*kraw-kumeni*), since it describes rotten flesh.

Classification of Animals

Tables 5.1 and 5.2 present the Suya classification of animals in terms of smell. The animals in each group have special properties and relationships with humans that characterize the groups as a whole. These characteristics are relevant to the ways in which the same categories of smell are used to classify certain types of persons and transitional periods. Odor classification is also central to the analysis of curing chants, myths, dreams and omens.

I did not realize the importance of the classification of animals by smell until the end of my first period of fieldwork, in 1973. Then I suddenly discovered that not only animals but also men and plants were so classified. My wife returned to the Suya in May 1973 in order to ask a number of questions on this feature of Suya culture, and the answers she obtained were central to my dissertation. In subsequent visits in 1975 and 1976 I considerably amplified my data and completely vindicated my emphasis on the importance of odor. A number of points that were suggested but unsupportable in my dissertation proved correct and can now be maintained with certainty.

Table 5.1 lists a fairly large number of animals according to their classification by odor. Variation among my informants or in special features of the animals themselves was slight and appears in the footnotes. Mammals are fairly evenly distributed in the three categories. Most birds are bland, as are most fish, but there are exceptions in both cases.

Table 5.2 lists the animals classified by the Suya as strong smelling and compares them on three variables: their diet, their edibility, and whether they were classified in the same way by the Eastern and by the Western Suya. Of the twenty-three animals listed in the table, fifteen are carnivorous—eating meat or fish. Three of the four herbivores are considered physically strong—the capybara as a swimmer, the deer species as runners, and the tapir strong in every way. These three may all be eaten, although there are restrictions on when they may be eaten and by whom. The sloth, which the Suya say acts as if it is dead, is dangerous for that reason and is never eaten. The lizards I am not sure about. The anaconda is an important animal in the Upper Xingu mythology. The Eastern Suya are ridiculed by the Upper Xingu groups for eating snakes, but significantly they no longer do so and classify these snakes with the strong-smelling animals. The Western Suya have always eaten them and still do. The *cobra azul* and pit viper are considered evil omens by the Eastern Suya and are not eaten. In general, however, poisonous snakes are eaten while the nonpoisonous ones are avoided. The electric eel is an especially fatty fish, which may be why it is listed as *kü-kumeni.* The *curimata* is considered the chief of the fish because it appears as a key figure in one of the Suya ceremonies. The smell classification of the fish itself may have something to do with the powers of the chieftainship as well.

The carnivores are considered inedible for all but the old people's age grade, and most are considered inedible even for that group. The tapir, the deer, and the capybara are eaten at certain times by the Suya, though not the sloth. The fish are eaten but restricted by age. In general, the animals classified as strong smelling are too powerful to be safely ingested by most people most of the time.

The jaguar, of all the strong-smelling animals, has a very special relationship to humans. This is true not only among the Suya but also among the Gê (T. Turner 1973) and throughout South America (Reichel-Dolmatoff 1975). According to Suya myths, men stole fire from the jaguar, and it taught the Suya the ceremony performed after killing an enemy in battle.[1] Hunted for its claws, teeth, and hide, used for necklaces, dancing belts, and most recently for trade, the jaguar is never eaten by any group of persons. It is said to be like man in that it is very smart, and its claws are likened to steel knives. Like man, too, it is said to

Table 5.1 The classification of animals by odor[a]

Strong smelling (*kü-kumeni*)	Pungent (*kutü-kumeni*)	Bland (*kutwã-kumeni*)	Rotten (*kraw-kumeni*)
Mammals			
Jaguar[b]	Wild pigs (Queixada, caitetu)	Mice[c]	Opossum
Wild cats	Giant anteater[e]	Small armadillo (*tatu bola*)	
Tapir[d]	Lesser anteater[e]	All bats[f]	
All species of deer	Giant armadillo	All monkeys except Howler[g]	
"Fox"	Lesser armadillo (*tatu galinha*)	Cutia	
"Wolf"	Coati	Paca	
Giant otter	Porcupine[d]	Kinkajou	
Capybara	Weasel		
Three-toed sloth[h]	Skunk		
Two-toed sloth	Howler monkey[g]		
Birds			
Fishing hawk	Hawk (*acauã*)	Hawk	Vultures
Storks[i]	Owl (*corujão orelhundo*)	Owls (*coruja de campo, murucutatu*)	
Heron	Macaw	Parrots	
Ibis		Mataica	
		Larger parakeets (do not eat smaller ones)	
		Toucans	
		Woodpeckers	
		Pigeons	
		Curassow	
		Tinamou	
		Partridge	
		Ema	
		Muscovy duck	
		Goatsucker	
		Swallow	
		João-conga	
		Cuckoo	
		Hummingbird	
		Thrush	
Reptiles and amphibians			
Lizards (*lagarto, calango do rabo verde*	Cayman (Western Suya)	Cayman (Eastern Suya)	Land turtle
		River turtle	
		Lizard (lagartixa)	

Table 5.1 (continued)

STRONG SMELLING (*kü-kumeni*)	PUNGENT (*kutü-kumeni*)	BLAND (*kutwã-kumeni*)	ROTTEN (*kraw-kumeni*)
Reptiles and Amphibians *(Cont.)*			
Snakes (boa, pit viper, cobra azul)		Snakes (rattlesnake, boa [Western Suya], anaconda [Western Suya], *surucucú*)	
		Toads (Western Suya)	
		Tadpoles (Western Suya)	
Fish[j]			
Giant catfish		All fish with the exception of those listed at left	
Electric eel			
Very fatty fish (Eastern Suya only)		Stringrays	
Curimata (Western Suya only)			

[a] A concordance of animal, bird, reptile, and fish names, as far as was possible to discover them, is given in appendix B in English, Latin, Portuguese, and Suya.

[b] The Western Suya say that the spotted jaguar is both *kü-kumeni* and also *kutü-kumeni* at the same time.

[c] A minority of informants said that all mice were *kü-kumeni.* In fact, very few were eaten.

[d] The tapir is *kü-kumeni* in general but *kutwã-kumeni* when cooked. It is both strong smelling yet edible even for people under moderate diet restrictions. The same is true of porcupines.

[e] The classification of anteaters was quite inconsistent. The *tamanduá bandeira* was said by two informants to be *kutwã-kumeni,* by two to be *kutü-kumeni,* and by one to be *kü-kumeni.* The smaller anteater was more generally agreed to be *kutü-kumeni,* as its name *hwat-kutü-ti* might indicate.

[f] A few Eastern Suya say that all bats are *kutü-kumeni.* Eastern Suya did not eat many. Western Suya, who ate them a lot, all said that they were *kutwã-kumeni.*

[g] Some monkeys have *kutü-kumeni* viscera but when cooked are *kutwã-kumeni.*

[h] There is some disagreement about the sloth; one informant considered it rotten (*kraw-kumeni*) while another said that he had never smelled it since it was a bad omen just to see one.

[i] This bird is classified this way because it eats so many fish.

[j] Most fish are bland and may be eaten almost any time by any person.

Table 5.2 The strong-smelling animals

ANIMAL NAME	ANIMAL DIET	EATING ANIMAL FORBIDDEN TO	SAME CLASSIFICATION BY EASTERN AND WESTERN SUYA
Jaguar	Carnivore	All ages	Yes
Wild cats	Carnivores	All ages	Yes
"Fox"	Carnivore	All ages	Yes
"Wolf"	Carnivore	All ages	Yes
Giant otter	Carnivore	All ages	Yes[a]
Deer (all species)	Herbivores	Postpartum	Yes
Capybara	Herbivore	Young people	Yes[b]
Sloths (two- and three-toed)	Herbivores	All ages	Yes
Tapir[c]	Herbivore	None	Yes
Fishing hawk	Carnivore	All ages	Yes
Storks	Carnivores	All ages[d]	Yes
Heron	Carnivore	All ages[e]	Yes
Ibis	Carnivore	All ages[d]	Yes
Lizards			
Legarto	?	All ages[f]	Yes
Calango do rabo verde	?	All ages[f]	Yes
Snakes			
Boa	Carnivore	All ages	No
Anaconda	Carnivore	All ages	No
Cobra azul	Carnivore	All ages	Yes
Pit viper	Carnivore	All but very old	Yes
Giant catfish	Carnivore	Young people	Yes
Electric eel	Carnivore	Young people	Yes
Curimata (Western Suya)	Berries	Young people	No
Fatty fish (Eastern Suya)	–	People on rest diets	No

[a] Eastern Suya ate these *in extremis,* once.

[b] Eastern Suya eat, Western did not before coming to Xingu.

[c] The flesh is bland (*kutwã-kumeni*) when cooked.

[d] Very old Western Suya ate these occasionally.

[e] Very old Eastern and Western ate these occasionally.

[f] Some informants said that "in the past" their ancestors had eaten these. Whether they meant the historical past or the mythical past is difficult to tell. The animals are not at present part of the Suya diet.

disembowel its game, leaving the entrails to one side. The Suya further say that underneath their skins the jaguars are like Indians, but they have not developed this idea to the extent that other groups have.

The tapir is the second most important animal in the Suya cosmology. It is the largest mammal in the jungle and an herbivore. In the fire myth it is the tapir that actually carries the fire into the village and drops it in the plaza. In another favorite myth the tapir has an illicit affair with a married woman who, enamored with the tapir, feeds it the largest sweet potatoes and gives only the small ones to her husband. The husband, discovering the deceit, eventually kills the tapir and feeds some of its flesh to his wife. The tapir's great strength is an important attribute, and sexually he presents a threat (a tapir's penis is huge). His classification reflects this mediation: the raw tapir is strong smelling but the cooked tapir is bland and entirely edible. The special association of the tapir with fire may be related to this feature. The tapir is one of the few animals whose smell classification changes through cooking.

The giant otter is known for its huge appetite for fish. It is considered inedible because it is strong smelling, although in times of famine, the Suya have been known to eat them. They say the experience of eating otter flesh was frightening.

The capybara is the world's largest rodent. It lives near the banks of rivers and streams and is quite at home in the water. The Eastern Suya eat it freely; the Western Suya say that only old men should eat it. The capybara does not appear in myths, its teeth and claws are not used for ornaments, and it does not appear in ceremonies. It is noted for its strength and its ability to hold its breath under water, which are both the subjects of curing chants intended to instill those attributes in children.

The sloth (in Suya, the "bad" or "ugly" anteater, *hwàt kasàgà*) is considered inedible because it moves so slowly. Any person eating the animal soon exhibits similar traits. Old persons may eat it (though rarely) since they already move slowly, but young persons should avoid it. The belief that the trait of the animal is ingested with its flesh is the rationale for many of the Suya diet restrictions.

All species of deer are classified as strong smelling. They are especially important in myths and ceremonies, particularly the savannah deer (*bawchi*). The bones of the savannah deer are used as ritual paraphernalia, and its flesh is forbidden to one of the plaza groups. The power of the deer lies in its swiftness and strength, traits that are important for the Suya. Although Suya avoid eating certain animals to avoid ingesting their traits (as with the sloth), they do not eat animals in order to obtain desirable traits. They do not eat deer to make themselves or their children strong. For that they use chants.

The birds in table 5.2 are all carnivorous. Only the vulture (which is rotten smelling) appears in myths. The fish are a mixed group. The giant catfish is never eaten, and to see one is an omen of death. It appears in several myths, omens, curing chants, and songs. Other large, bottom-dwelling fish, such as the *komdu-tendepti,* are forbidden during periods of diet restrictions and for certain persons altogether. The electric eel and the curimata are both eaten. The curimata appears especially in the *tep-kradi* ceremony and may be associated with leadership. The electric eel is a very fatty and rather powerful animal.

Members of the group of animals classified as strong smelling are thus carnivores or very powerful. They are thought to stand in a particular relationship to human beings, and many of them appear in myths. As a whole, the Suya guard themselves against members of this group by complete dietary avoidance or extensive restrictions on eating them. The carnivores are all forbidden. The herbivores, with the exception of the tapir, are forbidden to many people for long periods of time.

The animals classified as pungent form a fairly large group. Few birds and no fish are represented. Table 5.3 lists the animals of this class according to the same variables used in table 5.2 for members of the strong-smelling class. Members of this group are forbidden to people undergoing diet restriction (*sangri*) of almost any kind. Not many of these animals have particular symbolic importance. Queixadas appear in some myths and ceremonies and are occasionally used as a metaphor for non-Suya Indians because they travel in large herds. Some of the animals of this class may be eaten only by married or elderly men and women, but most of them are edible under normal circumstances by everyone. Animals of this category figure importantly in curing chants, but they are not felt to be endowed with as strong and dangerous traits as the members of the strong-smelling group.

Animals classified as *kutwã-kumeni,* or bland, are always among the first nonvegetable foods allowed to persons undergoing dietary restrictions. In the later stages of these periods people may eat most of the animals in the bland class with certain exceptions that depend on the purpose of the restrictions. The characteristics of this group are given in table 5.4.

Bland animals do not appear as important figures in myths, and they are not found in curing chants. The giant anteater does not appear in Suya myths, although its mythical importance in other Gê tribes may be reflected in its uncertain classification by the Suya (see table 5.1). Monkeys, because of their physical likeness to man, appear in dream symbols and in some ceremonies. All these bland animals are highly valued as food. When they are caught, they are usually given to men and women observing diet restrictions who cannot eat other flesh.

Animal attributes are contagious through the ingestion of animal flesh, and the classification of animals is paralleled by restrictions on the eating of their flesh. The criterion for prohibiting the flesh of certain

Table 5.3 The pungent-smelling animals

Animal name	Animal diet	Eating animal forbidden to	Same classification by Eastern and Western Suya
Wild pig (peccary)	Herbivore	None[a]	Yes
Wild pig (queixada)	Herbivore	None	Yes
Giant anteater	Ants	None	No[b]
Lesser anteater	Ants	None	Yes
Giant armadillo	Herbivore	None	Yes
Lesser armadillo	Herbivore	None	Yes
Coati	Herbivore	None	Yes
Porcupine[c]	Herbivore	Children	Yes
Weasel	Omnivore	None?[d]	Yes
Skunk	Herbivore	None?[d]	Yes
Howler monkey	Herbivore	None?[e]	Yes
Hawk (*acauã*)	Carnivore (?)	Children	Yes
Macaw	Herbivore	None	Yes
Cayman (Western Suya)	Carnivore	All but elderly	No[f]

[a] Sometimes forbidden, while queixada is not.
[b] Classified in several ways.
[c] Bland when cooked.
[d] Hardly ever appeared in Suya diet.
[e] Avoided after childbirth.
[f] Eastern Suya classify as bland.

animals is not simply smell, or simply the diet of the animal involved, or simply the size of the animal, but a combination of the three. Although the biggest, most physically powerful animals are among the most dangerous, others that are not big are dangerous.

Plants

I know very little about the Suya classification of trees and many plants. Learning about them presented several difficulities. I knew little about the plants, and it was not easy to identify plants in an unfamiliar region. I learned much of what I know about trees while paddling upstream with loquacious informants, so I was always some distance from the trees and thus unable to get a good look at them or even be sure which one was being described. Yet in the cosmology of the Suya, trees and plants are far less important than animals, and far less use is made of

Table 5.4 The bland-smelling animals

Animal name	Animal diet	Eating animal forbidden to	Same classification by Eastern and Western Suya
Mice	Herbivore	None	No[a]
Small armadillo	Herbivore	None	Yes
Bats	Insectivore	None	No[a]
Monkeys, except Howler	Herbivore	None	Yes[b]
Cutia	Herbivore	None	Yes
Paca	Herbivore	None	Yes[c]
Kinkajou	Herbivore	None	Yes
Birds listed in Table 5.1 are all herbivores and some are especially good in times of diet restriction			
Cayman	Carnivore	None	No
River turtle	Herbivore	None	Yes
Lizard (*lagartixa*)	?	?	Yes[d]
Rattlesnake	Carnivore	None	Yes
Surucucu	Carnivore	None	Yes
Boa (Western Suya)	Carnivore	None	No[e]
Anaconda (Western Suya)	Carnivore	None	No[e]
All fish except for strong-smelling ones: the blandest fish are minnows and very small ones which are the first to be eaten following restricted vegetarian diet characteristic of certain rites of passage.			

[a] Some Eastern Suya say this animal is pungent.
[b] Said to be especially good for people observing *sangri.*
[c] Heads eaten by old people.
[d] Rarely appeared in Suya diet.
[e] Eastern Suya do not eat these two snakes and classify them differently.

them, with only a few exceptions. My data are richer for medicinal plants and for some of the taste adjectives used for foods.

Suya plant medicines operate on several principles, which include metaphoric aspects of the plant: a plant with smooth white sap is used to "cool" a "hot" infection. Of the twenty-two medicines listed in table 5.5, however, thirteen are pungent. Indeed, one informant said that Suya medicines were all pungent. When I investigated further, I discovered that this was not strictly the case.

The pungency of plant medicines introduces a refinement into the Suya odor classifications. The strong-smelling, pungent, and bland distinctions are less important. There is only one strong-smelling

Table 5.5 The classification of medicinal plants by odor

Plant	Classification	Efficacy
1. *Hwin-krã sü*	Very pungent	The center pit of the piqui fruit is used to make an emetic (if swallowed) or burned and applied as a poultice to reduce local pain.
2. *Hwin sü sü krü*	Very pungent	A small seed infused as a potion for "liver" pains.
3. *Kangã-twa so*	Very pungent	The "snake tooth leaf," which resembles a fang, is boiled in a pot so that the steam rises to the patient. This is a very strong medicine for a child's fever, considered stronger than plant 5.
4. *Karen-tà-pòyi*	Very pungent	A leaf, like 3, soaked in water, boiled, and used to steam the patient. This is good for adult fevers, and quite strong. Another name for it, *waiyõ-kutü-ti,* includes the word "pungent" (*kutü*).
5. *Sak-tà*	Pungent	A pungent leaf soaked in water and boiled to make a vapor for people with fevers; also rubbed directly on the chest for congestion. Not as strong as 3 and 4.
6. *Mẽ swapo kande-ta*	Pungent	Literally "our convulsion fever medicine"; a plant with a thick taproot, which is beaten, mixed with water, rubbed on a healthy child's body so that he will not get convulsions when his parents begin to eat fish and game after postpartum diet restrictions.
7. *Rodn-krã*	Pungent	The nut of the Babassu palm; it is burned, its ashes are mixed with piqui oil, and the mixture is rubbed on painful and itchy swellings.
8. *Tugrĩ kande tà*	Pungent	Literally "shortness of breath medicine"; the sap of a vine, drunk by persons who feel weak and breathless to make them feel strong.
9. *Akro tügu*	Pungent	The "black vine"; this plant is cut, and its copious, bitter juice is drunk by children to make them strong winded and to keep their hearts from beating unusually fast after exertion.

Table 5.5 (continued)

PLANT	CLASSIFICATION	EFFICACY
10. *Hwin tuk tà*	Pungent, also sweet	A small plant with a root that smells like root beer; it is crushed in the hands, and the pulp is rubbed on children and adults who are weak or suffer from convulsions.
11. *Sipe tu kande*	Slightly pungent	A "vine" or ground creeper, which is dried, soaked in water, and drunk when a person feels weak.
12. *Kapa tügü*	Slightly pungent	An abrasive hanging vine which may be mixed with water and rubbed on the skin, especially on boys at the new moon to make them accurate archers. Also used as an emetic.
13. *Wañikot kande tà*	Strong smelling and cooling	Literally "our swelling medicine"; this plant has a milky juice very similar to semen when it is squeezed out. It is put on hot, infected places. It is somewhat strong smelling and is similar to semen. It is the only strong-smelling medicinal plant that I discovered.
14. *Hwintu sàni*	Sweet	This plant has an anise-flavored root that is crushed and rubbed on young children, or water is added and the infusion is drunk. Makes a person grow tall, broad faced, and beautiful.
15. *Waisaktà niatïktà*	Burning	A fever medicine rubbed on the brows and eyes. It stings a great deal.
16. *Kupentukande swachida*	Hot tasting	An infusion made from the fruit of a bushy, peppery plant; taken for influenza and called "the hot (spicy) Upper Xingu Indian medicine."
17. *kobñi sakratsi so*	*Si ra-chi*	I cannot translate this taste term; also said to be slightly strong smelling. It is a spiny plant whose juice is rubbed on the shaven heads of initiates to make their hair grow long and beautiful.
18. *Bontu kanda*	Bland	A poultice for the hair made from the fat of inajá palm nuts boiled in water.
19. *Hwin daw kïdi*	Slightly pungent	A small parasite plant that grows in trees. Mixed with water to make an infusion that is drunk as a pain killer.

Table 5.5 (continued)

Plant	Classification	Efficacy
20. *Mẽ swapo kandetà poyi*	?	A tree used to make an infusion against convulsions in children. Although all other convulsion medicines are pungent, I did not get an odor classification of this one.
21. *Krotchi iase sü*	No odor	A berry whose juice is squeezed on burns, said to have no odor.
22. *Me tuk iare*	?	The sap of this plant is put in the ear of a person who has a swollen ear which interferes with his hearing. It is supposed not only to improve hearing but also to be useful for learning songs well and learning in general.

medicine, and only one bland medicine. Instead, there are three degrees of pungency. These are *kutü-kumeni,* with heavy emphasis on the second syllable, *tü; kutü-kumeni* without heavy emphasis, and *kutü-re,* in which *re* is a diminutive. I would translate these as "very pungent," "pungent," and "slightly pungent." The efficacy of the medicines seems to parallel these distinctions. Thus the strongest medicines for fever are very pungent, while useful but less effective ones are pungent.

Medicinal plants, then, are classified in the same way that animals and human beings are classified. A single class is taken as particularly effective and subdivided into subclasses. Strong-smelling plants would be harmful; bland ones would be ineffective. Pungency is the locus of the power of these medicines.

Edible plants are classified far more by taste adjectives than by smell. Thus some plants are sweet-salty (*sàn-kumeni*), or bitter-acid (*swa-kumeni*), or not sweet (*sàn kïtïli*). Sweet-salty is used to describe foods that are either sweet (like honey) or salted to taste and therefore tastier than unsalted foods. Thus the water in which meat has been boiled is mixed with manioc flour and is "sweet" when a little salt is added. It is "not sweet" without salt. Bitter-acid refers not only to acidic fruits such as limes or to unripe fruits but also to spicy ones such as peppers and to some things that tingle in the mouth such as certain kinds of honey which are not considered desirable because they are bitter. "Not sweet" is used to describe things that might be sweet but are not. The attributes "hot" and "cold" occasionally appear in the consideration of foods, although they have little importance. Good honey is cold and sweet, while bad honey is hot and bitter-acid.

Sweet-tasting foods are highly valued by the Suya, who have only recently begun planting sugarcane obtained from the Kayabi. The important sweets are boiled manioc juice and especially honey.

Categories of taste are little used for talking about things other than food. The important exception is their use to characterize sexual intercourse, which among the Suya—as in many other places—is considered related to eating. Sexual relations can be sweet (*sàn-kumeni*) or, if not very enjoyable, not sweet (*sàn-kïtïli*). It is perhaps congruent that the ideal food gift for a lover is honey. It is a case of "sweets for the sweet" at a metaphorical level.

Cultivated plants have a special place in Suya life. Classified differently from wild plants and medicines, they are the subjects of chants to influence their growth, chants otherwise used only for humans. They are considered "children" of the people who plant them. In a ceremony that I never witnessed, a man who takes responsibility for the gardens advises everyone to obey the food restrictions until the crops are harvested. These restrictions are similar to those observed by the parents of newborn infants. The "father" of the gardens pierces his penis, does not have sexual relations, and is careful about food taboos. There is a kind of physical bond between people and their crops which is similar to that between parent and child. The distinction between wild and cultivated plants is important in understanding the diet restrictions of the Suya, in which garden products are edible but all wild products and animal flesh are avoided.

The Suya classification of animals and some plants according to their odor is more than simply taxonomic: the animals in each group have similar characteristics. Those in the bland group rarely appear in myths and other symbolic genres and are seldom prohibited as food. Those in the pungent group appear more often in symbolic genres and are more often prohibited in times of passage. Most of those in the strong-smelling group are central in mythology, curing chants, omens, and other genres and are generally not eaten. Odor is related to power and to a greater or lesser degree of naturalness as defined by the Suya.

6

Sex, Age, and Odor

HUMANS, LIKE ANIMALS, are classified by odor, but they are different from animals in an important respect. While animals are permanently classified in a given category (except for the tapir and the porcupine, which change after they are cooked), human beings have different odors according to sex, stage in the life cycle, and transition through certain ambiguous states.

It was only in the last month of my fieldwork in 1973, shortly after I had realized the importance of animal classification, that I discovered that smell applied regularly to humans. One of my informants was telling me how smart the jaguar is. He said that it sneaks up behind a hunter after he has gone by and smells his tracks. If the tracks are pungent (*kutü-kumeni*), the jaguar knows that a bellicose man has passed and

Table 6.1 The classification of body fluids by odor

SUBSTANCE	STRONG SMELLING (*kü-kumeni*)	PUNGENT (*kutü-kumeni*)	ROTTEN (*kraw kumeni*)
Blood (all)	X		
Breast milk	X		
Vaginal fluids	X		
Semen	X		
Sweat		X	
Feces			X
Unwashed female genitals			X

slinks away. If the tracks do not smell, the jaguar follows the hunter and steals the game that he shoots. Although I had heard odor terms applied to humans before, it occurred to me that perhaps there was a regular system.

In fact there is. The classification of human beings by odor shows the same correlation between strength of odor and dangerousness, naturalness, and power. The same adjectives used in animal classifications are also used in human classifications, and these reveal the extent to which certain human beings in certain states are in some respects animal-like and natural. Table 6.1 shows the classifications of body substances as described by a variety of informants.

Women and Sexuality

Distinctions of sex and age are fundamental parameters of Suya social organization. All human beings are either female (*mẽ-ndi-yi*) or male (*mẽ-mbü-yi*): literally "a Suya with mons veneris" or "a Suya with penis." This distinction between the sexes is fundamental economically, ritually, and ideologically. Unlike some other South American Indian groups, however, the Suya have not sexualized the universe (Reichel-Dolmatoff 1971). The sex of mammals is of some importance, but the sex of some birds, all fish, trees, and the like is not a matter of concern. The sex of humans most definitely is.

There is a sexual division of labor and a difference between the sexes in body ornamentation. What men *say* about women, their attitude toward them in times of ritual activity, and the roles of women in myths reveal that women are considered to be marginal to the center of society, "somewhat natural." They live in the arc of houses mediating the opposite poles of jungle and plaza; the gardens are theirs. Their names do not necessarily carry moiety and plaza group membership; they have no lip disks; with rare exceptions they have no formal roles in the political arena; and they are strong smelling.

The men tend to emphasize the opposition between men and women during rituals. On the first log race that I witnessed, when all the men left the village early in the morning and set up a daytime camp some kilometers away, they told me that women are "our bad belongings" (*wa iõ kasàgà*).[1]

There are several synonyms for women: our bad property (*wa iõ kasàgà*), our rotten-smelling property (*wa iõ kraw-chi-da*), our strong-smelling property (*wa iõ kü-kumeni*), our hot property (*wa iõ kangro-chi*), that which we follow (*wa kot tà*). The adjectives "bad," "rotten-smelling," "strong-smelling," and "hot" describe women in their sexual aspect. "Our bad property" is sometimes used to refer specifically to the vagina. This is even clearer in the classification of bodily substances.

Women are said to subvert the ideal men's society, the group of fully initiated men living in the men's house and associated with the plaza. Specifically, the vagina subverts the men's society. A man leaves the men's house only after he has fathered a child, which requires frequent and repeated intercourse. The men frequently said that when a man has a child and leaves the men's house, he no longer wants to sing. His companions call to him at the rise of the morning star and he says, "I'm coming right away." But he does not come until dawn because he has his hand in the entrance of his "bad property" (his wife's vagina). Men who are married and associated with their wife's household are no longer as active in singing as when they were unmarried initiated men.

Women, when they are sexually active and strong smelling, are considered dangerous. Sexual relations are considered dangerous for men. Intercourse is restricted for a long time after the birth of a child, after killing an enemy, after the death of a spouse, and during ceremonies or ceremonial periods. Sexual relations are also dangerous for women, since by having intercourse with a witch they may become witches too. Engaging in sexual intercourse at times when it should be avoided is as dangerous as eating meat during periods of diet restriction and for the same reason: a man's stomach will swell up and he may become a witch. The danger of sexual relations is a recurrent theme in myth and in instructions to young men and boys. Uninitiated boys should not engage in sexual intercourse because the vagina is so hot that it will burn off their pubic hair and it will not grow; neither will they. Somewhat older, initiated men should not have frequent or lingering sexual relations because it keeps them from learning songs well, it obstructs their hearing, and it weakens their legs so that they cannot race well. There is thus an opposition between hearing-knowing-understanding well and sexual relations.

Sexual intercourse with the wrong people, at the wrong time, or in the wrong place is a dominant feature of Suya myths and stories. Either the man or the woman may be at fault, taking the initiative in the seduction. Sexual relations begin a number of Suya myths, which in other Gê societies do not have such a beginning. The result of the improper intercourse provides one of the motivating factors of the myth. The myth of a man who puts his foot in a fire, burns it off, sharpens the legbone, and begins to kill people with it is found among most of the Gê. Only in the Suya version is there a motivating cause: the man's wife did not tell him she was menstruating before he had sexual relations with her. For that reason he became angry and sharpened his leg, eventually killing her and a number of her brothers (compare Nimuendaju 1939, p. 175; 1946, p. 248; Schultz 1950, p. 119, for Apinaye, Ramkokamekra, and Kraho variants). Similar motivations occur in other myths.

The ambivalent features of sexual intercourse are also present in stories about named, possibly historical people. These emphasize the incongruous, animal-like aspects of sexuality. In one, a man has sexual relations with his female name receiver in the men's house, but in the middle of it his wife shoves a brand through the thatch and burns his backside so that he screams and his penis pops out of the woman (a favorite Suya anecdote which they find hilarious). In another, a man goes into his house and sees his father and mother copulating next to the wall of the house. He says, "Father, father, what's up?" and his father only laughs—a high, whinnying sort of laugh which my informant said was "like a wild pig" (queixada). Another tells of a young man having sexual relations with his father's second wife, a captive. Her vagina gets so hot in the foreplay that they run down to a cold spring and make love there where the water can cool them.

Heat and smell and ambiguity characterize sexual relations, but the Suya also call women, and again especially the vagina, "that which we follow" (*wa kot tà*) because they like sexual relations. When relations are good they are "sweet" (*sàn-kumeni*). In this context the vagina may be referred to as "the sweet thing" (*sàn-tà*). For women a desirable man has a large, hard phallus. For men a good woman has a large, wet vagina. Women are said to be best from the time they begin to swell at their breasts (*hen sum hrü*) until they have had two children and are considered "already old." This does not mean that their sexual life stops. On the contrary, it merely means that they are stably married and have left the age grade of desirable young women.

The adult men are particularly fond of unmarried women, who are the potential wives of the unmarried men (*sikwenduyi*). The initiated but still unmarried men are the extramarital sexual partners most desired by the older, married women. There is thus some conflict between the married men and the unmarried men about women. The ritual specialist once orated about how a particularly desirable girl was refusing to sleep with older men because the young men were sleeping with her too much. Conflicts between age grades about women can arise especially in ceremonial times when women are taken by a group of men on a long hunting or fishing expedition for sexual and culinary purposes.

Adultery may be fairly common when a married man and an unmarried women are involved. It is less common, and not condoned, when a man has sexual relations with another man's wife. Men become angry when another man has sexual relations with their wives. The Suya have two different strategies for dealing with this kind of adultery. A man may make a public statement in the plaza or men's house to the effect that if the other man wants his wife so much, he can have her and have sexual relations with her whenever he wants. The object is to make the other man ashamed. He will then say, "No, I will not do it. I don't want her." A man may also beat his wife and sometimes threaten the other man. In one argument I overheard in the men's house, the aggrieved party finished by saying, "I won't beat my wife [for having sexual relations with you]. I will sleep with your wife right in front of you and you will beat your wife." In fact, that is precisely the second strategy when a man is confronted with his wife's adultery. He tries to seduce the other man's wife. I recorded several cases in which this was attempted or accomplished.[2]

Women may also be held responsible for political actions taken by adult men. At one point there was a rumor that one of the Western Suya was going to secede from the village with his companions. He was harangued at night by the ritual specialist. Addressing the ritual specialist as "father" (*ture*), he denied that he was going to leave the village. Finally he argued that the move was his wife's idea. Thus blamed on her, the move was not as much a political act, because women are "like that." Women are gossips, their political acitivity less clearly defined (though very important) and less social.

The men's house, the men's society, is considered ideal by the men. It is seen as subverted by women and sexuality. Women are strong smelling, and their sexuality is rotten smelling, strong smelling, hot, and irresistible. But to create a simple dichotomy between men and women on these grounds is to oversimplify. Just as there are degrees of naturalness in space and in smell, so there are two kinds of women, and discussions of women are contextual. The Suya distinguish sisters and mothers from wives and lovers. The first are close relatives (*kwoiyi*); the second are actual and potential sexual partners (*hronyi*).

Female Relatives and Sexual Partners

The Suya make a clear and omnipresent distinction between female relatives and sexual partners. Sisters, mothers, and sister's children form a group of relations (*kwoiyi*) called *whai-wï-ieni*. As a group these people play important roles in most ceremonies. Wives and lovers are referred to as *hronyi* (*hron*, wife; *yi*, indicating group). They rarely have important ritual roles and are usually rigidly excluded from performing the acts performed by the *whai-wï-ieni*. Most ritual relations are explicitly nonsexual. Name givers and receivers and a man and his ritual relation (*krãm ngedi*) are not supposed to have sexual relations.

The Suya say that sisters, mothers, and ritual relations are "for ceremonies" (*mẽ kïn katüwü*) once a man has left his natal household. These people appear in almost every Suya ceremony, their role varying from suppliers of food to merely holders of a brother's bow and club while he dances or runs. Almost always it is a sister who plays the dominant part. Where there are no sisters, a mother or a sister's daughter will do as well.

What distinguishes women who are "for ceremonies" from wives and sexual partners is the act of sexual intercourse, which is related to strong-smelling fluids. Women are defined precisely by their sexuality. But certain relatives may become sexual partners. The men agreed that it is especially enjoyable, and not too reprehensible, to have sexual relations with one's "distant" or classificatory sisters.[3] But if a man has sexual relations with all his sisters, he will have none left for ceremonies. This was raised as an issue before a ceremony. Once a man has sexual relations with a member of his *whai-wï-ieni*, she is no longer eligible to perform the tasks associated with her former status.

After the Suya log race a man receives a little food from all his uterine and classificatory sisters, close and distant. There is always interest in seeing whom he does not take food from, thus indicating a new sexual partner, at these times.

Suya ceremonies invert a number of the usual social relations, and invert them precisely around the distinction between female kinsmen (*whai-wï-ieni*) and sexual partners (*hronyi*). In nonceremonial times a man shares food primarily with those with whom he may have sexual relations—his wife and her sisters and their parents (with whom he may not). In ceremonies a man gives and receives prepared food from his mother and sisters. In ceremonies the collective society of the men is omnipresent and unconflicted by affinal relationships, while in secular life uxorilocal residence and a man's relationship with his affines are of great importance and some conflict. Sexual relationships are seen as interrupting the ideal men's society; affinal relationships attenuate natal family ties. During ceremonies both the male collectivity and the family ties are reestablished and relations with sisters are more important than those with wives. In ceremonies sisters are not "our bad property" and no sexual partner can be a sister. When the men take women on long hunting or fishing trips for sexual and cooking services, those women do not act as sisters to anyone during other parts of the ceremony. They do not, however, have sexual relations with their brothers: house exogamy is observed and at least two women are taken. During one savannah deer ceremony I was told that if a man's sister is one of the "wives of the savannah deer," she does not pierce her brother's mask at the conclusion of the ceremony (a ceremonial duty of sisters). This is because she was, during the early part of the ceremony, one of the "wives" of all the deer (men), the wife of the collectivity.

The feature that distinguishes a man's *whai-wï-ieni* (mother, sister, sister's children) from his *hronyi* (wives and sexual partners) is sexual intercourse. Sexuality itself is what makes women strong smelling, and it is a marginal, powerful, and decidedly ambivalent part of Suya life. The importance given to sexual intercourse is at least in part related to the role of sexual relations and procreation in the separation of a man from his natal household (and his *whai-wï-ieni*) and in his leaving the men's house to take up residence with his wife.

Age

Age, like sex, is an important feature of Suya social organization and one that is closely related to ideas about nature and society. Age is not marked by the number of years since birth. Instead it is marked by membership in age grades. Among the Suya, age grades follow stages in the life cycle; for example, one becomes a member of the grade "already with child" only after fathering or giving birth to a child. Age-grade membership determines an individual's status in ceremony, in politics, and in the household.

Table 6.2 shows the Suya age grades for men and women and the odor classification for each grade. The first column describes the approximate ages. The male term and the male odor are followed by the female term and the female odor. Reading this table horizontally, one can see that male and female age grades have the same names before puberty and after the first child. They have the same classification by smell as infants and as old people. But in the middle age grades, when men are active in ceremonial life and women are sexually active and bearing children, the sexes are distinct. Adult men have no odor while women are consistently strong smelling.

Reading vertically, one can see that male infants and boys are strong smelling, then become odorless until they are old and pungent. Females begin as strong smelling and then become very strong smelling, and finally pungent in old age. These classifications parallel Suya ideas about the naturalness or animal-like aspects of the persons in these age grades.

Infants (*titi*) are said to be born strong smelling and to remain so for some time. Although they are given names shortly after birth, they are addressed by the term *titi* until after the child can walk or until the birth of a younger sibling, who is then called *titi*. Because the fetus is created of semen, which is strong smelling, is sustained by mother's milk which is also strong smelling, and has not undergone the first major rite of passage of the naming ceremony, it is still natural.

From the time boys can walk until their first signs of puberty they are members of a group called the *ngàtureyi* (*ngàtu,* adolescent; *re*, a diminutive; *yi*, a class of persons). Although the boys have gone through the naming ceremony, they are still very much associated with their parental household and are still considered strong smelling, although some Suya said they had no smell. As a group they are in danger from certain supernatural beings and are extensively treated with herb medicines to make them tall, strong, and successful hunters and ceremonial performers.

Girls before puberty (*pureyi*: *pu,* adolescent girls (?); *re*, diminutive; *yi*, class of persons) are ambiguously classified according to their smell. Some Suya say they are strong smelling while others maintain that they

Table 6.2 Suya age grades and their classification by odor

Age, status	Male term	Male odor	Female term	Female odor	Undifferentiated age-grade term
Birth to walking	*titi*	Strong smelling	*titi*	Strong smelling	*titi*
Walking to earliest signs of puberty	*ngàtureyi*	Strong smelling	*pureyi*	Strong smelling or no smell	*Kra*[a]
Early puberty (to entry into men's house, for men)	*ngàtu*	No odor or strong smelling			
			puyi (*hen sum hrü*)	Very strong smelling	—
(For men, entry into men's house) to birth of first child	*sikwendyi* (*whukatügu*)	No smell (or bland)			
One child to several children	*hen kra* (*suyape*)	No smell	*hen kra* (*suyape*)	Strong smelling	*hen kra*
Several children to several grandchildren	*hen kwï ngedi* (*hen tumu*)	No smell	*hen kwï ngedi* (*hen tumu*)	Strong smelling	*hen kwï ngedi* (*hen tumu*)
Several grandchildren to death	*wiken*	Pungent	*wiken*	Pungent	*wiken*

[a] Female children may be specified by the optional suffix, *ndi-yi*, thus child with *mons veneris*. Males are simply *kra*.

have no smell. There is an important contrast between them and girls who have begun sexual activity, who are very definitely strong smelling.

When boys begin the sudden growth of adolescence, show some interest in sex, and begin to grow pubic hair, they are said to have become *ngàtu*. This term translates roughly as "newly of the center." Although still living in their natal households, these boys are incorporated to some extent into the social and ceremonial life of the plaza. The ambiguity of their position is marked by the ambiguity of their odor, as reported by my informants. Since they are still in their maternal house, they are strong smelling, but since they are already associated with the plaza they can be considered to have no smell. The *ngàtu* cut wood for the men's house fires, carry water, cut and wash meat for the men's house meals, and begin to learn to make their own bows, arrows, and artifacts. They undergo a number of rites of passage and have their ears pierced during this stage.

Girls whose breasts begin to swell are said to be *hen sum hrü,* or "swelling," "budding." The term does not refer to menstruation, since the first flow of blood occurs when a girl has sexual relations for the first time, usually well before puberty. Girls whose breasts have begun to swell and who are getting big are considered very desirable sexually and very strong smelling. They are then potentially *puyi*, or girls who in the past had certain ceremonial roles of an indeterminate nature, possibly similar to the *vute* girls mentioned by Nimuendaju among the Timbira (Nimuendaju 1946, p. 92). This group is marked by their sexual activity, their ripeness, and their very strong odor. Women's ears were pierced when they became *hen sum hrü.*

Boys of about sixteen or seventeen ("when they are big") have their lips pierced, and after elaborate rites of passage they enter the men's house. They spend their time making larger lip disks themselves, singing, and painting themselves. They are said to be bland (*kutwã-kumeni*) because they so often paint themselves with piqui-nut oil, which has that smell. They are the only group so classified. They are considered the ideal of manhood and socialness.

When a man has fathered a child, he leaves the men's house and takes up residence in his wife's house. He is less active in ceremonial life, but fully initiated, and without odor. When a woman has a child, she remains strong smelling and sexually active. Both sexes remain, respectively, without odor and strong smelling when they have had several children. Men of the *hen kwï ngedi* age grade are the most politically active. Women of the same age grade are not considered as sexually desirable.

A man or a woman who has had several grandchildren goes through a rite of passage and becomes a *wiken*—a member of the age grade *wikenyi.* These are clowns (*wiken,* to laugh; *yi,* a class of persons). Male *wikenyi* have ceased to be as active in political affairs and have special roles as clowns. Old men are less fully social than younger, more active men. Old women, on the other hand, cease to be as active sexually and are said to be merely pungent.

For both sexes the age grades are clearly divided into two parts, with an age grade of passage between them. For a man the two periods are before he is fully initiated (*titi-ngàtureyi-ngàtu*), when he still lives in his natal household, and after he has moved to his wife's house (*hen kra-hen kwï ngedi-wikenyi*). The stage of initiated man living in the men's house is an age grade of passage (as is *ngàtu* to a lesser extent). For a woman the age grades before puberty (*titi-pureyi*) are contrasted with those grades after the first child (*hen kra-hen kwï ngedi-wikenyi*). The age grade of passage is that of *puyi*. The difference between men and women is clear here: while young men in the men's house typically make larger lip disks and sing all the time (social activities associated with social faculties), women of the age grade of passage are especially known for having frequent sexual relations—their genitalia are stretched by foreplay, they are especially desired for ceremonial hunts and fishing expeditions. The men are the epitome of the social and have no odor; the women are the epitome of the nonsocial and are strong smelling.

Suya age grades are important ways in which persons are classified without individualizing them: personages in myths are often referred to only by their age-grade name rather than by an individual name. The same is true of descriptions of past events and rituals, where age grades are extremely active.

During the time that I was with the Suya, the age grades were important functioning groups. Their character has changed somewhat, since some initiation ceremonies are no longer performed. As men do not have their lips pierced and enter the men's house, no young men can become *sikwenduyi*. Instead they remain *ngàtu,* even after they marry and have children.

The distinction between male and female is unalterable. Men are considered, by themselves and in some contexts by women, to be more social than women. But the socialness of both men and women varies according to their age. Socialness is not a permanent state, but a temporary one. The transient aspect of the social and the natural is also quite clear in Suya humor.

Humor, the Odorous, and the Marginal

Suya humor can be very gross, bearing a strong resemblance to early cinematic slapstick. It can also be very subtle, relying on word play and speech style. Suya humor was one of the delights of living with them. Humor is important to the Suya themselves. It marks the relationships of certain individuals—mother's brothers (*ngedi*) and sister's sons (*taum-*

twü)—as well as groups of persons—old people (*wikenyi*)—to the rest of the village. One of the outstanding experiences in our life with the Suya was witnessing the pantomime farces that one old man would perform on request in the village plaza of an evening. His vivid portrayals of hunting, in which he played both hunter and hunted, would draw the entire village out in front of their houses and keep everyone in hysterics. As hunter he would pull back the bow, but his arm would tire before he could shoot and he would stop, rub his arm, and draw the bow again. Or he would run frantically in circles looking for a digging stick to root out an armadillo gone to its imagined hole right in the center of the plaza. As hunted, he would portray the strange movements of the prey, from the moment it sighted the hunter to its dying agonies, which were always exceedingly funny. Another time he mimicked his own experience of getting a thorn in his foot. Hopping around the plaza with one foot in his hand, he soon picked up a raggedy chorus line of young children hopping around after him.

I was often the butt of Suya humor, yet they were so democratic in their teasing that I rarely felt aggrieved. One evening when the men were feeling in need of some amusement, they picked on me by speaking very fast and then asking me what they were saying. When they tired of that, they asked a Western Suya to tell them a story about a man who got sick because his wife's mother was secretly farting in his face at night—when he finally discovered it he shoved a sharpened stick up her anus and killed her. They made fun of the storyteller's pronunciation throughout. Then they made a Western Suya *wikenyi* sing his repertoire of obscene songs and marched him toward the women on the periphery while he sang. The women attacked him, pulling his hair and genitals, sending him running, screaming wildly, back to the center, where the men marched him back out again. When even this palled, they measured the oldest Western Suya *wikenyi* for his grave. Then they turned his elliptical lip disk sideways, tied it over his nose, and marched him toward the women and then off to bed. That was the end of an evening of male "playing around" (*mẽ-mbü-yi aikràgachi*).

One form of Suya humor, the humor of joking relationships and that of old people, centered on sex, body exudates, and spastic movements. Strong-smelling and rotten substances are central features of Suya humor and are manipulated to create, or to augment, humorous situations. Incongruous behavior such as choking, animal and human death agonies (in the case of humans, always well after the fact), and the intrusion of any unexpected elements into the continuity of biological or social life was considered funny.

A Suya cannot joke indiscriminately. The people with whom a person jokes are distinguished from those with whom he would never joke. My informants said that a man jokes with his mother's brothers (*ngedi*) or with his sister's children and grandchildren (*taumtwü*) but not with his real or classificatory fathers, mothers, sisters, brothers, sister's daughters after they reach puberty, or with nonrelatives (compare Radcliffe-Brown 1924). He may not joke with ritual relations or affines toward whom he has shame. A man whose wife's father farts makes no comment or sign whatsoever; a man whose *ñumbre-krà-chi* (a ceremonial relationship) stumbles or falls is similarly unmoved. Although a man may joke with his same-aged ceremonial companions (*ñumbre*) and with other same-age companions, most of the sexual joking is between persons standing in the relationship of mother's brother-sister's son (*ngedi-taumtwü*). Ceremonies, especially those that involve taking women on a hunting or fishing trip, always stimulate a huge crescendo of sexual joking between pairs of joking relatives. People who lack a joking relative either joke out loud but directly at no one or vicariously enjoy the antics of the joking pairs.

The other important group of jokers are old men and women who have gone through a particular ceremony in which they became clowns (*wikenyi*). On ceremonial and often on secular occasions these old people behave in a farcical way. They are uninhibited and without shame (*whiasàm kïtïlï*) about things excretory or sexual. Old men pull up their penises and chase women, feigning copulation. Old women hop on one leg toward other women, saying "Smell me! Do you want a smell of my vagina?" When the "savannah deer dancers" died after being "wounded" by their sisters, one old *wikenyi* reveled in his dying agonies and was attacked by shouting women who poked his genitals with sticks and pulled his hair. All the other dancers died in a very stylized way by simply bending over. Groups similar to the *wikenyi* are found among other Northern Gê groups. The best described are the *iken* of the Ramkokamekra (Nimuendaju 1946). The Ramkokamekra clowns, one of a number of men's societies, consist of those with a special tendency toward buffoonery. Among the Suya, especially the Western Suya where every old person receives a new name with the prefix of *wiken-*, every elderly person with many grandchildren becomes a *wikenyi.*

For *wikenyi* and joking relatives anything sexual is the object of fun. Beeswax lumps used for arrows become phalli, bananas are equated with the partner's penis, and intercourse is mimicked with these objects. Beeswax vaginas are fashioned. Body exudae—blood, penis exudate, feces, spittle, and pubic hair—are rubbed on each other.

Blood is strong smelling (*kü-kumeni*). Animal blood is carefully avoided and washed off as soon as possible. The Suya believe that it causes permanent discoloration and moles if left on the skin. But when a man kills a mosquito on himself that is gorged with blood, he often carefully wipes the blood on his joking relative. The victim reacts with gestures and sounds of disgust and runs away. He may be chased with the intention of completing the job.

Penis exudate is also strong smelling (*kü-kumeni*). I saw this particular substance used only once, as the Suya now prefer to wear pants when they can get them, probably partly because of their own sense of humor, which is traditional and predates any clothes. One old man came into the men's house with a drop of something hanging from his penis which he tried to conceal with his hand. A young man took a stick, got the drop on it, and then chased everyone, threatening to wipe it off on them. Children ran in great fear. Without ever rubbing it on anyone, the young man threw the stick on the roof of the men's house, where it was left. The old man, a *wikenyi*, just looked foolish.

Feces are rotten smelling and disgusting. Yet it is always considered funny when someone else steps in them. One night a five-year-old boy put his hand directly in some dog feces in the center of the plaza. He fled to his house screaming with fear and disgust while everyone else thought it was hilarious. Joking relatives would try to push each other into piles of feces or pick up somewhat drier pieces on small sticks and hurl them at each other. After one savannah deer ceremony many years ago, the returning men were met by feces-throwing wives, a great hit with the women but not so much appreciated by the men who had to dance all night in smelly dance masks. Disgust about feces does not extend to mothers of small children. They are not alarmed when their children defecate on them; they find a leaf and calmly wipe themselves and the child clean. Perhaps they react this way because young children are still integrally a part of their mothers and feces are not foreign material in the same degree.

Spittle is occasionally taken from a person's mouth and rubbed on the hair or body of a joking relative. This is never appreciated.

Hair is also a little disgusting. A man would sometimes take a brand and singe the hair on his legs. He would then rub the singed hair on someone else (a joking relation). Or he might pull out some of his public hair and do the same thing. Both would draw expressions of disgust. But joking relations could be counted on to return the favor in kind.

Sweat serves the same purpose. It is rubbed on other people as a joke.

Spastic movements, or unusual movements, are either humorous or ominous. Tripping, slipping, hiccupping, moving strangely, and even shortness of breath accompanying intercourse all seem funny to witnesses. The stumblings of a child, incongruous behavior, and lack of body control among the young or the old are considered funny.

Perhaps the funniest movements made by men and animals are their death throes. The Western Suya would describe with great hilarity to fascinated listeners the deaths of Brazilians that they had killed. They would describe with equal hilarity the death throes of their own relatives, as long as the deaths had occurred a number of years before. The Suya sometimes brought wounded birds, such as storks, back to the village and killed them in the plaza. These were a source of great hilarity because of their spastic movements—they are uncoordinated-looking birds in the best of circumstances, with their long legs, long necks, and clacking beaks.

The marginal elements—blood, body exudate, and hair—which the Suya find humorous are not generally important in other contexts. They are not part of witchcraft or sorcery or any ritual symbolism. But they are all strong smelling (*kü-kumeni*), rotten (*kraw-kumeni*), or pungent (*kutü-kumeni*). The blood from mosquitoes is *kü-kumeni,* as is penis exudate. Feces are *kraw-kumeni* and sweat is *kutü-kumeni.* Most aspects of sexuality including sexually active women are strong smelling also. Some forms of Suya humor are thus the juxtaposition of a person and a strong-smelling or powerful object which is usually kept separate. In the same way, uncontrolled behavior also implies desocialization of the body. The discussion of or the actual conjunction of natural things and human beings is considered humorous. Humor thus includes teasing about sexual matters as well as the application of body exudae which are considered strong smelling. The importance of the strong-smelling and incongruous or natural behavior is another measure of the Suya concern with the danger of the natural, the sexual, and the odorous in general.

The Suya faculties are important in their organization of and perception of the world. Hearing, speaking, and vision and the related ornamentation of the ears and lips mark individuals as members of groups. Men and women have their ears pierced so that they will hear-understand-know; men have their lips pierced to make them bellicose and fully initiated. Odor characterizes the natural and the social worlds. The most powerful and important animals in the Suya cosmology are all strong smelling, while the less important ones are pungent or bland. Human beings are not all equally social. Men are socialized through initiation and lose their strong-smelling odor. Women, on the other hand, by their very sexuality are strong smelling. Old people are neither as fully social as adult men nor as sexually marked as young women, and old males and females are both pungent.

The Suya cosmology does not mark two distinct poles of nature and culture standing in permanent opposition. Rather there are degrees of naturalness and degrees of socialness. Social life is thus a constant socialization or naturalization of human beings, bodies, animals, and space. In humans the process is that of socialization and initiation. Humor, too, makes use of a process: elements that should be kept separate are joined, movements that are coordinated are suddenly spastic. It is precisely the linking of the domains of sex and age, the body, and humor with the domain of odor that makes the classification of animals by their odor so important, for odor is the hallmark of the natural and discriminates social groups as well.

Two important features of the Suya social organization are sex and age. Men are contrasted with women; and age grades, clearly and importantly differentiated, reveal some of the basic structures of Suya society. Two other central aspects of the social organization are the distinctions between "us" and "other" and between "substance-based groups" and "name-based groups." The relationship between the classifications of the natural and social worlds is close, because a limited number of principles operate in both the social organization and the cosmology.

7

The Principles of Kinship and Naming

TWO *KEY PRINCIPLES* organize Suya social relations: the relationship system and the naming system. The basis of Suya kinship is the identity of a group of persons who share bodily substance, a group that I have translated as "us" (*kwoiyi*), and their opposition to those who do not share bodily substance, translated as "others" (*kukïdi*). The substance group may also be contrasted with name-based groups. According to the Suya, at one time they did not have names but learned about the naming system from people living under the earth, one of whom they captured. The acquisition of names separates them from the animals and socializes the individual infant. Both features of person classifications are related to the distinctions between nature and society.

The Suya have several, different, crosscutting relationship and person classification systems. This feature has endeared the Gê-speaking societies to social anthropologists with an interest in social organization.[1] There is a kinship system, but it is impinged on by a naming and a ceremonial relationship system. The behavior of a given Suya with other Suya varies according to relationship. Joking, shame, diet restrictions, preferred marriage, and sexual prohibitions are culturally defined behaviors appropriate toward some people and not toward others, depending on the nature of the relationship: kinship, naming, ceremonial, or age grade. To make matters even more difficult, the systems of kinship classification are used and manipulated for political reasons.

The distinction between us (*kwoiyi*) and others (*kukïdi*) runs through the Suya social universe. The contrast between them has a variety of referents which depend on context. It can be used to indicate Suya as opposed to non-Suya, consanguines as opposed to affines, and close consanguines as opposed to more distant ones. The contrast between us and other involves varying distances from ego and is analogous to that of the center versus varying degrees of the periphery in Suya concepts of space. Figure 7.1 summarizes the types of context in which the terms are used.

The first distinction is that between the Suya and other Indian tribes. In this sense all Suya are *kwoiyi* of each other. All people in other tribes are non-*kwoiyi* (*kukïdi*). Any non-Suya who marries a Suya woman is a "sister's husband" (*wiyaiyõ* or *tukà*) to every male Suya. Similarly the Txukahamae, who stole a number of Suya women, are sometimes called "the brother-in-law people" (*mẽ tumbre: mẽ,* people like Suya; *tumbre,* sister's husband).

At the second level of contrast the *kwoiyi* are opposed to *mẽ kukïdi,* "the other people." I asked the Suya a number of times and in a number of ways what was different about people who were not *kwoiyi.* This question always brought a long silence and some thought. I twice suggested to my informants that people who were *kukïdi* had different blood (as among the Apinaye), but they denied it. One man offered this explanation: he said that affines were different, they were the other part of a pair, *ita tõra.* "It is like having two possessions that are alike [the example he used was feather armbands]. When one of them is missing, you say 'Where is the other one like this one?' [*ñita ita tõra*]. If there are many things [more than three], you do not say that. But if there are just two [he was insistent on this point], then you say *ta tõra* or *kukïdi.*" The dualism of the concept could not be more clearly expressed. *Kwoiyi,* at this sec-

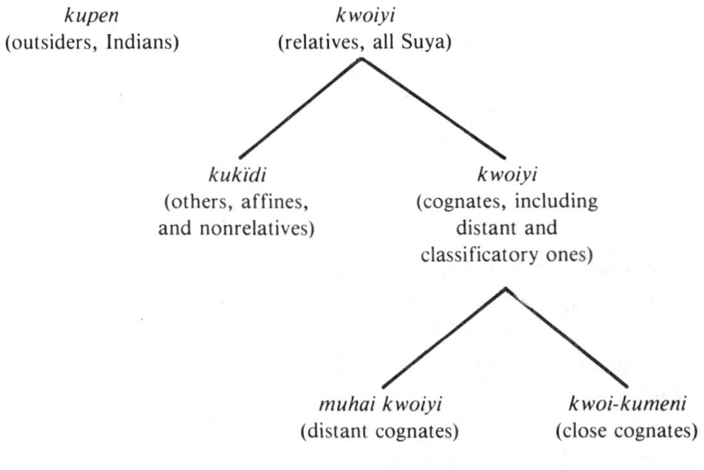

Figure 7.1 *Levels of contrast of the term* kwoiyi

ond level, are all those people who may be addressed with kinship, as opposed to affinal, terms. All affines, including the spouse, are non-*kwoiyi,* or *kukïdi.* Persons to whom no relationship of any kind is traced are also *kukïdi.*

At the third level of contrast the Suya distinguish between "distant *kwoiyi*" (*muhai kwoiyi*) and "real *kwoiyi*" (*kwoi-kumeni*). *Muhai* means spatially distant, and the Suya usually point across the plaza to indicate the actual physical distance that separates them from their *muhai kwoiyi.* *-kumeni* is a suffix used to indicate emphasis. Thus *kwoi-kumeni* are "really *kwoiyi.*"

The distinction between close kinsmen (*kwoi-kumeni*) and more distant kinsmen (*kwoiyi*) rests ultimately on ideas of physical or biological relationship combined with certain behavior toward other individuals. The Suya believe that a child is created through the repeated intercourse of the same man with a particular woman. Emphasis is placed on the repetition—it takes a lot of semen to build a child—and on the unitary nature of the genitor. A child has only one genitor, though that man may not necessarily be the mother's legitimate husband. With repeated and frequent intercourse the body is formed, then the forehead, the rest of the head, the arms, hands, fingers, and legs, in that order. The nose and teeth come last, according to one informant, the eyes are last according to another. It is important to note that the child is created entirely by the accumulation of semen, for which the female is a receptacle. The "real kinsmen" of a Suya always include those people with whom he has biological identity: full brothers and sisters, children, and parents.

Relations who are not full siblings, children, or parents are distinguished by the observance of certain types of behavior toward the specific individuals. The six important variables are (1) coresidence (during childhood, in the case of men) (2) diet restrictions observed for them when they are ill, (3) the use of kinship terms for ascending generations, (4) joking relationships, (5) an attitude of reserve, which the Suya call shame, and (6) sexual relations. Close kinsmen (*kwoi-kumeni*) are individuals with whom the first three variables, but never the sixth, are observed. Distant kinsmen are those adults toward whom the third and fourth are found and with whom the sixth is possible although considered a little wanton (*añi mbai kïdi*). Affines or *kukïdi* are those with whom the fifth and sixth are present but not the second, third, or fourth. These behaviors are summarized in figure 7.2.

Coresidence means residence in the same house or in houses of the same name. People who live in one's house are also called *tchï-yi,* "people who sleep in the same place." Houses are rigidly exogamous and sexual relations between *kwoiyi* living in the same house are considered extremely wanton. Behavior expected to obtain between *kwoiyi* is above all expected of people who sleep in the same house. The flexibility to be

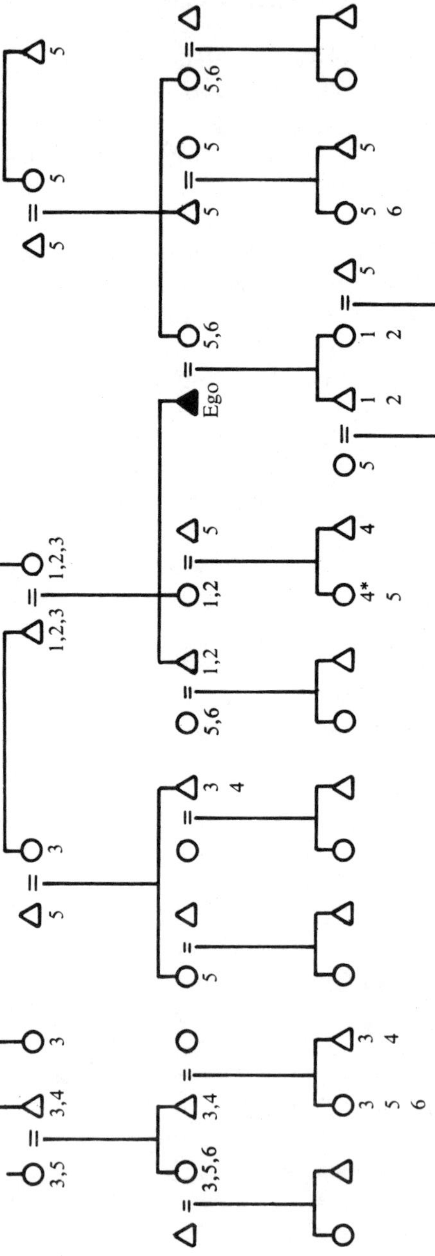

Figure 7.2 *Relationships among close kin and affines. (1) Coresidence in natal household. (2) Diet and activity restrictions when injured. (3) Use of kinship term. (4) Joking relationship. (5) Shame relationship. (6) Sexual relations are permissible. (4*) Joking relationship ends at puberty and is replaced by shame.*

found in kinship classification and behavior is found in relations with distant *kwoiyi* resident in other houses. In an uxorilocal residential situation the coresidents of a person's natal house are his mother, mother's sisters, father, mother's sisters' husbands, unmarried brothers, sisters, sisters' husbands and their children, mother's sisters' unmarried sons, and mother's sisters' daughters with their children. In the Suya kinship terminological system these are all classified as mother, father, brother, sister, and sister's children.

The Suya say that there is a physical identity between parents and children, which begins with the formation of the fetus and continues throughout life. In times of transition—birth, serious injury, death—certain relatives observe dietary and activity restrictions (*sangri*) to protect their biologically linked relative. A person observes these restrictions only for his close kinsmen (*kwoi-kumeni*). He does not observe them for adopted relatives. A man may choose not to observe them for children of his wife who he believes are not his own.

Terms denoting kinsmen (which are distinguished from affinal terms) are usually used for ascending-generation individuals who are *kwoiyi*. Names are used for same-generation and descending-generation *kwoiyi* and unrelated individuals. Affinal terms are used for the rest.

Persons standing in the relationship of mother's brother and sister's son (MB-ZS) have an institutionalized joking relationship.[2] My informants said that a man can joke with his *ngedi* (class of persons including his mother's brother), a sister's son (*taumtwü*), a companion, and a sister's daughter (*taumtwü-ndiyi*) before she reaches puberty. He does not joke with other people until he has many grandchildren and becomes a clown (*wikenyi*). There is some mild joking with grandchildren, not usually reciprocal, but there is no joking with affines or with coresidents of a house.

Shame (*whiasàm*) is the inverse of the joking relationship, and the relationship that should obtain between a man and his affines (*kukïdi*). A person with intense shame toward another does not look straight at him or her, nor speak to him directly, nor use his name, share cooked food with him, engage in sexual relations with him, or joke with him in any way. In addition certain modifications of normal speech are made when referring to a person toward whom one has shame. For example, when a man says "We are going" and he is going with a person toward whom he has shame, he uses a form of "to go" that indicates a large group (*maw*) rather than the word used under less formal circumstances (*tem*). Shame is exhibited in varying degrees toward affines, ritual relations, and older age grades. Of course a man has sexual relations with his wife, but during the early stages of marriage he does not often look straight at her, never uses her name, and employs a special relationship terminology of shame for her. Lesser degrees of shame are exhibited by young men toward older ones and by wrongdoers toward people whom they have wronged.

Sexual relations are of great importance in determining who is a *kwoiyi* and who is a *kukïdi*. The Suya say that it is extremely wanton to have sexual relations with any person from one's own natal house. It is somewhat less wanton to have sexual relations with distant *kwoiyi*. It is permissible for a man to have sexual relations with certain affines (wife, wife's sister, brother's wife, and sometimes wife's brother's daughter) and for a woman to have sexual relations with her husband, husband's brothers, sisters' husbands, and sometimes father's sister's husband. As soon as two individuals have had sexual relations they no longer address each other by name or kinship term, and they may no longer behave in manners dictated by former kinship or name-based relationships. The act of sexual intercourse requires the reclassification of the partner as an affine (*kukïdi*). It does not, however, require a reclassification of all the partner's relatives into affines unless there is an actual or arranged marriage and coresidence.

Within the group of coresidents, the members of the nuclear or restricted family are clearly set apart from other relatives by the presence of dietary and activity restrictions (2). Male members associated with the uxorilocal household (mother's brothers) are clearly marked by joking relationships (4). The marking of the relationships through special forms of behavior demonstrates several important principles: the distinction between kinsmen and affines (*kwoiyi* and *kukïdi*), the contrast between physical and nonphysical relationships, and the pivotal role of the mother's brother.

Figure 7.2 must be taken as a normative system of relationships. To a great extent these behaviors are observed, but the frequency and degree of the observance may be reduced by distance and increased by closeness. For various reasons an individual may want to change a distant relationship into a close one. He then begins to observe scrupulously the relationship as if the close genealogical relationship existed. If the other person reciprocates, they they have effectively reclassified each other. The transition can also be from close to more distant. In a small-scale, endogamous society there are usually several ways of tracing a relationship to any given person.

Kinship Terminology

Whether an individual uses names, kin terms, or affinal terms to refer to or address a particular individual is flexible. There are some rules: names are never used for affines, rarely for ascending-generation *kwoiyi*, almost always for nonrelatives and same-generation and descending-generation *kwoiyi*. Kin terms are used for ascending-generation *kwoiyi*, occasionally for descending-generation and same-generation *kwoiyi*. Affinal terms are used for close *kwoiyi* of a spouse and for any person with whom a person has had or is having sexual relations. Even though an actual kinship term may not be used between related persons, they are quite conscious of the relationship. Behavior is often explained using a kinship idiom: "I did such-and-such because so-and-so is such-and-such a relative."

I found rather quickly that I was not able to understand the regularities in Suya behavior until I understood how different individuals believed that they were related to each other.

I collected data on kinship terminology in two ways. The approach of W. H. R. Rivers (Rivers 1910), eliciting terms for positions on a genealogy, by itself, did not yield very good data. I also was able to obtain photographs of every Suya from Dr. Roberto Baruzzi of the Escola Paulista de Medicina. I asked a number of Suya to look at the photographs and to tell me how they addressed and referred to each individual. If the logic of the use of a certain term was obvious, I merely noted the usage in my notebook. When I did not understand the use of a term, I asked a person why he used it. This method was quite successful and quickly revealed the principles underlying the terminology.[3]

There is a definite pattern in the ability of Suya to use their kinship terms. Adults know how they are related to other people in the village better than nonadults; men know better than women. Children know the least and are frequently unable to give terms for people living in any house other than their own. Even teenage boys would sometimes be corrected by their elders in their use of terms. Young unmarried men were able to classify about 50 percent of the photographs, mostly as close and distant relatives, leaving a fairly large group of individuals whom they could not classify at all. Young men were also less able to discuss the reasons for classifying certain people as they did. After men are married and have entered the political arena, they are able to classify nearly every person in the village. The adult men from whom I elicited terms were able to tell their relationship to individuals in 94 percent to 98 percent of the photographs. They were also able to explain why they used one term and not another. Adult women in general were less able to look at the photographs and classify them according to kinship terminology; they were able to classify between 60 percent and 80 percent of the photographs. They did not appear to think in kinship terms as much as the men and had more difficulty with persons outside their own house. These patterns of familiarity with relationships to other members of the village clearly reflect the differences in age and sex roles. Adult men are more concerned with relationships outside their natal and residential household; women are more concerned with relationships within their own house and related houses; children are not integrated into the adult world and are mostly familiar with the members of their own house and with their parents' siblings.

The Suya kinship terminology is characterized by the similar classification of members of same-sex siblings, by an Omaha-type "skewing" of generation, and by the reclassification of individuals after having sexual relations with them. The distinction between "classificatory" and "close" kinsmen, which are sometimes analytic tools of dubious usage, is in fact paralleled by the Suya distinction between distant kinsmen (*muhai kwoiyi*) and really kinsmen (*kwoi-kumeni*).

The unity of the same-sex sibling group means that fathers' brothers are addressed by the same term as fathers and that their children are addressed by the same term as that used for one's own siblings. Mothers' sisters are addressed by the same term as mothers, and their children too are addressed as siblings. In the affinal terminology, a man's brothers' wives are all addressed as wives and their children are addressed as children. Since these relationships continue in genealogical time (a son's son is a "brother" of his grandfather's brother's son's son), after a few generations each person has many classificatory brothers and sisters who are not closely related in the Suya sense of the word. These are the distant *kwoiyi* who are distinguished from the *kwoi-kumeni* by various kinds of behavior.

The second way to gain classificatory relatives is through the reclassification of sexual partners. When a man has sexual relations with a woman, she becomes a wife (*hron*). If he suspects that a child of hers is his own, he may refer to the woman as "mother of my child" and to her child as "my child." In this way Suya who have no apparent genealogical connection or relationship in terms of sanctioned spouses have a genealogical relationship according to the Suya. All the children of a man's wife are usually called his children, since he is their mother's husband. However, some of them may simultaneously be classified as the children of another man who is believed to have engendered them. Of a sample of five adult men, two classified six women as sexual partners (*hron*), one classified eight, and two classified ten. This makes it possible to classify a large number of children in the village by more than one term, depending on whether one classified them as "wife's children" or as "children of that woman's husband."

Despite the flexibility in classification, the Suya have a clear and conscious system of kinship terminology. They are quite consistent in their usage of this terminological system for their closer kinsmen. The bare genealogical kinship figures and lists of terms are presented with some trepidation. They are intended for summary purposes and for comparative interest. Although the Suya observe genealogical relationships, their definitions of them are different from ours. They have their own theory of conception, of closeness and distance, and their own ways for reclassifying kinsmen. Suya villages have always been small enough to permit several ways of tracing relationships to any person outside the extended family. The charts represent an ideal that does not actually exist in the observed use of terms and behaviors; they are a type of genealogy that has never existed, although the principles operating in them operate in the Suya use of the terms.

As figures 7.3 and 7.4 show, the Suya have an Omaha-type cross-cousin classification. The sons of a mother's brother (*ngedi*) are addressed by the same term as their father (*ngedi*), while the daughters of a *ngedi* are addressed by the same term used for mother (*tire*). Children of a father's sister are addressed by the terms used for son and daughter when the speaker is a male. In addition to this generational skewing of cross-cousin terms, the Suya have a FZH-WBD spouse equation, a feature frequently found among groups with Omaha systems.

Among the Northern Kayapo and Apinaye the mother's brother is terminologically equivalent to the mother's father and father's father. Among the Suya there is one term for mother's father and father's father (*gitumu*) and a different term for mother's brothers (*ngedi*) and all male children of *ngedi*. The terms are in a sense derivative. The term *gitumu* can be reduced to two components, (*n*)*git*, a contracted form of *ngedi*, and *tumu*, or "old." Thus *gitumu* means old *ngedi*. The reciprocal terms for both *ngedi* and *gitumu* are identical (*taumtwü*). The behaviors of a man toward his *ngedi* and *gitumu* are somewhat similar. *Ngedi* are joking relatives, but one may also joke in a less riotous way with a *gitumu* or *taumtwü*. Although it is possible to show a derivation of one term from a modification of the other, the Suya say that *ngedi* and *gitumu* are definitely different terms and that they signify different sorts of relatives.[4]

Marriage and Affines

The Suya differ from other Gê tribes in their marriage norms. Preferential matrilateral cross-cousin marriage, a group of siblings marrying another group of siblings, and brother-sister exchange (the exchange of men between two houses) are all considered good or ideal marriages by the Suya and are not found among the other Northern Gê. The marriage ideals of the Suya are at first glance mutually exclusive. If a man marries his mother's brother's daughter, and there is a sibling exchange, the other man must be marrying his father's sister's daughter—a form of marriage that is supposed to be prohibited. In fact, according to my genealogies, such marriages existed. But they were more frequent among distant kinsmen of those classes. To make an exchange conform to an ideal, or good, pattern, it is sufficient to exchange any classificatory sister preferably, but not necessarily, from one's natal household.[5]

The most frequently stated marriage norm is that a man marry the real or classificatory daughter of a real or classificatory *ngedi*. When there is a matrilateral cross-cousin marriage preference in a Omaha kinship system which does not have a spouse equation terminology, a man must

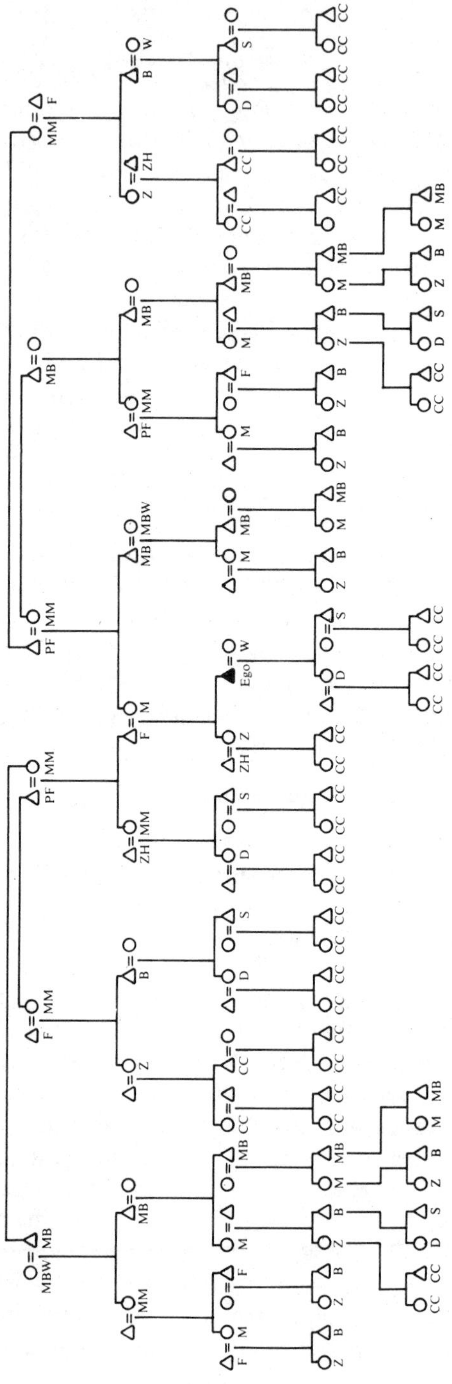

Figure 7.3 *Kinship terms for a male ego (M,* tire; *F,* ture; *MM,* tuwuyi; *PF,* gitumu; *MB,* ngedi; *MBW,* tuwuyi *(female speaker),* ngit-ta-teng-nã *(male speaker); B,* kambü; *Z,* kandikwoiyi; *W,* hron; *H,* mjen; *S,* kra; *D,* kra-ndiyi; *CC,* taumtwü)

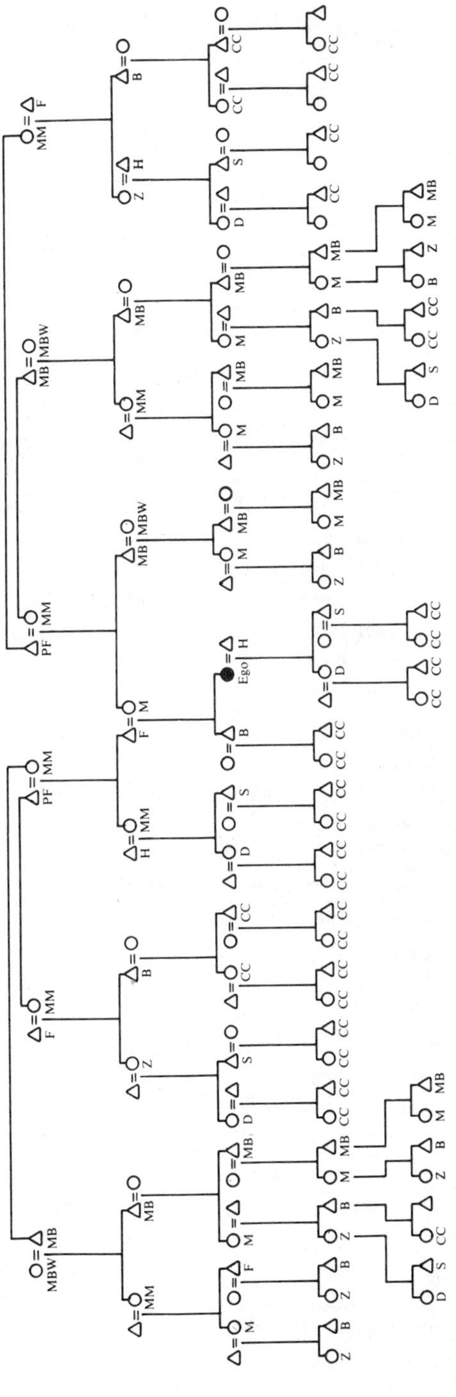

Figure 7.4 *Kinship terms for a female ego (symbols are explained in figure 7.3)*

marry a classificatory "mother." This is the case with the Suya. Knowing that the Suya believe it to be extremely wanton to have sexual relations with a father's spouse, and having been told some funny stories about men who actually had sexual relations with such women, I asked why it was acceptable to marry a woman addressed, before marriage, as "mother" (*tire*). My informants were unconcerned by the problem. They merely acknowledged that "of course we call them mother if we do not marry them." The distinction that appears to be important is between close and distant kin. Biological mothers, and father's spouses, are not potential wives. However, distant mothers and the distant daughters of a mother's father or a father's father are acceptable as spouses. Daughters of a *ngedi* are ideal. When a man marries, his wife's sisters and his brothers' wives are all his *hron* (potential sexual partners). The Suya say that a man may have sexual relations with his brothers' wives and his wife's sisters and that no one should be angry with him because these women are his *hron*.[6]

Tables 7.1 and 7.2 give the reference terms used for affines. These terms appear in myths and descriptions. For one's own affines an elaborate set of indirect and metaphorical references is used instead of these terms. The indirect affinal reference terms (tables 7.3 and 7.4) are used in talking to a person toward whom the speaker has shame when he is referring to a relative of the person to whom he is speaking. Some of the indirect terms appear in other Northern Gê languages as primary reference terms. An example is the use of *tukà-yi* by the Apinaye for wife's father. Other indirect terms appear to be metaphors for "people of your sleeping place" and refer to the important social units of houses and groups of houses having the same name.

The Suya guide for using the indirect reference terms is this: "When you see an affine go by and your spouse asks 'Who was that?' you are ashamed (*whiasàm*) to say the name of the person because it is a relative of his (hers), so you use these terms." These are, then, circumlocutions for the direct terms of reference.

The indirect affinal reference terms (given in tables 7.3 and 7.4) can be used as the basis of an interesting comparative analysis with the other Gê. Term number 1 *a-tukà-yi* appears to equate all inmarrying men for both male and female speakers, since *tukà* appears as a direct reference term for sister's husband and here for a wife's father as well. A similar situation exists among the Apinaye.[7] The terms for spouse's mother (2) are different for male and female speakers. For a man the terminology is a metaphor. For a woman the term is merely a formal form of saying "your mother" (*i-wa-nã-yi*). This difference may well reflect the greater degree of shame between a man and his wife's mother than that between woman and her husband's father. Term 3 is for both sexes merely a somewhat formal way of indicating a sibling of the same sex as the

Table 7.1 Affinal terms for male ego

SUYA TERM	RELATIONSHIP	RECIPROCAL
tumbre-ngedi	WF, father of jurally recognized wife	*wiyaiyõ, tukà*
tumẽ-ngedi (*twoi-ngedi*)	WM, WBW of jurally recognized wife	*wiyaiyõ, tukà*
hron	W, WZ, BW, WBD; any woman with whom one has had sexual relations	*mjen*
wiyaiyõ (tukà after several children are born)	ZH, FZH; husband of any woman referred to as sister (*kandikwoiyi*)	*tumbre*
wiyaiyõ	DH; husband of any woman classed as *krandiyi*	*tumbre-ngedi*
tumbre	WB, WBS of jurally recognized wife	*wiyaiyõ*
twoiyi	SW	*tumbre-ngedi*
wàtàn-puita[a]	Refers to wife before birth of first child	*neumda, wàtàna*[a]
màn-ngedi	F of woman with whom one is having sexual relations	—
tukà nã	ZHM	(?)
tukà pam	ZHF	(?)

[a] Literally, "what's-the-girl's-name?" (*watan,* what; *puita* from *puiyi,* adolescent girl). Young men are supposed to be ashamed to admit they have a *hron.*

Table 7.2 Affinal terms for female ego

SUYA TERM	RELATIONSHIP	RECIPROCAL
tumbre-ngedi	HF; father of resident husband	*twoiyi*
tumen-ngedi	HM, HZ, HZD	*twoiyi*
mjen	H, HB, ZH, FZH; any man with whom one has had sexual relations	*hron*
twoiyi	BW, SW	*tumengedi*
wiyaiyõ	DH	*twoingedi*
tukà nã	ZHM	?
tukà pam	ZHF	?
neumda[a]	Refers to husband before birth of first child	*wàtànpuita*

[a] Literally, "what's-his-name"; from *neumda,* "who."

Table 7.3 Indirect affinal reference terms for male ego

Indirect term	Direct term	Relationship	Semantic meaning of indirect term
1. *a-tukà-yi*	*tumbre-ngedi*	WF classificatory WF	*a,* your; *tukà,* term used for ZH with children. May mean a man married to woman of your house; *yi,* class of persons. Thus "a man married to a woman of your house."
2a. *wa-kato-jï* (when speaking to one's wife)	*tumẽ-ngedi*	WM classificatory WM	*wa,* first person plural, us; *kato* (?), might mean *kato,* birth; *jï,* form of *yi,* a class of persons. Thus may be "one of the class of persons who gave birth to you."
2b. *a-maito-jï* (to person other than wife)	*tuwoi-ngedi*	WM	*a,* your; *maito* (?), *jï,* class of persons. I cannot translate this term.
3. *a-tõno*	*hron*	WZ	*a,* your; *tõno,* means sister in this term, but it is not encountered elsewhere. Perhaps from *tõ,* a word used for male sibling.
4a. *a-kot-tchï-yi*[a]	*tumbre*	*WB*	*a,* your; *kot,* accompanying, going with; *tchï,* sleeping place, a family's part of the house; *yi,* a class of persons. Thus "one of the group of persons who is (was) of the same sleeping place or part of the house."
4b. *a-ka-tõ-yï* (an alternative to 4a used by Western Suya)	*tumbre*	WB	*a,* your; *ka-tõ,* brother; yï, class of persons. "One of the class of your brothers."
5. *ka-whai-yi*	*tumbre* *hron*	WBS WBD	*ka,* your; *whai,* a word for bed; *yi,* class of persons. Thus "people of your bed," with approximate meaning of *a-kot-tchï-yi.* Another referent for *whai-yi* is a roasting rack.

[a] *Tchï,* or sleeping place, was discussed in the description of space categories within the house; see chapter 3.

Table 7.4 Indirect affinal reference terms for female ego

INDIRECT TERM	DIRECT TERM	RELATIONSHIP	SEMANTIC MEANING OF INDIRECT TERM
1. *a-tukà-yi*	*tumbre-ngedi*	HF	*a,* your; *tukà,* a term used by a male ego for ZH, a female ego for DH with children; *yi,* a class of persons. Thus "one of the in-marrying men (of your father's generation)."
2. *i-wa-nã-yi*	*tumẽ-ngedi*	HM	*i-wa,* polite form of "your"; *nã,* mother; *yi,* class of persons. Thus "one of your mothers."
3a. *a-ka-tõ-yi*	*mjen*	HB	*a,* your; *ka-tõ,* brother; *yi,* class of persons. "One of your brothers."
3b. *a-tõ*	*mjen*	HB	This is not a special form, simply "your brother" in normal speech. *a,* your; *tõ,* brother.
4a. *ka-whai-yi*	*tumẽ-ngedi*	HZ HZC	*ka,* your; *whai,* bed; *yi,* class of persons. "People of your bed," also "people of your house," by extension.
4b. *i-wa-tõ-yi* (used by Western Suya in addition to 4a)	*tumẽ-ngedi*	HZ	*i-wa,* polite form of "your;" *tõ,* may mean sibling here; *yi,* class of persons. A polite form of "one of your sisters."

spouse. These individuals are potential spouses of the speaker, and the relation of shame is not as great as for the other affines. This is clear when term 3 is contrasted with the terms for cross-sex siblings of the spouse (4a, 4b). A man says "a person of your (family) sleeping place (*a-kot-tchï-yi*) or uses a formal way of saying "your brother" (*a-ka-tõ-yi*) when he is talking to his wife. A woman calls a man's sisters "*ka-whaï-yi*."[8] I have translated the term as "people of your bed." In the case of a female speaker that is literally true, since the man's sister lives in the man's natal household and slept on the same pole bed as a child. In the case of a male speaker, the woman's brother who has children no longer lives with his sister but rather with his wife in another house. The relationship between cross-sex siblings is stressed. The indirect terms for the children of cross-sex are the same. The Eastern and Western Suya groups use the same indirect affinal terms with the exception of 4b, which the Western Suya use in addition to 4a.

The indirect affinal reference terms include larger numbers of kinsmen than the direct reference terms. They tend to emphasize the unity of the named houses and the nuclear families within them as well as the distinction between us and other (*kwoiyi* versus *kukïdi*), which is fundamental to the ideology of kinship.

Suya Naming Practices

The relationhip terminology is not based exclusively on genealogically defined kinship, for naming relationships are extremely important and the terminology of naming relationships overrides kinship terms. Da Matta (1976) has argued quite cogently that the terminology of kinship can be understood only if the naming relationship is taken into account (see also Lave 1967).

In one sense the kinship and naming are quite different. Kinship is based on a biological identity with the parents, a corporeal similarity established through procreation and marked by diet and activity restrictions. Naming marks the socialization of the infant and identifies the public personage. This social identity is often represented through body painting according to moiety and sometimes even name-set membership. But name givers are also relatives, and the two systems are interrelated. A boy is supposed to receive his names from a *ngedi,* a girl from a *tuwuyi*.

Every Suya possesses a set of between one and forty-four names. The lower figure was the case for a number of women, and the higher one was the largest number of names that I elicited for any one name set. Each set is thought to be a separate entity, and each person receives only one set during his lifetime, although nicknames may be added. The names themselves usually have some semantic meaning, although these are apparently not of great importance to the Suya.

A man's name set is a complete social and ceremonial identity. It gives him automatic membership in one of the log-racing moieties (*Kren* and *Amban*). It gives him membership in one of the four plaza groups which appear in ceremonies in which the log-racing moieties are inactive and which are themselves really reducible to two moieties, *sàiko-kambrigi* and *sàiko-dnto*, each also including a small group painted with the same colors but with vertical instead of horizontal lines (*ponirekunawti* and *atàchi*).[9] In addition, each name set has certain rights and obligations which go with its names. Thus in a given ceremony the members of one name set are at the front of the line of dancers and the members of another always conclude the ceremony. Some have certain ornaments that only they wear. These specific features may apply to a single ceremony, or they may be more general. But the smallest unit, and the most basic one, is always that of the men who hold the same set of names. An individual, as distinct from his name set, holds no special ceremonial role (with the exception of the "controller of songs"). The members of the group are ceremonially identical.

Some name sets have associated women's names, and women with these names are affiliated with the same moieties as the male members of the groups. But they rarely act as part of the groups. Many women's names are not associated with men's name sets, and the women with these names have no moiety affiliation. My Western Suya informants said that sometimes women gathered by moiety and sang. They said that those women who had men's name sets assembled with the moiety group to which their names belonged. The rest joined the group to which their husbands belonged.

Suya names are individualizing as well as classifying. Nearly every person living in a village is addressed by a different name even though many of them share a single name set. Different members of the same name set use different names in it. Close relatives (mothers, brothers, sisters) may address one another by names different from those used by the rest of the village, usually another name from the name set. Certain relatives may use nicknames, usually given by an old person after an unusual event. One man was called "dung beetle" because when he was young he drank one in his manioc drink and his grandfather thought it was funny and called him by that term. Later most men of his age called him by the same term, in informal situations. Most of the time, however, a Suya is addressed by one of the names in his name set by most of the members of the village. My genealogies indicate that a given name is used in alternate generations. When men die, their names may be used by a living person. According to one informant, when all of the names in a name set are being used by living people, the name set is not given to any more people, a rule to which there are some exceptions.

The Western Suya differ in a few respects. Each name set appears to have a central, identifying name. In addition, each has a number of auxiliary names, which are used in daily conversation. In formal situations (including the collecting of genealogies, unfortunately) the identifying name of the set is always given. Individuals were differentiated by names that they were given at the conclusion of ceremonies, which always had the prefix of the name of the ceremony and a suffix referring to their particular performance of it, or by certain altered forms of the identifying name such as a diminutive.

Both groups of Suya could discuss naming more easily than kinship relations. Women, especially, knew a great deal about naming and name transmission, which contrasted with their relative unfamiliarity with kinship classification. This tendency may be due to the clarity of the naming system: either one is a member of a given name set, and therefore moiety, or one is not. In the use of kinship terminology there is considerable ambiguity and room for manipulation according to specific political situations.

The stated norm for giving names is that a *ngedi* (real and classificatory mother's brothers) gives his names to a *taumtwü* (sister's son) while a *tuwuyi* (real and classificatory father's sisters) gives hers to a *taumtwü-ndiyi* (brother's daughter). The genealogical mother's brother and father's sister are mentioned always as the ideal name givers, although more distant ones may do. A man often calls his sister "mother of my name receiver" even before she has a child, although the reverse form (father of my name receiver, female speaker) is never so used. Parents and siblings, real or classificatory, can never give their names to an infant. Furthermore, name givers should be chosen so that uterine brothers are in different moieties. Often the firstborn is given an *Ambàn* name set and the second-born a *Kren* name set.

The Suya comply with their norms to a considerable extent (tables 7.5 and 7.6). My information is most complete for the younger generation because I know exactly how parents address each other. I have less certain data for the first ascending generation, and my information cannot be used statistically for the second ascending generation. The Suya compliance with this norm is even more impressive in view of the population losses that they have suffered and the large-scale incorporation of captives without relatives into the population.

In the youngest generation, 47.5 percent of the boys bore the names of a real or classificatory mother's brother (*ngedi*). The total percentage for two generations is 28.5 percent. This is especially striking since the next most numerous name givers are grandfathers (*gitumu*), with only 18.5 percent together. (Some of these men may have actually received their names from a *ngedi* but have been named in memory of the *gitumu* whose names they also bear). Two men received names from female relatives who had male names sets and could pass their name sets to a

Table 7.5 Name-giving kinsmen in two generations, male ego

Generation	MB	FF	MF	FB	MMB	MFB	MZ	FZ	MMF	Unknown	Total
Lowest 001-042 in appendix A	10 47.5%	– 0%	1 4.75%	– 0%	2 9.5%	1 4.75%	1 4.75%	– 0%	– 0%	6 28.75%	21 100%
First ascending 101-155 in appendix A	2 9.5%	4 19%	3 14.25%	1 4.75%	– 0%	– 0%	– 0%	1 4.75%	1 4.75%	9 42.75%	21 99.75%
Total 001-155	12 28.5%	4 9.5%	4 9.5%	1 2.37%	2 4.75%	1 2.37%	1 2.37%	1 2.37%	1 2.37%	15 35.75%	42 99.85%

Table 7.6 Name-giving kinsmen in two generations, female ego

GENERATION	FZ*	MM*	FM*	MMZ*	FMBD*	MMM*	MB	MMB	MF	MMZH	UNKNOWN	TOTAL
Lowest 001-042 in appendix A	2 11.2%	2 11.2%	1 5.6%	2 11.2%	— 0%	2 11.2%	1 5.6%	— 0%	— 0%	1 5.6%	7 39.0%	18 100.6%
First ascending 101-155 in appendix A	1 3.7%	1 3.7%	2 7.4%	— 0%	1 3.7%	— 0%	— 0%	2 7.4%	1 3.7%	— 0%	19 70.3%	27 99.9%
Total 001-155	3 6.6%	3 6.6%	3 6.6%	2 4.4%	1 2.2%	2 4.4%	1 2.2%	2 4.4%	1 2.2%	1 2.2%	26 57.2%	45 99.0%

*All the genealogical positions marked with an asterisk are referred to by a single term, *tuwuyi,* by the Suya.

man. A large number of the name givers whose genealogical relationship is unknown are the result of the population decrease suffered in the recent past and their present rapid population increase. There are now many children, and the tendency is to name children after famous men of the more distant past when the complement of close *ngedi* has been exhausted. (Siblings should never have the same name set; thus a different *ngedi* is needed for each one).

Female name giving does not conform to as neat a pattern as that of the men. Female names are ceremonially less important. They often appear singly, unattached to any name set. One result is that there is a large imbalance in the number of name sets. The relationship between female name giver and name receiver is also less important than the corresponding male relationship. Members of a male name set dance together and play important roles in each other's ceremonial life, and the male name giver is an important mediating figure in the life cycle. But the female child receives her name from a broader group of relatives, and more often than a man she is given the name of a distant relative.

The male name receiver is said to be the exact replica of his name giver in all ceremonial affairs. They share membership in the same groups, and they share the same rights and obligations. The Suya maintain that there is an actual identity between the two, that in some senses they are one being. They address each other as *krã-tumu* and *krã-ndu*, which I have translated as "name giver" and "name receiver." Several researchers have translated identical terms among the Apinaye and Northern Kayapo as "old head" and "new head." This is the literal translation of *krã* (head) and *tumu* and *ndu* (old and new). The Suya were in general loath to indulge in folk etymologies and absolutely deny this meaning. They say that the term has nothing to do with heads but with names. The terms imply a definite identity between the members of the naming relationship but not in the sense of head. The upper, fainter arc of a double rainbow, is said to be the *krã-tumu* and the lower, brighter arc is called its *krã-ndu*. A man calls all people older than himself who share his name set *krã-tumu,* and all of those younger *krã-ndu*.

One of the ways in which the identity of the name giver and name receivers is expressed is in terms of taboos against sexual relations with a female name receiver. The Suya say that relations between such persons are bad because "they are of one name." When a man has sexual relations with a female name giver or receiver, she becomes an affine and can no longer behave like a ritual relation. Nor should a man have sexual relations with the wife of a male name giver or name receiver. If he was doing so before they married, he should stop when they are living together. Having sexual relations with the wife of a name receiver would be acting as though the name receiver were a brother, one of the relatives that can never give or receive names.

The identity between a name giver and a name receiver is not the same as the identity between a child and its parents. Name givers never observe diet or activity restrictions for a name receiver. Name sharers are not obliged to exchange food in the daily distribution unless the name giver is a close *ngedi* and receives food from his own sister. The Suya distinguish between relations with close kin (*kwoi-kumeni*) and naming relations. In an important naming ceremony a hostile opposition of the two groups clearly marks their contrast. Each type of relationship is relevant to a separate domain, and the interaction between the two domains is symbolically reiterated at every stage of a male child's transformation into a grown man, somewhat less so in the transformation of a girl into a woman. Naming terminology always overrides all other kinds of terminology, as does the ceremonial relationship terminology.

Ritual Relationships

Relationships established under ceremonial circumstances and for ritual purposes are an important part of the relationship system of an individual. As with naming relationships, there is a special terminology of address and a set of normative behaviors. There are four ritual relationships, summarized in figure 7.5.[10]

The first in ceremonial importance are the *ñumbre-krà-chi* bonds. These relationships may be inherited, and new ones can be formally established only in log races that use burity logs. The village in which the Suya were living during my stay had no nearby burity trees, and consequently not all the men had living *ñumbre-krà-chi.* The young men who had them had inherited the relationship. As a consequence, I was never able to witness the formation of the bond. According to my informants, the bond is established when a child is quite young, though after he can walk. In the case of a male child two men who are either good friends (often ceremonial friends, *ñumbre*) or who are ritual relations (*ñumbre-krà-chi*) themselves take their sons and say to them, "That is your *ñumbre-krà-chi.*" The terminology for the relationship is one of reciprocal address; each partner calls his male ceremonial relative and that man's sons, *ñumbre-krà-chi.* Although a *ñumbre-krà-chi* should not be a close relative (*kwoiyi*), the relationship can be inherited: the sons of a man's *ñumbre-krà-chi* are *ñumbre-krà-chi* to him and to his own sons.

The relationship is actually established when, for the first time, the *ñumbre-krà-chi* actually perform the ritual act of painting each other for a burity-log relay race. Once established, they also cut and decorate each other's dance masks in the mouse ceremony and play small roles in other ceremonies. Among the Western Suya an important function of *ñumbre-krà-chi* was to give each other water in certain ceremonies and to play some role in the induction of a man into the men's house. These ritual activities are undertaken in silence and with solemnity. Under most circumstances *ñumbre-krà-chi* behave with intense shame (*whiasàm*) toward each other. They do not use each other's names; they do not directly address each other or make eye contact. The Suya say that a *ñumbre-krà-chi* is the same as a wife's father in the degree of shame exhibited toward him.

In addition to these male ceremonial relations, a man also has a female ritual relationship with women he calls *kràm-ngedi*. *Kràm-ngedi* are the

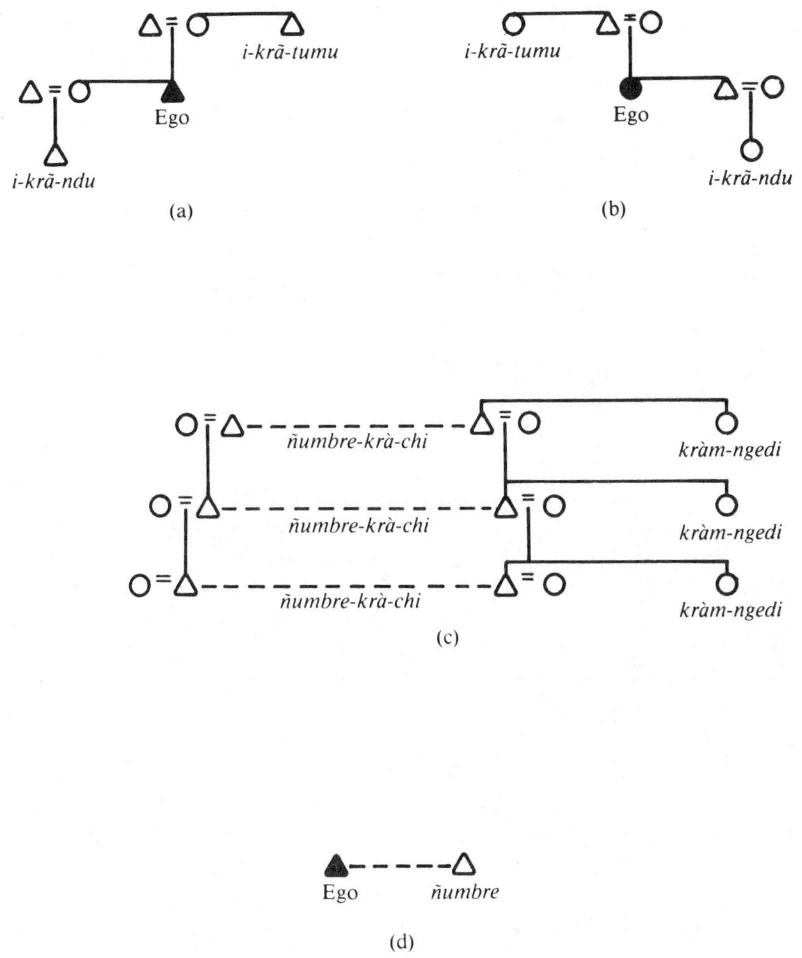

Figure 7.5 *Naming and ceremonial relationship terms. (a) Naming relationship terms for male ego. (b) Naming relationship terms for female ego. (c) Ceremonial relationships. (Terms are reciprocal.* Ñumbre-krà-chi *bonds established for a child are usually with an older man.) (d) Friendship terms (reciprocal).*

sisters and daughters of his *ñumbre-krà-chi. Kràm-ngedi* also help to paint dance masks and, ideally, paint the corpses of their *ñumbre-krà-chi.* Ceremonial relatives of both sexes are necessary. In the mouse ceremony, for example, *ñumbre-krà-chi* cut each other's masks and apply black paint to certain parts of the mask and apply white bird down. A man's *kràm-ngedi* paints the red on parts of the mask and on the dancer's feet. The relationship of a man with his *kràm-ngedi* is also supposed to be formal, although the solemnity is not as great as with a *ñumbre-krà-chi.*

The relationship of a woman with her *kràm-ngedi* is marked by little shame. They do not perform many duties for each other besides painting each other's corpses.

The duties performed by the *ñumbre-krà-chi* and *kràm-ngedi* occur inside each person's natal household. They are involved in developing the social identity of the child and in maintaining the social identity of an adult. Although a name giver (*krã-tumu*) bestows his name and social identity on a child, the *ñumbre-krà-chi* and *kràm-ngedi* enter his house and paint him and prepare some of his ornaments for the ceremony, especially for those ceremonies involving rites of passage. The *ñumbre-krà-chi* and *kràm-ngedi,* chosen by the parents and sometimes inherited from them, to some extent mediate between the family (*kwoiyi*) and the fully developed name-based ceremonial groups and ceremonial relationships (*krã-tumu, krã-ndu.*)

Another ritual relationship is that of *ñumbre. Ñumbre* are male companions who have established a "bosom friend" relationship in the men's house. They may be either of the same or of opposite moieties. The friendship is established, however, during a young man's residence in the men's house before he fathers a child and moves to his wife's residence. A man always shares food with his *ñumbre,* addresses him by that term, sings with him, and travels with him. The relationship is not hereditary. It has fallen into disuse among the younger men with the discontinuation of a period of residence in the men's house.

Another relationship, less formal than that of *ñumbre,* is that of *kràm.* A *kràm* is a companion. One informant said that when two men do things together all the time, people call them *kràm.* They are usually about the same age, and they hunt, sing, and share food with each other, like *ñumbre.* But the relationship is not established ceremonially, and there is no special term of address. The term *kràm* is restricted to third-person and second-person usage; one can say "his *kram*" and "your *kràm*" but not "my *kràm.*"

One of the interesting features of this terminology for ceremonial relationships and friends is that similar terms are used. The companion of the men's house is a *ñumbre*; the male ceremonial relation is a *ñumbre-kràchi.* The informal companion is a *kràm;* the female ceremonial relation is a *kràm-ngedi.*[11] This indicates that these ceremonial relatives are "formal friends" (as similar ritual relations have been called in the literature). They have a special kind of relationship. they are like friends in that they are not relatives, and they are individual relationships (rather than name-set relationships). They do not imply an identity (as in both kinship and naming relationships) but act as mediators between kinship-based groups (the nuclear family and residential houses) and name-based groups (the ceremonial activity of the plaza). They are mediators, too, in that they concern themselves with the physical aspects of their ritual relations in moments of ceremony; they paint each other and among the Western Suya give each other water. At one moment they act as representatives of the ceremonial life (painting), at another as representatives of a family group (providing water).

Like the naming relationships, the ritual relationship terms (with the exception of *kràm*) override the kinship terminology. Even young Suya who could not say what their kinship relations were for most of the village always knew who their ritual relations were.

The complexity of the social organization of the Gê societies is increased by any attempt to interrelate the principles operating in the commonly differentiated domains of kinship, terminology (not only vocative and referential, but indirect reference as well), naming, and ceremonial relationships. But in fact they are all related. The structure of the kinship terminology is closely related to the ideas of what a relative is and what a name giver is; and friends and highly respected ceremonial relatives are interrelated. Part of the complexity can be reduced by analyzing them as interrelated, but after considerable difficulty.

Understanding the importance of the group of people who share a kind of physical identity is fundamental to understanding Suya kinship. There are no lineages and no clearly defined intermarrying groups. Instead there are core groups of people whose bodies share a substance, groups of people who observe diet restrictions for one another. I have called these corporeal groups (Seeger 1975). This emphasis on the body is a recurrent feature in Suya society. The importance of this group is clearly revealed in the indirect reference terminology.

There is a gradual process of attenuation of the close physical bonds with the natal family, for a male, and an increasing identity with the life of the plaza and of an adult. This socialization of the physical entity that is born is reflected in the ornamentation of the body and in the classification of the members of different age grades by odor.

Some of the same principles that are important in other spheres of Suya life are clearly discernible in their social organization. In fact, the social organization itself can be better understood by examining the operation of these principles than by a separate analysis. The pattern of these institutions and relationships becomes clear in the context of the life cycle.

8

The Process of the Life Cycle

S*UYA INFANTS ARE BORN* unornamented and are not considered socially alive. They go through a series of rites of passage in which they and their bodies are socialized. When they die they are buried painted and ornamented, along with all their ceremonial paraphernalia. Socialization is a process of becoming. Most age-grade denominations may be phrased as "already become such-and-such." Each age grade is marked by a rite of passage, the most elaborate of which occur in the transitional age grades, the *sikwenduyi* for men and the *puyi* for women.

The linear description of the life cycle emphasizes important features of Suya society. First, it gives dynamics to the static analysis of kinship, naming, marriage, and aging. Second, the descriptions of rites of passage reveal the importance of the domains of space and their manipulation. Third, it restores the general emphasis of Suya society: that of transition and becoming, rather than that of categorization and being. This description of the life cycle is also useful in a comparative perspective, since the data given here may be compared with that described for the other Gê, for which similar data are available, and the variations from society to society in rites of passage covary with a number of other features of these societies (T. Turner 1973).

Conception and birth, walking, ear piercing and puberty, lip piercing, men's house residence, parenthood, and old age are all part of the ongoing process that represents the idealized operation of Suya society—as a continuing exchange of men in the men's house as individuals are born, age, and die. From birth until marriage, times of passage emphasize the attenuation of the intense ties that unite the corporeal group, the "really kinsmen" (*kwoi-kumeni*). These are attenuated at birth, naming, walking, certain children's ceremonies, induction into the men's house, and again at marriage. The close identity of brothers is attenuated by their social identities. Brothers should belong to opposite moieties, and there is a statistical tendency to give male siblings names belonging to alternate moieties. Brother-sister ties remain important through most of their lives, and these ties may be reinforced through naming each other's children or the marrying of their children. The attenuation of nuclear family ties does not extend to all ties with the kinsmen (*kwoiyi*). But daily relationships become those typical only of ceremonial occasions.

The Suya retain a balance between the ties to their natal family (family of orientation) and their family after marriage (family of procreation). The close identity and conjunction of the nuclear family gives way to a moderate disjunction which is not complete until very old age because of the importance of kinsmen in rituals and in dietary observations. Sisters are for rituals, and wives are for sexual relations. Each has its domain. But marriage is not a weak bond; there is no case of divorce of a man with more than two children in my genealogies.

The role of the mother's brother (*ngedi*) is pivotal. He is at once a name giver, a joking relation, and a possible wife giver. Thus he may not only provide the social identity of the boy which counteracts the boy's corporeal ties to his nuclear family; he may also be the very figure who draws the child from his natal residence into uxorilocal marriage. He is the focus of ritualized hostility in the naming ceremony, in which the parents of the child threaten him. No other Northern Gê society utilizes the mother's brother as both a provider of social identity and the provider of women.

Periods of Transition

A number of periods mark transitions between statuses for a Suya man. There are also a few for Suya women. Not all these rituals mark so-called biological life crises. The argument that all societies elaborate biological life crises is true for the Suya, but it is by no means an adequate enumeration of the times of passage. In addition to birth, puberty, and death, the Suya mark the time when the child can walk, when he has fathered a child, certain illnesses, the state of a man after he has killed an enemy, and life after death. Certain restrictions are imposed on food, sexual activity, and other activities at these times. The individual's status at the end of these times is always altered.

The restrictions on diet and activity are called *sangri*. The restrictions vary in intensity. Usually a person observes the most intense restrictions for just a few days; then he gradually relaxes the observations. However, if something untoward should happen, he usually reverts to a more severe form. The Suya take a very pragmatic attitude toward the restrictions: they are expected to work. Thus if a man is avoiding all the restricted animals and his newborn child gets sick, he may add to the list of foods to be avoided the food that he believes to be responsible for the sickness. To observe dietary and behavior restrictions is also a symbolically important public act. As such, certain individual motivations and specific situations alter the actual observance. A person who is afraid of being accused of being a witch may scrupulously observe the restrictions to show that he hears-understands-behaves well (*añi mbai mbechi*). A man trying to enlarge the number of his real kinsmen (*kwoi-kumeni*) may observe the *sangri* restrictions for a person who was formerly a distant kinsman (*muhai kwoiyi*). Finally, a man who believes that his wife's newborn is not his child may observe diet restrictions very severely until the child gets sick; then he knows the child is not his, since the child became sick in spite of his observing the restrictions. Or he may not observe any restrictions and note that the child stays healthy. This last, however, is considered a bad procedure by the rest of the village, and wanton (*añi mbai kïdi*).

Five intensities of restriction can be discerned. The most severe is the restriction to eating only manioc cakes made from the finest of manioc flour, a sediment that settles after the straining process, and a drink of water mixed with that same fine flour. This is the ultimate degree of culturally processed comestibles. This diet usually continues for several days. Later, a person may begin to eat other garden products, especially yellow sweet potatoes and *cará*, avoiding "black" (purple) sweet potatoes and dried dark-colored corn. Later he usually eats all the garden products but still no meat. Certain honey species are restricted. After a couple of weeks of this (in the case of the longer diet restrictions as for a child or after killing an enemy) a person may begin to eat small fish. After a month or so he may begin to hunt for game and eat those animals listed as bland. Later still the diet is enlarged, and some of the pungent animals are tried. Those that are strong smelling are avoided. Finally, when the restrictions are over, a person can eat anything appropriate to his sex and age grade.

In addition to diet restrictions the *sangri* includes restrictions on activity. A person in strong restriction lies still, does not get overheated, does not participate in plaza activities, does not paint the body, does not make anything especially beautiful (no arrows or well-made artifacts), and above all must avoid sexual intercourse.

The purpose of the restrictions is usually twofold: to benefit another person, usually a close kinsman (*kwoi-kumeni*) and to protect oneself. *Sangri* are observed for a biological child in the Suya sense, for biological relatives, for the dead, and on other occasions. Failure to observe the restrictions can lead to a swollen belly—a sign of being a witch—and to being considered wanton (*añi mbai kïdi*), also a sign of a witch.

Diet and activity restrictions are important means of marking periods of passage. They may be used as a social symbol: observing or not observing them may be a public act affirming or denying a relationship. Almost all the rites of passage involve some kind of diet and activity restriction.

Birth

Birth is an important time of passage for the parents as well as for the child. The restrictions apply only to the parents, but the ill effects of their failure to observe them are shared between parents and child.

Prepartum restrictions are the fewest. The child grows through the accumulation of semen, and intercourse must be frequent. A woman knows that she is pregnant when she no longer menstruates, feels nausea, and is tired. The Suya say that the fetus has a spirit, or *mẽgaron,* even while it is inside the womb. Should it die there, its spirit goes directly to the village of the dead. The only restriction usually described is that a man should not fell large trees when his wife's belly is large. The child may be harmed by the great crashing of the tree when it falls. A man and his wife may eat everything and do anything. During this period either parent may have dreams that symbolically indicate the sex and some other attributes of the child.

Birth itself is a woman's province. If labor begins at night, the woman's husband is told to leave the house. The Suya say that if the husband stays in the house, the child will refuse to come out. The husband must do nothing strenuous, in what has been called the *couvade.* He may even simulate birth himself. One Western Suya whose wife was beginning labor came out to the men's circle and lay down and groaned, saying that he hurt and was weak. The rest of the men laughed when I asked what hurt and said that there was no medicine of mine that was good for him; it was his wife who was having the child. If the birth is difficult, the father unstrings all his bows, for the tension of the string may be holding the child in the womb.[1]

If labor begins at night, the birth takes place inside the house. If it begins during the day, the mother goes into the bushes and gardens in back of the house (the *atuknumu*) and gives birth there. In a night birth it is common for female kinsmen to gather in the house. In those witnessed by my wife the group of women carried on wide-ranging gossip sessions among themselves, occasionally talking supportively to the woman in labor. She would lie in a hammock and cry out only in a high, stylized cry: "*aga*!" One older woman was usually in charge and supervised. There is no secrecy about birth. Most of the village knows when labor pains have begun and may listen for the crying of the newborn infant.

When the child is about to be born, the woman gets out of her hammock and squats on the ground, usually holding on to something. The child falls out onto a mat or leaves on the ground and is picked up.

Picking up a newborn child is an important social act. It indicates acceptance of the infant and the intention to take responsibility for it. Deformed children, twins, and children who are not wanted are not picked up but are buried near where they lie. Twins born to a young woman may both be buried. Those of an older woman may be treated differently, one being allowed to live. Children whose mothers die in childbirth may be buried as well, but in most cases attempts were made by some relative to raise them. If the child is born alive but not breathing, as happened in one case witnessed by my wife, the older women send a girl outside to find a hot pepper which is put in the infant's mouth. It is soon crying lustily.

If the child is picked up, it is most often the maternal grandmother who does so. Any person other than the mother who picks the child up is known as the "person who picked up the child" (*kra mbü kande*). She has a special relation toward both the parents of the child and toward the child.

The child's umbilical cord is cut with anything handy—a stick, knife, or bamboo sliver. Then the child is washed by the person who picked up the child. The rest of the women leave, and the husband is allowed back inside the house. The blood is covered with dust and the afterbirth is thrown outside on the refuse pile (in the *atuknumu*). In an outdoor birth, they are left alone. The Suya are not concerned with these parts of the birth process.

The father returns to the house, and both he and the mother spend the ensuing days in their hammocks observing the strongest form of dietary and activity restrictions. Both parents are in a dangerous state immediately after the birth of the child. They are filled with "child's-blood" (*ngàtureyi kambro*). The mother continues to bleed for several days, and her child's-blood drains out. In order to rid himself of the child's-blood the father takes a fishbone or fishtooth and pierces his glans penis. On the morning following the birth, at light (*agachi kït*), the father goes to the gardens or to the bank of the river. There he rolls back the prepuce of his penis and jabs it so that it bleeds. I have heard this described as producing a jet of blood and also as being just a scratch. This procedure should be repeated on each of the following two mornings. Eastern Suya parents also take an emetic, a custom they learned from the Upper Xingu Indians. Perhaps because of the emetic they pierce their penises only occasionally. The Western Suya pierce their penises more frequently, preferably in the predawn, at noon, and in the evening. One man did so on the predawn following the birth, the next day at about sunrise, and at midday. The following day he pierced his penis at midday and at sunset. Note that the times used for this are the ritually most important.

In addition to letting out the child's-blood, penis piercing makes a man strong. Because it hurts so much in the ensuing days, it is sometimes described as a preventive against engaging in sexual relations, which are restricted during the postpartum period. Since both parents have child's-blood inside them, they must avoid all meat, fish, and sexual relations. The food, if eaten, mixes with the blood inside them and swells their stomachs during the first month. Once the blood has fully drained, breaking the diet restrictions may give the child fever and convulsions but will not harm the parents.

Neither parent is supposed to have sexual relations until the child can crawl or walk. Men usually said until the child could walk; women usually said until it could crawl. I suspect that the first is the ideal and the second a more common compromise. A man often does not wait, but sleeps with his other classificatory or actual wives after his penis has healed. His wife is supposed to accept that without recriminations. A new mother should not have sexual relations with any man, or the young child will become very weak and light in weight. The Suya women say that they have the longest postpartum sex taboo of any tribe they know. They also say that they have no medicine to prevent pregnancy.

When a man is again able to hunt and eat bland meat, he goes hunting for a fairly large animal—capybara, wild pig, or giant armadillo are often mentioned—which he brings back to the village and drops in front of the house of the person who picked up the child. That woman then gives a ritual bath to the entire family.[2]

The principal danger for a young child, according to the Suya, is high fever and convulsions. The extreme restrictions of the first weeks when both parents are filled with child's-blood, are followed by more than a year when certain animals should not be eaten. These include all the strong-smelling animals, except for the tapir (which is bland when cooked), and those mammals, birds, and fish that have dramatic death convulsions regardless of their odor classification. During the year following the birth of a child the animals listed in table 8.1 are either particularly restricted (the left column) or especially recommended (the right column).

The avoidance or recommendation of particular animals for parents of newborn children goes according to the perceived traits of the animals.[3] If the parents eat the animal, the child will have the animal's characteristic. To protect the child, these natural traits should be avoided. A number of the fish, for example, are bland in odor but have violent death spasms. Male monkeys should not be eaten because they scream so much; it is good sense not to eat them—no parent wants a screaming child. The cayman is said to be especially good because it lies so still in the water and has white, or cool, flesh. The list does not include all animals. Some, such as the otter, were not even worthy of mention. Others are not particularly notable either way; for example, the wild pig (peccary) is eaten unless the child gets sick.

Suya birth restrictions reinforce the identity of the members of the nuclear family. It marks them as a group separate from other groups, and it also marks the close identity of both parents with the child. Both father and mother must bleed. Both must observe diet and activity restrictions. Both parents contribute to the child—the mother with her milk, the father by his semen, which has created the child. Children are said to look like both parents. The complete identity of the nuclear family with the child has already been tempered, however, by the person who picked up the child (*kra mbü kande*) and the socialization that occurred at that moment. Even shortly after birth the child is more than just the physical extension of his parents. Their physical identity is further moderated by the giving of names, which occurs within several days of birth.

For a boy (and a girl with male names) the receiving of names has two distinct parts. The first takes place shortly after birth, and the second when the child can walk. For a girl without male names there is only the first stage.[4]

Under normal circumstances (sometimes the name giver is temporarily absent and the parents postpone the ceremony until his return), the child is named the day after his birth. The parents are said to choose the name in the following way: After the child is born the father and mother sit on their bed and say, "What will the child be called?" Then one of them says, "Let's give it "uncle so-and-so's (*ngedi*) name," and the other agrees. One of them goes to tell the mother's brother (*ngedi*) who has been chosen. He, in turn, agrees. Then the *ngedi* sings inside his house.

Table 8.1 Food restrictions for parents of young children

Forbidden	Especially recommended
Jaguar[a]	Small fish[b]
All species of deer[a]	Cayman[b]
Large paca[a]	Giant anteater
Capybara[a]	Lesser armadillo[b]
Coati	*Salariakachi* (bird)[b]
Male guariba monkeys[a]	*Atorochi* (bird)
Mutum (tinamou)[a]	Female monkeys
Striped *mutum* (tinamou)	Wild pig (queixada)
Macaw	Tapir
Snakes[a]	
Eels[a]	
All large fish (a question of degree)	
Cachorra (fish, Portuguese name)	
Wariwari (fish)	

[a] Should not be killed even if they are seen by a father with young children; also forbidden for a considerable time.

[b] Especially bland and may be eaten by parents as soon as they are off an all-vegetable diet.

All the other people who have the same name set are told. Then the *ngedi* goes and "picks up" (*ku mbü*) the child. Each of the other people with the same name also comes during the ensuing days and picks up the child.

I observed a name-giving ceremony only once, for a Western Suya boy. It illustrates the way in which the giver of the names takes the child and mediates the extremely close bond between a mother and her child.

Between 7:00 and 7:30 A.M. an old man began to sing an *akia* (an individual song) in his house. I was told that he was singing a "name-receiver *akia*" (*krã-ndu tàktiri*). He was sitting in the house facing the plaza and singing. He sang several songs in this fashion, some of which were funny (obscene) and the listeners laughed. Finally he stood up, said "I will pick up my name receiver," and walked over to the bed where the mother (a classificatory sister) was seated holding her newborn child, which had been painted with red *urucum*. He sat down on the bed facing her across the width of it. He extended his arms. The mother held the child out to him, and he put his hands momentarily under the child. He barely held the child, if at all. The motion was that of being given the child symbolically. Then a boy of about three years of age who had the same name set was brought over by his mother to put his arms under the child. He was afraid and cried and struggled. Only with great effort could his mother get his tightly clenched fists under the baby. Then she let him go. Later that morning other people with the same names also put their arms out to the mother and had the child placed in their hands.

The spatial movement is important. The name giver starts singing in his own house (in this case, sleeping area) goes to his sister's house (sleeping area), and there gives the child his names. The child is placed briefly in his arms. The child is socially identical with the name giver and now has a social, as well as a physical, identity. This is reinforced as all the other members of the same name set come and hold the child briefly.

Although the child has a name set, he is not addressed by any of his names for several years. He is called *titi*, or baby, until he can crawl and often until a younger sibling is born. Like his name, a child's social identity is also incipient. The child is in constant physical association with the mother and is held and carried most of the time. During the first two years of life a child knows mostly his mother's sisters, his own siblings, and his mother's sisters' children. This changes when the child begins to walk and talk, and it is then that social identity ceases to be potential and becomes actual: the child is addressed by name and participates in an important naming ceremony.

Walking

At about the time that a child can walk, complete identity with parents is lessened. The child participates in the "mouse ceremony"(naming ceremony) with other members of his name set, his parents can eat most animals without harming him, and they may resume sexual relations. It is not a coincidence that these all occur at the same time. When the total physical involvement with and dependence on the mother and father diminish, the social identity given at birth is asserted both ritually and socially.

In the mouse ceremony, which may be performed every year, all the men wear palm-leaf dance costumes painted according to their plaza group membership. The name giver makes a tiny costume for his name receiver; the child's ceremonial relations, *ñumbre-krà-chi* and *kràm-ngedi*, cut and paint it, respectively. Starting in the child's house, members of his name set dance and sing together. If the child is too young to walk well, he is carried by the name giver. They dance out to the forest, where the mothers of the young children take food out "for the child," and the food is eaten by his name givers as well. Then the men march back into the village and sing over the prostrate body of each child who is participating in the ceremony for the first time. The child is then picked up by his actual name giver and is danced with until he goes to sleep. When the children go to bed, each one's name giver hooks the child's costume over the top of his own and the costumes continue to dance together the entire night. The dancing and singing continue all night without stopping until dawn, when the sisters of each man (the mothers of their real and potential name receivers) push arrows through the crown of the dance costume and "wound" the dancers. The groups dance together a while longer and then, name group by name group, they "die." A sister of every dancer strips him of his costume and pours cold water on him. The men bathe, throwing their ornaments in the water, and the ceremony is over.

The ceremony stresses the taking of the boy out of the maternal household, and his identity with his name group in the central plaza. The name group also eats the same food together. In addition, there is some hostility between the name givers and the mothers of the name receivers, who wound the men and end the ceremony, taking the dance masks to their houses and retaking their children as well. The Suya say that formerly all the close kinsmen of the child participating in the ceremony for the first time would come out at dawn and threaten the name givers with bows and arrows. They say they do not do so now because there are so few of them. It is only with a show of hostility that the parents accept the attenuation of their ties with their child.[5]

Ngàtureyi

Boys from the time they can walk until they reach puberty (*ngàtureyi*) leave the very close relationship with their mother for a peer group and a closer relationship to their father. Much of their day is spent with the peer group in play and imitation of adult male pursuits. Boys are also taken fishing by their fathers and mother's brothers and learn to shoot tiny bows and arrows at small fish. It is the father who makes most of the toys for his sons. *Ngàtureyi* are expected to do little more than play and are given little responsibility either inside or outside the house, in contrast with girls of the same age, who take care of their younger siblings and classificatory siblings.

The relative isolation of the *ngàtureyi* from both parents and the rest of the adult world is revealed in beliefs about sickness. One informant told me that *ngàtureyi* have no illnesses. Infants get sick because their parents do not obey the dietary restrictions. Adults (beyond puberty) get sick because of witchcraft. He maintained that *ngàtureyi* did not get sick. In fact they did, but the Suya are unable to explain their sickness because they are unaffected by either their parents or the society at large, and their sickness has no repercussions in the adult world. *Ngàtureyi* are marginal in another sense as well. They are said to be *kü-kumeni,* or strong smelling, like tapirs and jaguars. They are unsocialized and do not hear-understand-know or speak well or sing. Nor are they expected to. Herb medicines and chants (*sangere*) are applied to boys of this age to make them grow well and become good hunters and fishermen. But they are not instructed much.

When the *ngàtureyi* are eight or nine years old, they are subject to greater control by the adult men. They are harassed in certain ceremonies to make them bellicose (*sàgri*) and to make them grow quickly. They are also expected to run errands for the men. They cut and wash meat, which is then cooked in the men's house. They bring fire from the houses to the men's circle at night. They may be asked to do most of the work in repairing the men's house or building a new one. And they are suffered to come into the men's circle at night instead of either staying with their mothers or lighting a small fire of their own as the younger *ngàtureyi* usually do. In the men's circle they are occasionally subjected to humorous inspection of their genitals to see whether they have been having sexual intercourse. When this happens the boys are becoming *ngàtu.*

Puberty

Ngàtu fish and hunt quite regularly with their fathers, brothers, or some other adult. They no longer sit in the middle of the canoe with the women, the *ngàtureyi,* and the aged, but take the bow or stern paddle. They also begin their ceremonial life. The first ceremony in a boy's life might be the *pe-hrò.*[6] This ceremony has not been performed within the lifetime of any living Eastern Suya. The following abbreviated description is from informants whose fathers described it to them.

At the beginning of the ceremony, boys between the ages of about eight and thirteen (within the lower range of the *ngàtuyi* and the upper range of the *ngàtureyi*) were secluded on high platform beds in their houses. The high beds were built and walled in with thatch. The boys could not leave the houses during the day but urinated through the walls of the house. The belief was that if the boy was not seen, he would grow faster. Every night the boys would go to the river and bathe and sing in the water, hitting it with their hands to make a crashing sound. Late at night (*akatwa*) they would return to their houses. After the rise of the morning star (*agachi sülü*) the boys would return to the water. Harassment similar to that described by Maybury-Lewis (1967, p. 115) occurred. The boys would try to light fires against the morning chill, but older men would run down and throw the fires in the water and the boys would scramble back in.

During this period of isolation a lesser ceremony, the *pensogtagü*, or "rubber ball game," is performed.[7] Latex is spread on the boys. Rubber balls are made by peeling the dried latex off the bodies of the boys and wrapping it into round shapes. Two large balls, maybe eight inches across, and a number of small balls are made. When they are completed, the adult men come out of the men's house in moiety groups and the "controller" of the balls brings the balls out. First he brings small ones, thrown across the plaza for *ngàtureyi*. Then he throws one of the larger ones to a name receiver in the circle of the singing men. The name receiver throws it to another man, and they begin to bat the ball around with their hands, paddles, sticks, or stools—anything that makes the ball move well.[8] The boys do not participate. The game ends when the *bokàyi*[9] begins to hit the ball out of the circle of dancers. Then the balls are taken and put in the men's house. Later they are returned to the controller who gives them to his mother or sister to be washed and stored until much later when the men want to play again.

The *pe-hro* ceremony itself ends in the "wild pig (queixada) ceremony" (*angro-chi ngere*). The boys bathe at night and before dawn while the men sing the *angro-chi ngere* songs in the plaza. At last, instead of bathing in the river, they stand in the plaza all night while the men sing, and they have water thrown over them by their mothers and sisters while the men sing *angro-chi ngere*. By dawn the boys are shivering and miserable, and the ceremony ends. Following the ceremony the oldest boys, who are big *ngàtu*, may have their ears pierced.

The spatial pattern is significant. Boys are first isolated in their maternal houses, completely forbidden to take part in plaza activities. In the ball game the balls are made from their skin and taken to the center where the men play with them, but the boys do not participate. At the conclusion of the ceremony they are taken to the plaza and bathed by their *whai-wï-ieni* (mother and sisters) in the presence of all the singing adult men. These plaza baths are a common ending to Suya ceremonies and are an act of reincorporation. It is a rite of passage from the privacy of the maternal house, emphasized by the seclusion, to the public arena of the plaza.

A number of elements in the *pe-hrò* ceremony are related to ceremonies among other Gê societies. Boys of early puberty are secluded inside their maternal houses, similar to the Apinaye as described by Nimuendaju (1939, pp. 58-68). It is quite different from the Northern Kayapo custom in which boys of this age are initiated into the men's house. Suya boys do not enter the men's house until late adolescence, at the equivalent of the Kayapo *mẽ-noro-nu-re.* The seclusion of the *pe-hrò* on a high platform bed has a parallel in the Timbira and Apinaye custom of building platform beds for nubile girls (Nimuendaju 1939, p. 100), but in an inverted form. The ball game is similar in general outline to that described by Nimuendaju for the Apinaye except that no paddles were used (Nimuendaju 1939, pp. 61-64). Among the Apinaye, however, the ball game was part of the second phase of the initiation while among the Suya it was the first of the ceremonies involving boys and precedes the piercing of the ears. The importance for this age group of bathing in the water as a means of growing strong is found throughout the Gê tribes.

Ear Piercing, Lip Piercing, and Induction into the Men's House

A boy's ears are pierced when he is a "big *ngàtu*" and shows signs of having been engaging in sexual intercourse. It is to this end that his genitals are examined by the older men in the men's circle. If the prepuce rolls back easily, it is a sign that he has been having sexual intercourse (not that he has been masturbating, as Nimuendaju claims holds among the Apinaye—1939, p. 74). Then the old men say that he should have his ears pierced. That is done without much ceremony. The ear lobes are heated and pierced with a thorn or with a deer or jaguar bone because those animals run fast and strong (*mbrai tüt*). A small piece of wood is then inserted and after the wound has healed the hole is gradually enlarged. The ear piercing takes place at daybreak (*agachi kït*), and there are no diet restrictions other than the prohibition of "hot" foods to keep the ears from swelling.

The boy continues to live in his maternal household and continues to learn about hunting, fishing, and ritual tasks from his father. When his ear disks are big, and he is big enough, his lip is pierced before he enters the men's house. The lip piercing is not part of a ceremony but can happen at any time. It is usually undertaken by the Eastern Suya by the water's edge. The boy is taken down to bathe by his father and his *ngedi.* He washes his lip carefully, and then it is pierced. There is much blood. A small piece of wood is pushed into the hole, and his lip is wrapped with bark. The boy returns to his house and lies in his hammock. He does not have diet restrictions, but he eats very slowly and carefully.

After his lip is pierced, the boy continues to live in his maternal house until the next rainy season ceremony, which includes a log race. Then he enters the men's house. Often he plays an important part in the ceremony, being the "controller of the *akia*" (*tàktiri kande*) or "controller of the ceremonial telling" (*iaren kande*).[10]

On the last day of his initiation ceremony the initiate is brought in front of the men's house. His head is shaved, and he is given the special head ornament of the *sikwenduyi,* made by his name giver. This woven straw headdress has short tassels if the boy is a member of the *Kren* moiety, long tassels if he is a member of the *Ambànyi.* His father, mother, *ngedi,* and mother's lovers (if they are genitors) stay inside their houses. Then the initiate's mother brings his hammock out and hangs it in the men's house.[11] After that, the Suya say, a man never goes into his mother's house. That is an exaggeration, but he does not sleep in her house again.

The Western Suya performed complete initiation ceremonies until quite recently, perhaps 1965. The following description of a man's initiation into the men's house is based on a recorded description of his own initiation by Bentugarürü, who entered the men's house in the *tep kradi* ceremony.

> When Bentugarürü was a *ngàtu,* his ears were pierced following the conclusion of a ceremony. His father went to the men's circle and said, "My child is big." The men talked together and one said, "Yes, he is already big; he has probably been having sexual relations with women already." They decided that his ears should be pierced. Bentugarürü was painted in his mother's house, and in the late afternoon (*hwara mbedïli*) the adult men came into his house. He lay on his mother's bed, his mother holding his head. His ears were pierced with small sticks by a nonrelative who was a kind of specialist. His mother, sister, and father did ritual wailing. His ears swelled only a little, and he began to insert larger and larger pieces of wood in the perforation.
>
> He continued to live in his mother's house until he was quite big (sixteen or seventeen probably). Then his lip was pierced. The adult men came again to the house. He lay on his mother's platform bed. They sharpened a deer (*niatü*) legbone, carefully measured his lip, and shoved the bone through it so that it came up in front of his eyes. His parents and sister cried. He had no diet restrictions (*sangri*), and after his lip healed he made larger and larger lip disks until the disk was big enough to paint the circular design on the bottom known as the *ngroro,* or Pleiades, and the top surface red with *urucum*. Then he said he was ashamed (*whiasàm*) to stay in his mother's house.
>
> His ritual relative (equivalent of a *ñumbre-krà-chi*) went to the men's circle and said, "There is a companion of ours over there with a *ngroro* on his lip disk." The men, especially the *sikwenduyi,* said, "Let's bring him out." It was the end of the *tep kradi* ceremony. His ornaments for initiation had already been prepared by his parents, and he was ready. In the afternoon

the men left the men's house and trotted counterclockwise around the village. They entered the house. Bentugarürü was again lying on his mother's bed. The bravest, strongest men chewed a little food, took it out of their mouths, and put it in Bentugarürü's mouth. He ate. Then the men sang inside the house and left to go to another house. This was repeated two days later. After the singing, the *sikwenduyi* grabbed an arm or a part of him and as a group marched him to the door of the house; they made him stand just outside it. His mother cried. All the men shouted. There was a great deal of excitement. His mother keened a verse, "I am lying here crying."

That was the conclusion of that part of the ceremony. Bentugarürü stood in front of the house while the *sikwenduyi* went to another house and brought another boy out.[12] Then he went back in and lay down again. The men came in at night and sang again inside his house.

The next day, before dawn, he got up and was completely painted and decorated inside the house, with the exception of his moiety face paint. Rattles, gourds, and strings were tied on, and his wristlets of burity fiber were made. Then he went to the men's house accompanied by his mother and father who then returned to their house. He sat in the men's house and began to sing an *akia*: "*Tep swasiti,* I shake my *tutwä* (a dance ornament), I become belligerent (*kwï sà*), I become belligerent (*kwï sà*)."[13]

As he sang the old people did their characteristic *wikenyi* shout. When he finished singing, the men said "Let's get going." They painted his face with *genipapo* stain according to his moiety membership, which was *Ambànyi.*

When the sun was high, his wife's mother came to the men's house door with his wife. His wife chewed a little manioc and gave it to Bentugarürü to eat, just as the old men had done the day before. Then his wife's mother held him and sang a little herself. The she returned to her house with her daughter. Bentugarürü sang again. Then he went to his maternal house to lie down. In the late afternoon he was again called to the men's house, where his hair was completely cut off by all the adult men. He went to the water, washed off his head, and returned to the men's house. His mat was brought out, and he never returned to sleep in his mother's house again. He had *kwï sikwenduyi.*

This condensed description gives some idea of the richness of Suya ceremonial and of the importance of the spatial domains used. The mother's bed is quite important, and the initiate keeps returning to it. Members of the nuclear family are referred to as "people of your bed." In the initiation proper he is taken from the bed to the door by all the adult men, he goes to the plaza, and finally his head is shaved and he does not return to his mother's house. The whole rite of passage emphasizes spatial removal from the mother's bed through several zones—the doorway to the house, the men's house, and so forth. Each step of the process is accompanied by ritual wailing, or keening, of the parents and sisters. Keening is part of all rites of separation.

Another feature is the importance of the body ornaments, especially the lip disk. It is not the lip piercing per se that initiates the boy. The shame that he feels when he can paint the circular design on the underside of his lip disk is the result of the contradiction between having a full-sized lip disk and being still in his mother's house. The role of the body ornament in the actual passage from maternal house to men's house is quite clear.

Another feature is the importance of the ritual relation who arranges for the initiation of the boy. He plays a role reminiscent of the *pam kaag* of the Apinaye and Northern Kayapo as described by Da Matta (1976) and T. Turner (1966). There is a progression of mediators between the nuclear family and the boy. In the various ceremonies so far described it includes the person who picked up the child, the name giver (*krã-tumu*), the ceremonial relation (*ñumbre-krà-chi*), and finally all the adult men.

The initiation is a double process. First the boy's ritual relative and all the adult men acting together feed him from their mouths and take him from the natal house to the men's house. But the process is only partly accomplished. It is only after his wife feeds him and his mother-in-law sings and holds him that he is finally and irrevocably taken from his maternal household and inducted into the men's house. This may be seen as a movement by force: collective male force brings him to the plaza; future affinal ties keep him there. But he is not required to reside in his wife's household until he has a child. He has become a *sikwenduyi*.

The Eastern Suya initiation seems to involve only the action of the men and does not have a part for the wife and wife's mother. However, the second stage of the rite of passage appears in an Eastern Suya ceremony in which the *sikwenduyi* (initiated, unmarried men residing in the men's house) are the most active participants.

Sikwenduyi

The *sikwenduyi* represent the ideal of Suya masculine life. A *sikwenduyi* is supposed to sing frequently and perform collective activities such as fish with *timbó*. Otherwise he has no responsibilities. He does not cut a garden, hunt or fish much. He should make lip disks and sing. *Sikwenduyi* are sometimes called "controllers of Suya song" (*mẽro-ngere-kande*) because they sing so much. They are not supposed to have sexual relations with women, which prevents them from learning new songs quickly.[14] Men enter the men's house to hear-understand-know, to become belligerent, and to learn to behave correctly (*añi-mba*).

Sikwenduyi are not supposed to admit to having sexual relations with women until their hair grows out. They receive food from their mothers and sisters in small quantities. *Sikwenduyi* are supposed to eat and sleep little and to sing all the time. Men of that age I noticed were full of shame about eating and served themselves last. They were the last to bed and the first up in the morning down by the water. But they did so little during the day that they could catch up on their sleep then. They spend little time in their maternal houses and at night visit their lovers in amorous adventures undertaken with circumspection and shame (*whiasàm*). Young Eastern Suya men of that age are known for their virility but pretend to be entirely unattached. There has always been conflict between the ideal of a *sikwenduyi* who is strong and sings a lot because he learns easily as a result of not engaging in sexual relations and the actual *sikwenduyi* who is proud of his attractiveness and engages in surreptitious affairs.

The *sikwenduyi* play important roles in a number of ceremonies. One of these is the "dance of the turtles" (*kahran ngere*) which is also called *pebyitugü*, or "black *pebyi*." Unlike the *pe-hrò*, this ceremony has a part for wives and wives' mothers to play. These figures, important to *sikwenduyi* and adult men, are not important to the *ngàtu*. The ceremony thus shows the importance of those figures among the Eastern Suya, though not connected with the actual induction into the men's house. Variations on this ceremony have been described among other Northern Gê by Nimuendaju (1939, 1946), T. Turner (1966), and Melatti (1970). Turner, who witnessed the ceremony among the Northern Kayapo, describes a ceremony with some of the features of the Suya ceremony but with different sociological significance due to a different makeup of the groups.

The ceremony is called the *pebyitugü* because all the adult men except the *bokàyi* paint themselves black from head to foot. It was a ceremony that I never witnessed. Only two living Eastern Suya men had witnessed it. The two oldest Western Suya had also witnessed it among their group. The ceremony begins at the start of the dry season and concludes at the beginning of the rainy season. My descriptions cover only the final days of the ceremony, which are the climax. The first months involve the singing of the *kahran ngere,* a numerous group of songs, and preparing the paraphernalia for the final days.

There are several important groups of persons. The *pebyitugü* include all the initiated men (*sikwenduyi* and older) with the exception of those who by virtue of their name set are members of the *bokàyi,* a ceremonial group appearing in ceremonies having to do with the *pebyi.* The *bokàyi* and the *pebyitugü* paint themselves differently and sing different songs. The *bokàyi* conclude the ceremony just as they concluded the *pentagü* ball game, by literally breaking it up. The *sikwenduyi* play an important role; one of them is the controller and singer of the *akia* (*sàktiri kande*). There are also four "turtle girls" (*kahran-ndiyi*) who are female associates of the two moieties, have songs of their own, and provide sexual services at certain times.

The sequence and timing of the various parts of the ceremony are difficult to clarify. The singer of the *akia*, who is chosen from the *sikwenduyi*, must have an elaborate beeswax headdress made for him. Large gourd rattles are prepared for all the dancers. People are taught their songs, and there is a great deal of singing of the *kahran ngere.*

One night, while the men are singing, a man goes to the house of one of his sister's children (*taumtwü-ndiyi*) and brings the girl out to the men's house. She should be just around puberty, *hen sum hrü.* She becomes a woman of the ceremony. The man who brings her out never has sexual relations with her, since he has shame toward her. Other men, however, do. Usually four girls are brought out, two for each moiety. They are taught their songs.

At the start of the final period all the men pierce their penises with fishbones or teeth so that the blood runs out (*añi sagü*) in the entrance (*saikwa*) of the men's house. Then the women and the *pebyitugü* sing. The *bokàyi* do not sing, but just shout *huaaaaaa* from the men's house. The *pebyitugü* are not supposed to eat or drink except at certain times. If they are caught doing so by the *bokàyi* they are chased, all the pots and gourds near at hand are broken, and the *bokàyi* act very belligerent. Dancing begins before dawn and continues until late afternoon when people bathe, eat a little, and then sing again at night. This schedule continues for several days. On the last day the *pebyitugü* dance by moiety affiliation, exchanging places on the north and south ends of the plaza. First the *Ambànyi* sing in the north, the *Krenyi* in the south, and then vice versa. Then they sing together. The *bokàyi* go to the woods, sing their own songs, and gather wood for a huge fire which stretches across the plaza. The *pebyitugü* paint themselves black with charcoal, even their feet which are otherwise always painted red in ceremonies. Then they dance out to the north and south into the forest. One informant told me that the wives and mothers-in-law then go "looking for the *pebyitugü*," but I never could find out more about this section of the ceremony.

Later that night the pebyitugü return to the village and dance around the big pile of wood, which the *bokàyi* have collected. It is lit and there is a huge fire. The *pebyitugü* dance around the large fire with the *ngàtureyi* in front of them in a row, and in front of the *ngàtureyi* are the *kahran-ndiyi,* or female associates. The *bokàyi* sing their own song in the men's house. When at last the fire dies down, the *bokàyi* emerge from the men's house and chase after each *pebyitugü* and break his rattle with their clubs, ending the ceremony.[15]

The *pebyitugü* ceremony would be repeated the next dry season, and then not for a long time. It does not appear to have been an essential part of initiation among the Eastern or Western Suya. It was but one of the dry season ceremonies, along with the *tep kradi, bentü kradi, kwa kradi,* and others in which men could receive ceremonial names and enter the men's house.

The Suya *pebyitugü* emphasizes the importance of the wife and wife's mother, just as the induction into the men's house emphasizes them among the Western Suya. The wife and the wife's mother are important to a *sikwenduyi* because the next important step in the life cycle is paternity and residence with the child's mother in that woman's house. Marriage, with uxorilocal residence, is another step in the attenuation of bonds with the nuclear family. It, too, has ritualized aspects.

Marriage

Among the Western Suya some kind of marriage may have accompanied initiation, since a wife's mother plays a role in the entry into the men's house. However, I suspect that as among other Gê societies, the wife in the ceremony is for the purposes of initiation and the boy is not necessarily expected to father a child and live with her. Among the Eastern Suya marriage was not necessarily a part of initiation. Child marriages were occasionally arranged, but I knew of only one actual case—between 105 and 117. The husband said that when his wife was very young his father arranged the marriage with her mother. From that time on, the two principles did not use any address terms for each other, and the parents used affinal terms. There was no intense shame until they began to have sexual relations. My informants said that this kind of marriage was much more common in the past and may at one time have resembled the Western Suya ceremonial marriage. They said that marriage and postmarital residence are not the way that they should be, and they attributed this to the absence of living parents who would make the young men live in their daughters' houses.

It is possible that the Suya do not regularly live uxorilocally today because the initiation, complete with men's house residence which has been seen as a crucial step in the movement from natal household to wife's household, has ceased to occur. Men who were initiated live either uxorilocally or neolocally (227, 122, 120). Men who were never initiated live virilocally. This evidence tends to underline the importance of the men's house in the marriage and residence arrangements. In 1976 the situation changed somewhat, with two young men marrying uxorilocally. In that case some of the parents of the couple were living and uxorilocality without initiation may have begun.

Eastern Suya marriage ceremonies in which residence was virilocal are not very elaborate. I did not happen to witness any marriage ceremonies among the Suya. The kinsmen of the girl decide that the marriage should occur. They form a kind of procession and accompany her to her husband's house. Children go in the front, the girl next, and the older kinsmen behind. Once in the house, the couple are exhorted by the girl's older brothers who tell them to be good (*añi mbai mbechi*). She then takes up residence with him. This early period is the time for divorce. If she does not like him, she refuses to have sexual relations with him or cook food for him. If he does not like her, he does not eat the food she cooks but only his mother's food.

Marriage is always thought of as being "across the plaza." Informants usually pointed to the house opposite their own when discussing marriage in general, although the only exogamy was the house exogamy. The tendency to point across the plaza includes the men's house in the process. Indeed, under the ideal system the men's house acts as midpoint between residence in the natal household and residence in the wife's household. The double attenuation of a man from his natal household is symbolized by the keening of his mother and sisters when he enters the men's house and again when he enters his wife's house. The following description of a Western Suya marriage, the marriage of Bentugarürü, reveals a symbolic complexity not found at present among the Eastern Suya.

> A girl's ears were pierced.[16] Some time passed. Then she was painted. Bentugarürü, already resident in the men's house, was also painted. He put in new ear disks and a new lip disk with a new *ngroro*. He had a spotted design on his upper cheeks and up to his forehead. Then one of his *ngedi* (mother's brother, real or classificatory) came out and said to him, "She is there, her head is painted. You may have sexual relations with my daughter, she is there." Bentugarürü began to have sexual relations with the young woman. He did so for a long time. Then she got "lazy" [one of the signs of pregnancy].
>
> The girl said to her mother, "Mother, there is a child in me." The mother replied, "Are you pleased? [Do you like the child's father?]" The girl said, "I had sexual relations with him a lot." The mother: "Is he sitting there in the men's house? [Is he a *sikwenduyi*?]" The daughter: "He is there."
>
> The mother then told the older women, and all the old people knew that her daughter was pregnant and that Bentugarürü was the genitor. Then the girl's mother painted herself and went out to the men's house. She entered the men's house. She asked Bentugarürü if the child was his and he vigorously denied it. "It is not my child." Then the *Krenyi* [members of the opposite moiety of Bentugarürü] shouted, "Here comes your mother and chief!" The *sikwenduyi* were all painted, and the chief came in and said, "Well, what about it?" "Umm, it is not my child. It is someone else's semen. It is not my wife. It is not my child. I will go with you, and I had sexual relations with her, but it is not my child." He repeated his denials of paternity. The chief listened and then asked, "Will you go over there and live over there [in the girl's maternal house]?" Bentugarürü replied, "I will go. But it is not my child." Bentugarürü sat in the men's house and said to his companions. "*Sikwenduyi,* I guess I am going to live with a wife." They all said, "Go ahead and live with your wife."
>
> Bentugarürü went to his maternal house. Then his wife's brother came and talked to him. He left his maternal house and went toward his wife's house. His mother and sister cried for a long time. He still did not sleep in his wife's house.

The next day before dawn his wife's mother grated a lot of manioc. She went looking for her daughter's husband's mother (*tukà nã*). She said "*Tukà nã*, here is manioc for you." She repeated "*Tukà nã*, are you there?" Bentugarürü's mother replied, "I am here." "Will you eat some manioc?" Bentugarürü's mother replied "Yes." "Let's go." They went and processed manioc. Finally one of Bentugarürü's *ngedi* said, "That is enough." He said to Bentugarürü, "My daughter is inside the house. She is sitting there. Come with me." The young man accompanied his *ngedi* and his wife's mother and went and sat inside the house for a while. He ate some food there. When he finished eating, he did not stay there. In the ensuing weeks he had frequent sexual relations with the woman and the child grew.

Finally his wife's child was born. She called her Gaimbedi. Bentugarürü pierced his penis (*añi sagü*) repeatedly until finally his wife stopped bleeding. While he observed *sangri* in the men's house, his own sisters' husbands (he said he had many) brought him garden food—manioc, corn, sweet potatoes, cara—in the men's house. But he only ate a little. Then it was time to end his *sangri* and leave the men's house.

He went to the river and rubbed earth on himself, and he scraped himself with the claws of a young pigeon, two "medicines" to make him strong. Then he returned to the men's house and lay down. In the afternoon he ate his first fish. After he finished eating, the child was washed (by its *kra mbü kande*). After the bath a paca tooth-scraping tool was brought to the men's house and Bentugarürü was scraped with it to lose even more blood. More medicines were rubbed on him. Then he put on his decorations. His name giver (*krã-tumu*) came to the men's house and said, "Our wife is over there.[17] You go see her. If you are happy, if you like it [her], do not stay [here] living with the men in the men's house." At dusk Bentugarürü went to his wife's house. He walked to it, went in it, and stayed there. He continued to live there until she died, poisoned by some ranchers.

This text, considerably condensed from the original, taped, first-person description, reveals a number of interesting events. The repeated denial of the young man of his paternity of the child is characteristic of the *sikwenduyi* and something of the ideal behavior. Young men are supposed to want to stay in the men's house. Bentugarürü denies paternity but agrees to the marriage, which would have been unlikely if he had not been having sexual relations with the girl. He returns to his natal household before making a symbolic move from his house to that of his wife's in the company of a wife's brother.

Economic cooperation of some kind between the two families begins on the second day of the ceremony. Eating inside the wife's house is an important step as well. But it is the birth of a child that effects the final move from the men's house to the wife's house.

Bentugarürü married the daughter of a *ngedi*. She resided in the natal house or house group of his name giver. That is the reason his name giver appears at the end of the description. It is interesting that his name giver used the plural possessive form which implies their identity: "our wife" instead of "your wife." As his name giver had done before him, the boy must leave the men's house and take up residence with a wife. The role of the name giver here is mediator between the ties holding the boy to his natal household and the men's house, and his affinal relations with his wife, her mother, and her father.

A young man's relations with his affines are difficult. His ties with his father are greatly attenuated by his marriage. He hunts with his wife's unmarried brothers and her father. He must make a large garden and construct his wife's house when a village is moved. The Suya perceive these as obligations to the kinsmen of the woman. Bentugarürü said that his wife's father was a glutton and that he always had to go hunting for him. He did not have many nice things to say about his wife either. But divorce was extremely rare if it existed at all. I have no recorded case of it. When a man did not like his wife, he could return to his mother's or his sister's house. That occurs in the myth of the man whose wife had sexual relations with a tapir. What circumstances less than those would induce a man to do so are not apparent. The Suya claim that after two children a man does not leave because the children are too "valuable" to him. Eventually a man's children are old enough to marry, and he himself becomes a wife's father and eventually a *wikenyi*, entirely associated with his wife's house.

The Kupen Kande Ceremony

Some time between induction into the men's house and old age, a man might kill an enemy and undergo another important passage, the *kupen kande* ceremony. The restrictions imposed on a man who has killed an enemy Indian (not a witch but a member of a different tribe) are similar to those imposed on the parents of a newborn child. In Suya war raids and war tactics the ideal was for older men to grab and hold down an enemy until a *sikwenduyi* could club him to death. The *sikwenduyi* would then undergo the most severe restrictions and the *kupen kande* ceremony.

When a man kills an enemy he leaves his weapons, his lip disk, his ear disks, and his feather head ornament with the body. Upon his return to the village the killer goes to his house and lies down. Lying or sitting down on his hammock, he sings an *akia* until the late afternoon. Then he goes to the men's house and sings a little there. Then all the adult men hold him while a specialist scrapes his body with a sharpened paca-tooth tool. The tool is first tried out on his right arm, the "killing thing." Then horizontal scrapes are made on his chest, back, legs, and arms, perhaps an inch apart. Vertical scrapes are incised on his sides. The scrapes are not deep, but they are painful and bleed. Then kinswomen (*kwoiyi*) wash his body and spread on a medicine which cools the scrapes and forms welts of scar tissue, signs of a *kupen kande*. The killer then must observe stringent diet restrictions. He may eat no meat until the next moon, and then only "good" game (*kutwã-kumeni*). He does not paint himself or leave his house much. Sexual relations are forbidden for three or four moons. During the first days after his return, the killer also pierces his penis (*añi sagü*). At the end of his period of restriction the killer is painted with vegetable stain (*genipapo*) in a special design called *añi-ropti*,[18] or "the jaguar body design." Although the killer observes all these restrictions, no relative (*kwoiyi*) need observe them.

The Suya say that a killer is full of his victim's blood. For this reason he pierces his penis and "throws out" the bad blood and is scarred. The scarring further rids him of the "enemy Indian blood" which fills his whole body. Should he eat meat before the next moon or have sexual relations with a woman during the next three moons, the Indian blood inside him swells up and he could become a witch. With the proper observations a man avoids becoming a witch.

The *kupen kande* ceremony was especially important among the Western Suya in recent years because they were constantly fighting with invading Brazilians. Every adult man I saw had the scars of a *kupen kande*. Von den Steinen saw body scars among the Eastern Suya on his visit, and the older members of the group had seen a number of different *kupen kande*. From a Western Suya description of the ceremony I was told that a man's name giver held him and that his sister washed his wounds. The *dramatis personae* of the ceremony are the same as in other rites of passage.

The Eastern Suya stopped performing the *kupen kande* ceremony after the Juruna and rubber tapper combined attack. They thereafter concentrated their energies on capturing women. When a man killed a person on a raid, he did not usually marry any women he captured. Instead he gave them to a relative to marry. If the raid involved only capture, a man might marry the person he captured. The Suya preferred capture and escape to killing enemies in recent years.

When a man has killed a witch, the restrictions on eating and sexual relations are the same as for a *kupen kande*, but there is no need for the scarring or the ceremony. The killer lies still, does not eat meat for the first month, does not have sexual relations for several months, and does not paint himself. In the case that I witnessed the witch killer was also a bereaved husband. He did indeed just lie around the house for a number of months and was not linked in gossip with any women until five months after the death of his wife and his slaying of the witch. At the official conclusion of his restrictions he was painted with *genipapo* but in a design reserved for those who have not killed enemy Indians, the *kuntẽtẽ*.

Old Age

A man's increasing integration into his wife's household as he grows older and his children marry is expressed in several ways. One of these is the rite of passage which all old persons undergo.

When a man has a number of grandchildren and one of his descending-generation relations is going to do an all-day singing of *akia* in the plaza, the old *wikenyi* say, "Let's *wiken*." They gather in the men's house and shout for the old man whom they want to induct into their age group to come to the men's house. He goes there and everyone jokes with him and he responds in kind. Then the *sikwenduyi* sing and the *wikenyi* give their characteristic high shout of *kwü-kwü-kwü-kwü*. After that much food is brought to the men's house, and the newly inducted *wikenyi* is forced to eat as much as he can. Then he is given a special name with the prefix *wiken-*. He may be called "tall *wiken*" (*wiken hrikti*), or "strong *wiken*," "short *wiken*," and so forth. In the second part of the ceremony the new *wikenyi* sings an *akia* with his young relative. The young man makes a lip disk for the new *wikenyi*, but it is without a *ngroro*, or circular design, on the underside. It is hung along with other ornaments by the *wikenyi's* bed. The *wikenyi* puts on the lip disk and other ornaments. During the ceremony the young man calls the *wikenyi* "my child" (*i-kra*), and the *wikenyi* calls him "my father" (*ture*). When the old man is decorated, the two men leave the house simultaneously and the old man follows the young man around the plaza all day singing. That concludes the ceremony, and the old man has become a *wikenyi* (*kwï wiken*).

All old people become *wikenyi*. They are expected to do obscene and funny things both in ceremonies and in everyday life. They do not have the shame (*whiasàm*) expected of younger men and women, and they can eat foods that young people cannot eat.

The lip disk is an important symbol of a man's aggressivity, adulthood, and verbal ability, and the design of the Pleiades (*ngroro*) on the lip disk makes a young man ashamed to stay in his mother's house. In the induction ceremony the *wikenyi's* lip disk is made by a descending-generation *kwoiyi* and it has no *ngroro*. Simultaneously, when he becomes a *wikenyi*, a man ceases to sing unison songs and *akia* and sings only the high shout of the *wikenyi*. *Wikenyi* do not come to the center of the village as often. The inversion of kinship terms in the ceremony in which the old man becomes a "son" to the younger one, is partly an expression of Suya humor, saying the opposite of the obvious. But it is also partly an expression of dependency. Old men who no longer hunt depend on the younger men in the way that a son depends on his father. The young man makes the ornaments for the old man as a father makes ornaments for his uninitiated son. Becoming a *wikenyi* is a kind of retirement from the active affairs of village and ceremony. Old persons are appreciated for their knowledge of myth and ritual, but they cease active participation. There is also an interesting change in the relationship of the two groups that provide social and biological identity. The important person for inducting a *wikenyi* is a son, a grandson, or (rarely) a sister's son. It is a descending-generation relation, not a name receiver or a ritual relation. The *wikenyi* may cease to have such important ritual relationships with his sisters and become more associated with younger *kwoiyi* and in-marrying men who reside in his house.

There is a complete inversion between the roles of *wikenyi* and the ideal behavior of the *sikwenduyi* resident in the men's house. Table 8.2 summarizes these differences.

Old age is related to witchcraft, illness, and sexuality. Old people become more natural and animal-like in a number of ways. Food taboos are relaxed. Shame relations are relaxed. And old people are prime candidates for witchcraft accusations.

When a man has grandchildren and a woman ceases to menstruate, certain food restrictions cease to be observed. Old people may eat giant otter, large carnivorous birds, cayman eggs, and other animals prohibited to younger people because they are bad for them and because of their taste and smell classification. Old people are also given the heads of certain animals—paca, porcupine, capybara, anteater—that no one else eats. When a person eats the heads of those animals, his head becomes covered with scales. The Suya say that old people have scaly heads anyway, so they might as well eat the heads of those animals.[19] Old men

Table 8.2 Normative roles of inititates and old people

Sikwenduyi (INITIATED MEN IN MEN'S HOUSE)	*Wikenyi* (OLD MEN AND WOMEN)
Shame about sexual relations	No shame; obscenity and humor are mandatory
Eat very little, sleep little	Exaggerated appetites, sleep a lot
Strong, exaggerated ceremonial activity	Weak, not much activity
Sing in unison, *akia*	Do not sing, just shout
Emphasis on ritual relations in ceremonies, also on mediators	Emphasis on biological relations and inversion of F-S relationship
Enter men's house because can paint *ngroro* on lip disk	Cease to have *ngroro* on lip disk
Activity in men's house is above all to make lip disks	Does not make his own lip disk but has it made for him
Not yet established in a residential household	Completely established as oldest male in house

are also given some of the less desirable organs such as the tripe, the penis of the tapir, and other undesirable cuts.[20] Women past menopause are given any food that appears as a multiple or unnaturally twinned. For example, the fetus of certain animals is given to older women, as is any fruit, like a banana, which has grown double. A young woman who eats them might give birth to twins.

The quality of their foods is only one of the ways in which old people's relation to food changes. A man also eats a lot in public. The appetite of old men is emphasized to be humorous. Old men's contribution to the singing is to utter a piercing shout of *kwü-kwü-kwü-kwü* which means (among other things) "I'll take some, I'll take some, I'll take some." After the ceremony they are given food, which they eat before engaging in humorous play. In the induction of a new *wikenyi* he sits in the men's house and eats as much as he can eat. This contrasts strongly with the behavior of young men who are supposed to eat very little and are the last to take food.

Wikenyi are figures of Rabelaisian persuasion. In addition to making much of eating they cease to have shame about sex. *Wikenyi* humor is generally ribald. Old men chase women holding their penises in front of them. They sing obscene songs. They simulate sexual relations. *Wikenyi* shamelessness extends beyond ceremonial times. I was repeatedly told stories about old men who would go in broad daylight and bang on the thatch of a house. When a woman came to the door, they would say, "Let's go have intercourse." Old people are said to be without shame (*whiasàm kïtïlï*).[21] In this, too, they contrast with the young men. The sexuality of the old men may be partly bravado. The women would gossip about older men and maintain that so-and-so had run out of semen or had a soft phallus.

Old people, also in contrast with the *sikwenduyi*, sleep a lot. Old people are not very active during the day and may sleep more then.

These excesses, which are the hallmarks of age among the Suya, are also signs of being a witch. Witches are selfish and do not obey the norms of society. Old people eat, but they are unable to work very hard to get their own food, especially old men. They must live on what they are given. Old people are shameless and do things that are *añi-mbai kïdi*.[22] Witches are so busy flying around at night, the Suya say, that they sleep a lot during the day. So do old people. Age is seen as a transformation to a less social state, and one in which a person may easily become a witch.[23]

Old men are also transformed into members of their wife's house. Old men cease to belong in any real sense to their family of orientation and become completely involved in their family of procreation. The house in which they were born is forgotten by their descendants. Though important to a young man, the house in which he was born is less important to an older one. When an old man dies, he is buried inside his wife's house.

Both men and women become *wikenyi*. When someone is so old that it is impossible to perform economic duties even in moderation, other people will say, "Old man (woman), go ahead and die, you are too old." This is apparently taken with good humor by old invalids who are also the subject of pranks. Old people are supposed to be sad, because they miss their relatives who are already in the village of the dead and want to go there too.

Death

The final passage on earth is death. When a person is severely injured, very weak, or fainting, mourning begins. This usually takes the form of a high, songlike keening which is repeated many times. It appears to have a melodic section punctuated with brief periods of sobbing. Often there is a repeated cry of "my grandchild, my grandchild" or the appropriate term for the deceased. More highly structured keening may relate the events causing the keening to be performed, for example describe bad dreams of impending death. When a person faints the Suya say that he has died. A person can die more than once. But there is no question about the final signs of death: cessation of breathing after a last gasp, extreme paleness and coldness, and stiffness.

Corpses are usually buried with all their belongings, their gardens may be destroyed, and the close relatives go into mourning. Corpses are buried fully decorated because the principal activity of the spirits (*mẽgaron*) in the village of the dead is the performance of ceremonies. Death is a passage very similar to puberty for girls, and of entering the men's house for boys, for a person's spirit leaves the body looking like a young man or a young woman. Young women are received into their mother's house in the village of the dead, the men are taken into the men's house.[24] The following is a description of a burial that I witnessed.

> Roptindi (155) died in Diauarum in childbirth, and her child was stillborn. She was brought to the village in the motorboat belonging to the post. Above the sound of the engine could be heard the shrill cries of keening. The Suya waited on the bank for the boat to arrive. Finally it arrived by the predawn light of the morning star. Many people got out. The bereaved husband (142) was crying "My child, my child" as he came stumbling up the bank. I was surprised to find that not only the child but also the wife had died. The bodies were taken to the house in which she had resided (her husband's mother's house).
>
> In the house the dead mother and child were lying in a hammock with the husband lying across it, crying. There were many women in the house crying. Young men looked on soberly. Suddenly the bereaved husband got up, strode toward the door, and picked up the bow and arrows of his sister's husband, shouting that he was going to kill someone. His mother followed him and held the bows and arrows, and eventually he allowed them to be

wrested from him. His mother took them to another house. At this time, since I was not sure whom he had wanted to kill, I left the house to watch the digging of the grave. The grave was dug in the girl's sister's house. The atmosphere there was somber but not as tense. A classificatory brother of the girl (120) was digging directly inside the door of the house. His brother (121), the bereaved husband's sister's husband (227), whose sister had been killed the last time a woman had died in childbirth only a few months before, and a couple of Western Suya were watching. The grave was dug to a depth of about four and one-half feet in the sandy soil. Then the grave digger dug a groove into the walls of the grave. A sister's son of the grave digger (who was also a classificatory brother of the deceased, 110) brought sticks, and they were cut to fit into the grooves and across the top of the grave about eighteen inches below the surface. Then they looked for and found an old blanket and two mats for covering the sticks.

Meanwhile, inside the other house, the husband had gone out in back of the house after the bow had been taken from him. Later he came back in and said it was almost dawn.[25] The wailing intensified when he said that, and the face of the dead woman was uncovered. One of the older women (234) cut her hair. First it was neatly parted, then three knots were tied in it, and then the center hair of the forehead was cut and shaved.[26] While this was going on, the girl's older sister (152) went and got water and the girl was washed. The same woman (152) painted her with *urcucum*, covering her entire body, with special attention to her head and feet. Another sister (153) made cotton yarn out of some finer string and wrapped the corpse's knees and ankles as for a ceremony. A waist belt was put on her and all her bead necklaces were hung from her neck. Her sister destroyed the burity fiber string that the dead woman had been making and cut up her dresses. When the grave preparation had been completed, the men filed out, went into the house where the mourning was taking place, and without a word untied the hammock and carried it and the corpses lying in it into the house where the grave had been dug. Mourners both preceded and followed them into the house, crowding into the fairly small space. A young man who was a classificatory husband of the girl (148) was told to get into the grave with the body and help it down. The corpse was set in the grave in a sitting position, wrapped in its hammock. It was facing approximately northeast. The young man climbed out of the grave, and the grave digger began to place sticks across the top of the grave, a few inches over the top of the corpse's head. The husband was leaning into the grave, crying and holding onto the corpse, while other women knelt on the sticks and held onto the corpse as well.[27] The grave digger had to stop for a few minutes. Everyone was crying, now the young men as well as the old and the women. After a time the grave digger began to lay the sticks again. When he completed that, he put the cloth across the top of the sticks and began to pull dirt on top of the cloth-covered sticks. When he completed that step, all the nonrelated mourners left.

Later that morning, at about sunrise, the grave digger straightened his arrows as he made a short oration about witchcraft. But he made no specific accusation. A little later the deceased woman's brother made a short oration as well, walking with his bows and arrows. Again there was no specific accusation. Eventually the death was blamed on a nonresident Indian of another tribe who was the husband of the witch that had been assassinated by the Suya a few months before.

This is a description of a relatively simple burial. The preparation of the corpse of a woman is much simpler than that of a man, especially an adult man who has a full set of ritual paraphernalia. The description I received of such a burial is that the body is washed by a *kràm-ngedi* who also paints the entire body with *urucum.* (The girl whose burial is described here had no living *kràm-ngedi.*) Moiety face paint is applied. The hair is cut back from the forehead as for certain ceremonies and in the same fashion as was done in this burial. The back hair is knotted around itself, as for singing *akia* and doing hard work. White down is stuck to the body. the man is buried with all his dance ornaments, which were traditionally his most valuable belongings: macaw and parrot feather headdress with a beeswax base and long or short macaw feathers according to moiety membership, feathers tied to the back of the head, arm bands of cotton with feathers hanging from them, rattles on the back of the knees, jaguar skin belt with macaw feather pendants, and any other ornaments, such as jaguar claw necklaces, are also put on. The grave should be dug by a relative, preferably a distant brother.

There are two types of grave, one for those who are *mẽropakande*, or "chiefs," the other for people who are not. *Mẽropakande* graves are dug so that a corpse sits in the grave. The Suya say they learned of this type of grave from Upper Xingu Indians. The graves of *mẽropakande* can be located in the village plaza or in the houses. Usually the chief and his wife are buried in the plaza, and their children who never exercised the role in the houses.[28] Everyone who is not a *mẽropakande* is buried in a rectangular grave inside the house. The body is carefully protected from any contact with the soil. It is wrapped in mats or cloth. It is buried facing east if it is sitting, or with its feet to the east if it is lying down, so that its spirit can see the way to the village of the dead.[29] Many of the belongings of the dead are broken and thrown into the grave. Pets belonging to the deceased should be killed and thrown in also.

The day after the burial, in the afternoon, all the man's possessions that have not been buried with him are taken to the men's house. The grave digger can take any possession he wants. He may be given a wife by the relatives of the deceased, sometimes the wife of the deceased, or his sister, or his sister's daughter.[30] Any remaining arrows and bows of the dead are broken. A woman's garden is rooted up.

The reasons for this large-scale destruction are hard to ascertain. The object is partly to make sure that nothing particularly valuable to the deceased is left in the village. When it is broken or destroyed, the "spirit" of the belonging goes up to the sky as well. A myth of the origin of death tells of a man who said that he was going away for a while but would come back the next day and instructed his relatives not to destroy his belongings. But they destroyed his belongings, and the man who came back to life said they did not like him and that he would go away and never come back, just as human beings would always do. Thus the purpose of the destruction is partly to make sure that the person's spirit leaves the village and goes to the village of the dead.

Relatives of the deceased go into mourning. Close relatives shave their heads, more distant ones cut a little hair off the back of their heads. In the cases that I saw the husbands and mothers shaved their heads. The sisters cut only a little, if any. People in mourning are not to leave the house much for a month or so. A man does not hunt, fish, or participate in ceremonies for at least a moon. Widows or widowers do not engage in sexual relations for a month or two—until their hair is grown out again and the flesh of the corpse is "soft" in the grave and the spirit "hard" in the village of the dead. There is no need for penis piercing, just abstinence.

The *sangri* is for the benefit of the dead person. When a dead man's spirit arrives at the village of the dead, his moiety membership is recognized by the length of the macaw feathers on his headdress. The members of his moiety run out to him, and everyone talks to him. He visits his parent's house, and then goes to the men's house where he lies down and is covered by a bark mat. He stays under that until "he gets hard," until his earthly flesh is rotten. Failure of the survivors to observe mortuary restrictions may prevent the hardening of the man's spirit so that the spirit becomes rotten and is sent to the village of the witches. Once hard, the spirit continues forever in the village of the dead.

The restrictions continue until the village decides to perform a ceremony. The mourner is painted after having water poured over him in the plaza, and though he may decide not to participate in the ceremony, the mourning is officially ended.

Western Suya practices are somewhat different. The hair is not cut, just parted. The grave is dug by a nonrelative. Children and women are buried in their maternal houses, *sikwenduyi* in the plaza, and adult men (possibly only aged men) are buried in their wife's house. A man's face painting—his moiety paint—is applied by a brother. A mother, sister, mother's mother, or father's mother, rather than a *kràm-ngedi*, puts on the *urucum*. All a man's ornaments are put on his body. The rest of his belongings are destroyed, but his gardens are not dug up. Women are buried without any ornaments except for a waist string.

Relatives of the dead person observe diet and activity restrictions. Brothers, sisters, mother, father, and also grandparents, wife, child, grandchildren, and, according to one man, wife's brothers and sister's husbands observe *sangri*. The grave digger also observes diet restrictions, but a wife's parents and one's ritual and name-giving relations do not.

Among the Western Suya the relatives have greater responsibility for the body, and they all observe diet restrictions. The observation of *sangri* by affines is the first time that nonrelatives (*kukïdi*) observe restrictions for each other. Among the Eastern Suya it is a relative who digs the grave, and nonrelatives do the painting and the washing.

The Female Life Cycle

The female life cycle is less ritually and symbolically elaborated. At birth a woman is given a name. The name need not carry moiety affiliation, for she does not take part in those groups. Girls before puberty never form semiautonomous peer groups like those of boys. They spend more time with their mothers, helping with younger siblings and playing with girl's toys, which are more domestic in nature. They sometimes play house with boys, but their independence is noticeably less, for they begin much younger to learn their economic tasks. The time between birth and marriage, when a person must be able to perform most economic tasks adequately, is much less for women, who set up hearths as soon as they have their first child (around sixteen), than for men who should be "old" before they leave the men's house (perhaps twenty or more).

At her first menstruation the Western Suya girl observes a long period of diet and activity restrictions. Eastern Suya girls are sometimes secluded in a fashion that they say they learned from the Upper Xingu Indians but which serves the same purpose: a ritual marking of the girl's entry into adult status. At the same time a girl's ears are pierced, usually at the end of the rainy season but not accompanying any particular ceremony. Girls between puberty and their first child were most often those taken on ceremonies by the men for sexual purposes, or chosen as *kahran-ndiyi* in the *pebyitugü* ceremony.

The ceremonies in which young girls might be taken could be simply a collective hunt, or the savannah deer ceremony, or the *pebyitugü*, or others. After such ceremonies the girls taken usually receive names with a *koko-* prefix. A girl taken on a collective fishing expedition in 1972 was given the name Koko-sàgri (the angry *koko*) because she refused to leave her hammock to cook the men fish the next morning. The men return from a hunt or fishing trip with a lot of food for the girls' relatives.

There was another ritual role, but one which I could learn very little about. There were certain girls, called *puyi* by Eastern Suya (*wuyi* by the Western Suya), who sang special songs in some ceremonies. Among the Western Suya they sang in their houses in a characteristic style. The institution may have been similar to the *Vutu* girls described by Nimuendaju among the Ramkokamekra (Nimuendaju 1946; see also Melatti 1970; pp. 357-360).

The most important role of women in ceremonies is as an audience and as relatives (*whai-wï-ieni*, sisters and mothers) of the male performers. Women are the stable points between which the men move with such ceremony. They are born in their mothers' houses, remain there for their entire lives, and are buried there. Their ties to parents and sisters are not as much attenuated. Besides birth and death, the most elaborated passage is that of puberty, which marks the beginning of their real sexuality. At puberty a girl begins to be *kü-kumeni*, takes on lovers, and eventually gives birth to a child. Her husband moves in with her. She sets up a separate hearth but always acts in cooperation with her mother and sisters. The house is an economic unit, in which women share the tasks of preparing and distributing food, and the groups of closely related women who make up such houses are important social groups.

The wives of chiefs play important political roles in the village, calming disputants, taking food to nonrelatives, and often prodding their husbands to act. The wife of a politically active adult man is also important. When women cease to menstruate, they are no longer as strictly identified with sexuality. They become merely pungent smelling and may enter the old people's age grade (*wikenyi*). As with old men, they know a great deal of oral history, myth, and ceremonial lore. In most of the ceremonies that I witnessed, the oldest women were consulted about details of performance. They also helped the children by accompanying them, something that younger women never did. The importance of old women appears to have been a feature of the Western Suya as well. But it is an importance related to their knowledge and to their identity as wives, sisters, and mothers. Their rites of passage are fewer and less elaborate; their direct participation in plaza affairs is fairly small.

The processes by which an infant is transformed into an adult, an old person, and in death to a resident of the village of the dead consist of a number of steps involving an attenuation of the complete physical identity of the individual with his parents and ending with an identity with his offspring. Each stage is accompanied by dietary and activity restrictions. Each also has a particular mediator who helps effect the transition.

Space, body ornamentation and faculties, odor, and kinship are all involved in the transitions. In a purely spatial idiom a man is born in his mother's bed, leaves it for a period of residence in the men's house as a *sikwenduyi*, moves to his wife's house (ideally located across the village), and becomes fully integrated into his wife's house; in his last years a very old man particpates little in plaza affairs. There is a kind of similarity between young boys and old men—each participates little in plaza affairs—but there is an asymmetry as well, because the old men have participated and have a special role in the ceremonial and social life of the village. Each of these spatial transitions is highly elaborated in Suya ritual, being frequently repeated. Social relations often have a spatial expression.

Body ornaments and the development of the faculties are also an important part of the life process. When boys begin to have sexual relations, their ears are pierced so that they will "hear" and behave morally. When they are big, their lips are pierced. When the lip disk is large enough to paint a *ngroro* design on the underside, a young man is ashamed to remain in his natal household and goes to the men's house, where he makes his own lip disks. When he becomes a *wikenyi*, he ceases to make his own lip disk, and the one that is made for him has no design on the underside. He has less shame and spends much more time in his wife's house than in the center of the village or in the men's house. Thus in terms of body ornamentation as well, the very old (*wikenyi*) are identified with still uninitiated men. A similar situation occurs with women, whose ear disks are made for them in the *wikenyi* induction ceremony.

The relationship of odor to sex and age is another process of transformation. Infants are strong-smelling and, in the case of males, are socialized through a series of rites of passage which end in their having no odor. When they become *wikenyi* they again change odor, becoming pungent. Here a lessened association with the plaza and with affairs of the men's house and a weakening of the physical body are associated with a stronger odor. Women are strong smelling until they become *wikenyi*, passing then to a different, less powerful and less dangerous stage.

The child is born and identified with its corporeal group, its *kwoi-kumeni*. These ties are attenuated by a number of mediators of increasing genealogical distance from the child. It is usually his maternal grandmother who picks him up. His mother's brother names him. His ceremonial relations cannot be close relatives, and they are involved in his rites of passage. Then his wife is involved in his induction into the men's house, and later his own child is involved in his move from the men's house to his wife's house. One corporeal group is altered in order to form a different corporeal group. But the ties with the natal family remain and are especially important in rituals.

The close physical ties are attenuated first through ceremonial relationships and then through affinal ties. The ceremonial relationships involve name group, plaza group, and moiety membership. One can see, then, in the life cycle of a man, the shifting weight of certain relationships. In his early years his close relatives are the most important to him. In his most active ceremonial life the ceremonial groups are the most important; there he forms special friendships, exchanges days of singing, and so on. When he has several children, the weight shifts to those children. When his children marry, a man's position in his wife's household shifts radically, and his relations with his descendants (children and children's children) gain ascendancy.[31]

The natural world has been defined as associated with the periphery, with unaltered body parts, with strong odors, and to some degree with the corporeal sharing group of close kinsmen. A man's life cycle, then, begins as an infant associated in various ways with nature. But from birth begins a process of socialization that identifies the child increasingly with the plaza life and men's groups. The *sikwenduyi*, living in the center without odor, without strong ties to either family of birth or to affines, and spending their time making lip disks and singing, are the epitome of the social. It is the opposition between *sikwenduyi* and strong-smelling animals that the opposing poles of society and nature are to be found.

But the static nature of the opposition is illusory. The *sikwenduyi* are created by society. It is the adult men, who have been *sikwenduyi* but no longer are, who induct men into the men's house. Through its elaborate ceremony Suya society is continually recreating itself, reaffirming the distinction between society and the surrounding natural world. Thus one man saw the pattern of men exchanging places with other men in the men's house: the *sikwenduyi* continue even through individual *sikwenduyi* leave the center for the periphery and eventually become old men, belonging to the periphery and smelling pungent.

The female life cycle is quite different. Spatially she moves only laterally, setting up a hearth of her own in her natal household. In terms of body, a woman becomes only partly socialized: she is expected to hear-understand-know and behave morally, but she is not expected to orate or sing. In terms of odor she changes little. Kinship relations change little. Her names do not necessarily have plaza group and moiety affiliations. If they do, the ties are rarely activitated. Women do not tend to know their kinship relationsips with all the other members of the village, remaining more in their own residential segment. An important change occurs when a woman becomes a *wikenyi* and is pungent instead of strong smelling. But in terms of the basic parameters of Suya society—by which nature and society are defined and parts of it transformed—women go through fewer alterations and remain somewhat natural beings. They are above all associated with sexuality, and to some extent with the subversion of the ideal masculine order, the *sikwenduyi*.

Society thus transforms nature. Specifically, collective male ceremonial groups transform children into adults, and adults into old people. The dead are transformed through death, back to the age grade of transition: men arrive in the village of the dead as *sikwenduyi*, women as *puyi*. Thus men transform nature, but nature also transforms society. The presence of natural features in the social universe is a strong force, and a creative one.

9

Political Leaders, Ritual Specialists, and Witches

IN ADDITION TO RELATIONSHIPS of Suya with various categories of kinsmen and affines and the characteristics of groups distinguished by sex and age, Suya society has certain social roles that are to varying degrees achieved rather than ascribed. These offer opportunities for individual manipulation. In the society described so far all actions occur at the right time and in the right place; all adults hear-understand-know and behave correctly; all members of a given sex and age are homogeneous. But in fact factionalism exists, and political leaders manipulate their resources to obtain support for proposed collective action. Some men are better singers than others. Some have the important ability to compose music so that Suya ceremony is always innovative and always a reenactment of obtaining ceremonies from nature. And some people are considered witches and curers; the ambivalent position of the *wayanga* includes both curing and aggression.

The roles of political leader, ceremonial leader, and witch-curer give the social organization a special dynamic and once again reveal the importance of the "natural" in power. Although it would be a serious error to see Suya society as individualistic in the Western sense (L. Dumont 1966, 1977), there are certain domains in which the individual Suya may express his own style. Music is one of them. In the recently deceased generation about 30 percent of the adult initiated men could understand the language and songs of a natural species. Politics is another. The Suya have always had at least two factions, usually three, each with its political leader. And witchcraft-curing is another, though as one man said, no one wants to admit being a *wayanga.* All three roles, each in its different way, are considered powerful and associated with the natural domain.

The concept of "owner-controller" is central to any analysis of power. The ideal attributes of political leaders have often been listed (Clastres 1962), and the Suya leaders are within the pattern for American Indians. But these ideal qualities are the objects of considerable manipulation, as demonstrated by an extended case of factional conflict presented in this chapter. Only when the role of political leader is seen in the light of the conflicts in which he is involved is it possible to understand the ambivalance of the Suya toward their leaders.

The most important concept in Suya thinking about power is the word *kande*, which I have translated as "controller," although "owner" is also a possible translation. A *mẽropakande* is an owner-controller of the village (*mẽro,* Suya; *pa* village, or group of people together in a certain location; *kande*, owner, controller). A *mẽrokïnkande* is a ritual specialist who knows all the songs and is therefore a controller of ceremonies (*kin*, Suya ceremonies). A person who makes an artifact for his own use is the *kande*, or owner, of that artifact. A person who knows a certain curing chant that no one else knows is the *kande* of that curing chant. A hunter who has particular success with a certain kind of animal is the *kande* of that animal, which implies that he is able to control it. All things that are owned are owned by *kande*. Women are the *kande* of gardens and houses.

The word *kande* refers not only to physical property, but to esoteric knowledge as well. It includes the ability to do something or to make something as well as its ownership. It is control over goods and resources, where the goods may be intangibles and the resources symbolic. It may be potential ability: the *mẽrokïnkande* can teach songs to people. The small black bird known as the "controller of the rain" (*nda kande*) has control over rain; when it is killed, rain will fall for a long time without stopping. *Tu-kande* are plant and animal medicines that have some control over the body or the disease. Bad omens, called *sàwhiri-kande*, or "things that control death," are important presages.

The concept of *kande* resembles some of the more recent sociological and anthropological theories of power in which power is seen not as force but as control over the collective goal-seeking behavior of a group. Goal-seeking behavior may be controlled through symbolic as well as coercive resources (see Swartz, Turner, and Tuden 1966). Not only humans but also certain animals have power and control. The concept of the owner-controller permeates Suya society, even though there is relatively little property in the material sense of the word. Hunting areas, potential garden sites, and fishing spots are all collectively controlled.

But it is a fallacy of ethnocentricity to maintain that ownership and property are unimportant. From the Suya perspective most things have owner-controllers: villages, ceremonies, songs, houses, gardens, belongings, pets, and so forth. The importance of *kande* is pervasive.

The chief of a village (*mẽropakande*), the ritual specialist (*mẽrokïnkande*), and witches (*wayanga*) are all different kinds of *kande* with different powers.

Suya Leadership

Before the Suya entered into prolonged contact with the Upper Xingu Indian societies—indeed probably until the time of the Juruna raid sometime after 1915—their leaders were warriors, known for being extra brave, or extra belligerent, *sàgri-kumeni.*[1] First as a result of contact with the tribes of the Upper Xingu, and more recently from contact with members of the Brazilian national society, especially Claudio Villas Boas, certain aspects of leadership among the Suya have changed. The consistencies through the change are revealed through comparison with the Western Suya patterns of leadership. There is every reason to believe that leadership has always been hereditary, ideally in the patriline from a father to one of his sons, but that consent of the members of the village was essential. Leadership has always involved oratorical skill, and sanctions have always been few.

Traditional Eastern Suya leadership was described to me by informants who were themselves only told about it by men now deceased. Leaders were *mẽ-sàgri,* and were called *waropakande*,[2] or "controller of our village." *Waropakande* who had taken part in the important fish ceremony (*tep kradi*) were called *gaiontòni,* possibly because only they sang the *gaiyi ngere*, an important name-giving ceremony which I never witnessed but which I was told was reserved for leaders.[3] The obligations mentioned for those leaders were mainly initiative in war and in certain ceremonies. Because of their prowess and aggressiveness they were sometimes referred to as *mẽsisekande*,[4] or "controllers of the village circle." They were always the first to suggest making a raid, and they led raids. They also looked for enemies around the village. As one informant said, if there were belligerent Indians to the north, the *mẽsisekande* would always be hunting and fishing in the north, going out early in the morning and late in the evening looking for signs of the enemy. If there were belligerent Indians in the south, he would always go out to the south. He was always walking around the edge of the village.

Waropakande were also belligerent and volatile inside the village as well. Boys and young men were often the objects of harassment. There were ceremonies in which the leaders would carry boys on their shoulders and put peppers in their mouths, beat them with bones, sticks, and banana stalks. Harassment was not confined to uninitiated boys. One famous leader of the past liked to shoot arrows at the men's house and the *sikwenduyi* had to duck and dodge them. All such leaders were described as being frightening because they were so belligerent.

In addition to guarding the village and harassing the boys and young men to make them grow up to be belligerent, *mẽ-sàgri* orated in the plaza. They would walk in circles around the assembled men and orate loudly enough to be heard by women assembled in front of the houses. They coordinated community efforts. They had no control over anyone except their own kinsmen, but they could exhort, cajole, or shame people who did not cooperate as well as frighten certain timid souls by their characteristically uncontrolled belligerence. In the long run, if a person failed to follow the suggestions of a strong leader he could be accused of being a witch. When no one followed the leader's advice, the leader ceased to be effective.

Leadership among the Western Suya was quite similar but unaffected by Upper Xingu Indian influence. Their leaders were called *waropakande* and were belligerent and frightening. They were orators who called all the men to the plaza in the morning and evening and coordinated group activities. Only they could sing the *gaiyi ngere*. Although my informants said that a *waropakande* could be of either moiety, all four that I was able to obtain information about were *Krenyi*. The office was hereditary, several informants emphasizing that it went to the youngest son of a *waropakande,* though they may have been generalizing from a recent important case. They also said that there were always a number of *waropakande* who did not orate (*kaperni-kïtïlï*) and who did not lead but held the position through heredity. My informants also seemed to say that all the men in the village were involved in the choice of a leader, that only when people agreed to follow them could they lead. There is always considerable difficulty reconstructing political realities from people's memories and ideal statements. When they were in the process of being contacted (and killed) by Brazilians, the Western Suya had two chiefs. Both had taken part in the fish ceremony (*tep kradi*), were *Krenyi,* lived in houses of the name "black house" (*kikre tugü*) and had very large gardens of food which they distributed to the rest of the tribe.

Mẽropakande

One of the results of contact with Upper Xingu Indian tribes was that new responsibilities were taken by the Suya leaders and more obligations were placed on those led. Among the Upper Xingu tribes every ceremony has an owner. In Suya these are called the *kande,* or owner-controllers, of the ceremonies. Only Upper Xingu ceremonies have individual owner-controllers among the Suya. Strictly Suya ceremonies may be controlled by a moiety, but not by a single person. As a result of the performance of

Upper Xingu ceremonies by the Suya, certain men became *kande* of particular ceremonies. These men tended to be *mẽ-sàgri*. The leaders who were also controllers of ceremonies were called *mẽropakande*.

Mẽropakande did not have to be belligerent warriors. Their office was to perform the traditional Suya roles of leader and also to give out food in return for which the rest of the men would perform their Upper Xingu ceremony. My informants said that as a result of the addition of ceremonial responsibilities, more emphasis was placed on the hereditary nature of the office, just as they say there is in the Upper Xingu. Again, a man is a *mẽropakande* only if the village performs his ceremony. If it does not, then he is not a leader.

My informants agreed that Ndemonti (337) was the first real *mẽropakande* and the last real *mẽ-sàgri*. They always commented on how he gave food to the rest of the village, a sign of a *mẽropakande*, and fought all the time, a sign of a *mẽ-sàgri*. The obligations of a *mẽropakande* are (1) to give food publicly to all the men and to distribute food and objects given by other people (usually other *mẽropakande*) to the rest of the village, (2) to officiate at certain ceremonies such as those at the end of mourning, (3) to orate in the plaza (*ngà-ihogo kaperni*), (4) to coordinate group projects, and (5) to lead raids. The rest of the village has certain obligations to a *mẽropakande*. They help cut his garden, help build his house, make canoes, and perform his ceremony. *Mẽropakande* are buried in the village plaza in a special type of grave. The wives and children of a *mẽropakande* are buried in a similar manner, though possibly inside the house, because they too are said to have become controllers of the village (*kwï mẽropakande*).[5]

While most Suya distribute only to their kinsmen and affines as far as their obligations indicate, *mẽropakande* distribute to all members of the tribe beyond their kinship obligations. One of their most important tasks is to give food to the men in return for the performance of the ceremony of which they are *kande*.[6] They must also supply the paraphernalia. With their relatives they kill fish for the dancers. Their wives cook the fish and process huge amounts of manioc (or corn in season) to make sweet manioc drink, manioc cakes, and fishpaste for all the people in the ritual. When the ceremony has been performed the men shout, "Bring on the food! Bring on the food!" When the *kande* of the ceremony brings it out to the congregated men in the men's house, they say "Oh, it is so little." To this he replies, "You are so lazy; you hardly danced." Then another *mẽropakande,* not usually the one who brings out the food, divides it with great care so that everyone gets some, including orphans and widows. Married men get a share, which they take back to their families or send back with a child. *Mẽropakande* also take part in or supervise the distribution of raw meat when a large animal or several smaller ones have been killed on a collective men's hunt. They usually supervise the distribution of cooked food in men's house meals, when the men eat food that has been cooked by the young men in the men's house. A *mẽropakande* is supposed to be primarily a distributor known for his fairness which transcends his kinship ties. The Suya say this feature was not found among the earlier leaders, the *mẽ-sàgri*, but was learned from the Upper Xingu and distinguishes *mẽropakande* from *waropakande*.[7]

Only *mẽropakande* are able to perform certain semiritual duties. Only a *mẽropakande* calls members of the village to bathe in the plaza in the ceremony performed at the end of a mourning period, not as the representative of a particular group (he never does this after the death of his own kinsman), but as a representative of the entire village. Similarly, only *mẽropakande* can sing the *gaiyi ngere*. A *mẽropakande* has no special body paint or paraphernalia. Apart from supplying food and paraphernalia specific to his own ritual, a *mẽropakande* plays no special role in ritual affairs.

The ownership of rituals, the office of *mẽropakande*, and the ritual relationship of *kràm-ngedi* and *ñumbre-krà-chi* are the only statuses or property inherited patrilineally. When a *mẽropakande* dies, his oldest son (according to Eastern Suya informants) may become *mẽropakande* if the rest of the village gives him such power. If a *mẽropakande* has only very young sons, his brother may become one. If he has no sons and no brothers, he may pass the ownership of ritual or office to his sister's son (*taumtwü*). One *mẽropakande* (122) inherited one ceremony from his father (220) and another from his mother's brother (218) whose child was captured by Northern Kayapo raiders.

The agreement of the rest of the village about a man's claim to being a *mẽropakande* is important. My questions about whether a particular man's particular son would become a *mẽropakande* when he died were always answered vaguely. "When the father dies the people (*mẽ*) will know." There are at present three *mẽropakande* in the Suya village. Two of them are direct descendants of former *mẽropakande* (FFF-FF-F-ego). One of them is at the same time a *mẽropakande* through his mother's brother (MBF-MB-ego). The third case is the present *capitão*.

Only *mẽropakande* are supposed to use certain types of oratory in the village plaza. Plaza speech in general is a politically important act and is restricted to older men. There are several types of plaza speech (*ngà-ihogo kaperni*). The more restricted type, called "everybody listens speech," is generally spoken only by *mẽropakande* and *mẽrokïnkande*. It may be an exhortation, an announcement of a collective activity, or an announcement of special news of general importance. Another kind of plaza speech, specifically addressed to a *wayanga* (witch), may be spoken by any adult man and is not directed to everyone (although all can hear it) but specifically to the witch in question. When a relative is sick, or when a man or his relatives have had a nightmare, or when women's gossip has precipitated a crisis, a man may use this speech. He usually uses angry speech (*grutnen kaperni*) in which the words are clipped, shouted in short bursts, and in which tone contours are more jagged than in other types of plaza speech.

Plaza speech addresses not only the men in the center but the entire village. It is highly structured in both words and tone formulas. As he speaks, a man usually walks counterclockwise around the plaza. He always invokes the deceased ancestors of the villagers as examples: "Our fathers, our mother's brothers, our name givers, our grandfathers . . . did such-and-such a thing." They all exhort people to behave correctly. The phonetic and rhythmic features of speech are altered, generally by exaggerating rhythms and stressing unstressed syllables. All plaza speech is also highly repetitive. While one man is orating, other men may talk to themselves, paraphrasing or agreeing, although only one person orates at a time. *Mẽropakande* used to orate every day at dawn and dusk. When Amadeu Lanna was with the Suya in 1963, the village leader (204) used to orate every night. When I was there, partly because of the youth of the present *capitão* (105), the lameness of another *mẽropakande* (151), and the nonaggressiveness of the third (122), plaza speech was heard only occasionally. The ritual specialist (120) did most of the oratory during my stay.

Mẽropakande coordinate collective behavior. They coordinate group hunts, fishing expeditions, garden clearing, house building, and the like. They may coordinate ceremonies, but that is usually left to the *mẽrokïnkande*. The *mẽropakande* speak in the men's circle, exhorting the men to stay in the village the next day so that they can all do something collectively. If they agree, the men say *hããããã* when he has finished speaking. If they do not agree, they do not stay in the village the following day.

Mẽropakande used to initiate raids. This has not happened in recent years when the Suya were trying to avoid their enemies and then when the administration of the Xingu reserve forbade warfare. But they play important parts in conflicts with local ranchers.

The Capitão

Leadership today differs from precontact leadership as a result of the politics of indirect rule practiced by the administration of the Parque Nacional do Xingu. Claudio Villas Boas led the expedition that contacted the Suya and remained intimately associated with them until 1975, influencing almost every aspect of their lives in some degree. The Brazilians call the Indian who mediates between the Villas Boas and the rest of the tribe the *capitão* (captain). This term indicates a leader without implying anything about heredity or type of leadership. Every tribe in the Xingu reserve has a *capitão* through whom the Villas Boas (and now the administration represented by Olympio Serra) distribute gifts and communicate with the respective tribes. These men may be groomed for the position through instruction in Portuguese and favored status at the posts.

Among the Suya the present *capitão* is also a hereditary *mẽropakande*. Since all trade goods are distributed through him, his position as mediator and distributor of largesse undermines the status of the other *mẽropakande*. For this reason I would say that among the Suya there are at present three active *mẽropakande*, one of whom is a *capitão*. His additional function is as a mediator between Suya and Brazilians.

Some aspects of leadership have not changed through the decades. These include plaza speech and exhortation, the leader's position as mediator, a person who transcends kinship obligations and is supposed to reduce tension and prevent strife. He has always been responsible for relationships with other tribes, either by leading raids and protecting the village or by negotiating with Brazilians. None of the leaders described was necessarily a ritual specialist, which is clearly distinguished from political leaders.

The Making of a Mẽropakande

Norms are always flexible and manipulable by determined and ambitious men. The present *capitão*, Niokombedi, manipulates certain supports to justify and improve his position as leader of the entire Suya tribe.[8] In spite of general Suya reluctance to discuss the issues involved in past strife, I was able to trace a line of conflict back for two generations.

Before the Juruna raid in about 1915, the Suya were led by Ndemonti (337), already referred to as the last *mẽ-sàgri* and the first *mẽropakande*. He had killed several men, undergone the *kupen kande* ceremony, been wounded twice and recovered, and was very strong. He organized the first raid on the Waura tribe because he discovered that the Waura were trading old pots in exchange for good Suya arrows, feathers, and axes. Ndemonti had a daughter and two sons by his first wife, a daughter by another. He was not killed by the Juruna, but some years later he and a number of his family were killed or captured by a group of Kayapo (see genealogy, appendix A).

After the death of Ndemonti and before the Suya moved to the village on the *ngo saka* (village 9a in figure 2.2), the chronology is hard to determine exactly. The Suya raided the Waura for women again and captured three. Later they captured two Northern Kayapo women and a Juruna woman. One of Ndemonti's sons, Tebnti (244), was killed as a witch. His assassination was unusual, for he was at the time only a *sikwenduyi* and Eastern Suya say that only old people are witches. Niokombedi (105), the present *capitão*, said that Tebnti was killed because he had caused the death of Takuti's mother (325). Takuti (227) denied this, and said that

Tebnti had caused the death of Ndemonti (his own father) at the hands of the Northern Kayapo. Both agreed that he had become a *wayanga* because he pierced his penis and then had sexual relations with a woman.

As the years went by, one of the Suya named Waraku (204) began to establish himself as a strong leader. He was (or claimed to be) a descendant of Ndemonti also. He said that Ndemonti had had sexual relations

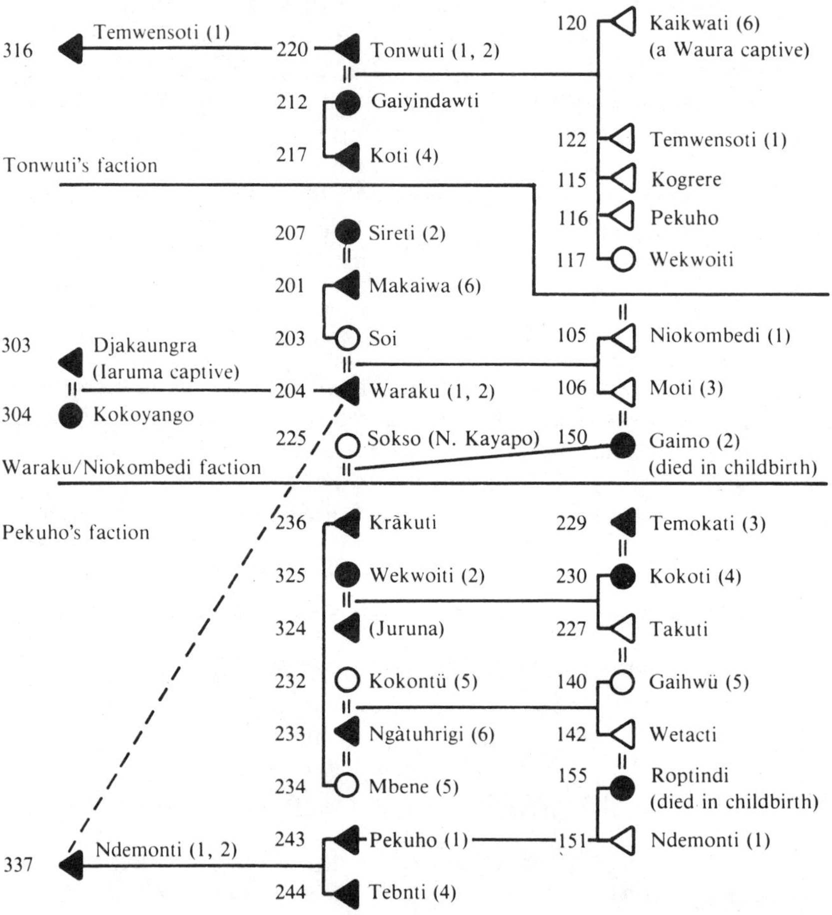

Figure 9.1 *Suya factions. (1) An important* mẽropakande *(political leader). (2) Death attributed to a particular witch. (3) Killed as a witch. (4) Principle killer in a witch assassination. (5) Individual accused of being a witch by members of Niokombedi's faction. (6) A* mẽrokïnkande *(ritual specialist). A complete genealogy of the Eastern Suya is in appendix A.*

with his mother and was in fact his genitor.[9] At the time there were two other important *mẽropakande*, Pekuho (243), the remaining biological son of Ndemonti with one of his resident wives, and Tonwuti (220).

One year when the piqui fruit was ripe (around November), Tonwuti died of fever. It was said later that he told his *taumtwü*, Temokati (229), that it was his wife's brother Koti (217) who was making him sick (Figure 9.1 gives the principal actors and their relationships; appendix A is more complete.) In the height of the rainy season that year (February or thereabouts) the men were off on a hunting expedition. There was some argument whether to kill Koti because of his reported responsibility for the death of Tonwuti. Temokati and Pekuho wanted to kill Koti, and Waraku opposed it, saying "Let him lie." Suddenly Temokati jumped up, grabbed his bow, and shot Koti who ran off into the woods. They followed him and shot him again. He was difficult to kill, however, and they had to return later to club him to death.

The Suya were then living in a single village in a maze of waterways on a tributary to the Suya-Missu. A plane flew over the village in 1954 or 1955. At that time Waraku's wife's brother's wife (207), who was also his mother's brother's daughter, died. There was apparently considerable acrimonious talk about this, because Waraku cut distant gardens and the next year moved to a village site some eight hours away by canoe from the rest of the village. He was accompanied by the wife of Tonwuti (212), whose brother (217) had been killed by Temokate, and all her children including Kaikwati (120), who was an adopted son, and Takuti (227), whose mother may have been killed by Tebnti (244), assassinated some time before. Waraku was also accompanied by his wife, her brother, and his children. Remaining in the other village were Pekuho (243), Ngãtuhrigi (233), Temokati (229), Krãkuti (236), and their families (see figure 9.2).

The two villages continued to perform ceremonies jointly, and there was no open hostility between them. One informant admitted that there was a lot of "bad speech" (*kaperni kasàgà*) between them. In 1959 the Suya were first contacted by the Juruna, who prepared the Suya for a visit by the Villas Boas and a Brazilian pacification team. Because Waraku's village was closer to the Suya-Missu and because the water was too shallow for a motorboat near Pekuho's village, it was agreed that all the Suya would congregate at Waraku's village and wait for the arrival of the Villas Boas.

At the request of the Villas Boas the Suya moved closer to Diauarum, settling at Yamaricumã, which had been a village site some decades earlier. The two groups did not set up camp together. A comment by Harold Schultz (1960-61) indicates that Pekuho was a more belligerent, less cooperative leader. Schultz camped near Waraku's camp. Waraku was the more important liaison with the Villas Boas. It was only during

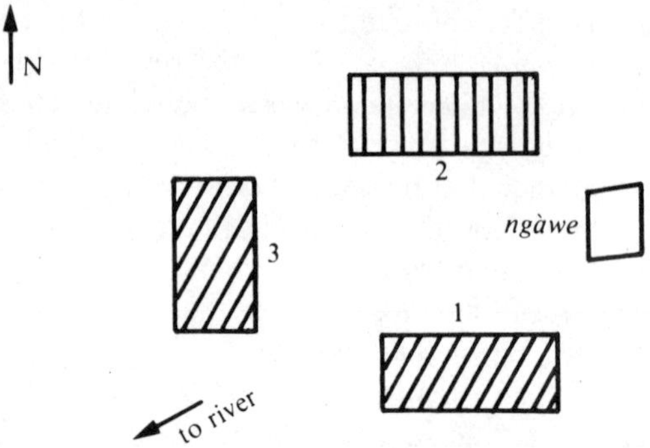

Waraku's village (9b in figure 2.2)

House 1: 204, 201, and families
House 2: 212, 120, 122
House 3: 222, 227
ngàwe: men's house

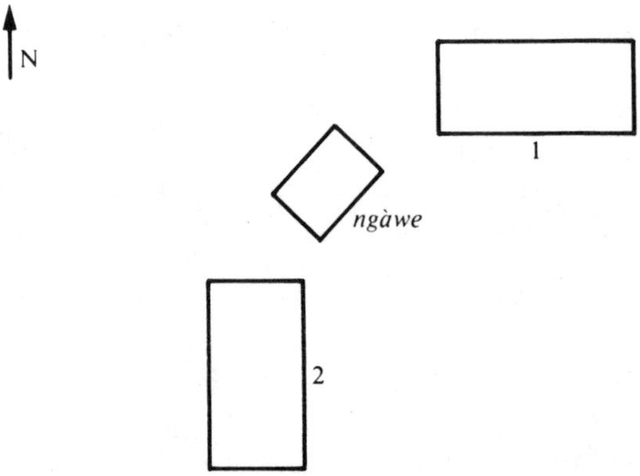

Pekuho's village (9a in figure 2.2)
after fissioning in 1957

House 1: 233 and family
House 2: 243 and family, also 229, 230, and family
ngàwe: men's house

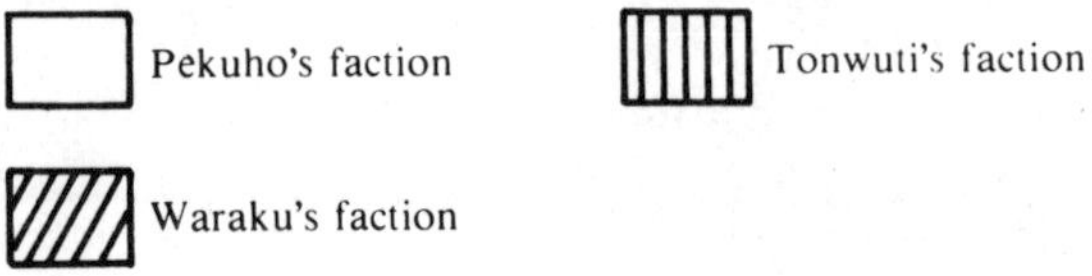

Figure 9.2 *Waraku's and Pekuho's villages after fissioning*

Amadeu Lanna's visit that the Suya formed a single village—in 1962 after the death of Pekuho and Ngàtuhrigi from disease.

When the two groups moved together, there was considerable intermarriage. Two sons of Tonwuti (120, 122) married four daughters of Ngàtuhrigi (144-147). Takuti (227) married another daughter of Ngàtuhrigi (140). Within three years of their move to Yamaricumã, all the older men had died with the exception of Waraku. The children of Pekuho moved in with Waraku, who was their classificatory father. The ensuing years saw many of the members of Pekuho's faction leave the village. Two of his daughters married a Trumai man who resided in the village until he was killed by a Kayabi (possibly at the request of the Suya who believed that he was responsible for Pekuho's death). Another daughter married a Trumai and lived out of the village. Temokati died of unknown causes, and his wife remarried a Trumai. By the time that I arrived in the village, she was living nearly full-time at Diauarum. Her children by Temokati, married to a Kayabi and Trumai, were also living out of the village. The second wife of Ngàtuhrigi (232) had to flee the village with her children because of witchcraft accusations after the death of her husband. These finally subsided and with time and with the intervention of the Villas Boas, they were able to return to the village.

The most recent events occurred during our stay in the village. The descendants of Waraku's faction were living in houses 1, 2, 3, and 6 (see figure 9.3). Descendants of Pekuho's faction were resident in houses 4 and 7, and spread out at both Posto Diauarum and Posto Leonardo. While we were out on a fieldbreak, in May 1972, the wife of one of Waraku's sons (150) died in childbirth. That man and his brothers (105, 106, 110) went to Diauarum and clubbed to death the widow of Temokati, Kokoti (230), who they claimed had caused the death of the woman in childbirth. She was also now accused of causing the death of Waraku, previously ascribed to the Trumai killed by the Kayabi. Some months later the wife of a son of Ngàtuhrigi (155) also died in childbirth. Her husband (142) was a member of a very diffuse and weakened faction, and no particular person was thought to be responsible.

In 1973 it was unclear what would happen. Takuti was clearly unhappy with the sons of Waraku who killed his sister (230), and they were ill at ease with him. Takuti's wife (140), his wife's mother (232), and his wife's classificatory mother (another wife of Ngàtuhrigi) are all thought to be witches by women of Waraku's faction. In 1976 the tension had eased, the events being futher in the past. Takuti's eldest son (133) had married a granddaughter of Waraku (006). The village was quite united against the surrounding Brazilians. The factionalism may well reappear, however, when new deaths bring new suspicions.

Waraku and his son Niokombedi became the strongest *mẽropakande* by manipulating a number of resources to justify and promote their claims as the dominant leaders of the tribe. There are at least eight resources that they and other controllers of the village have consciously manipulated during two generations. The first six are related to the ideal attributes of a *mẽropakande*; the last two are of a different order, but equally important.

Descent. Niokombedi repeatedly stressed his biological descent from the strong *mẽropakande*, Ndemonti. His father, Waraku (204), had called Ndemonti "father" because Ndemonti had been having sexual relations with his mother (304). Thus Niokombedi traces his inheritance

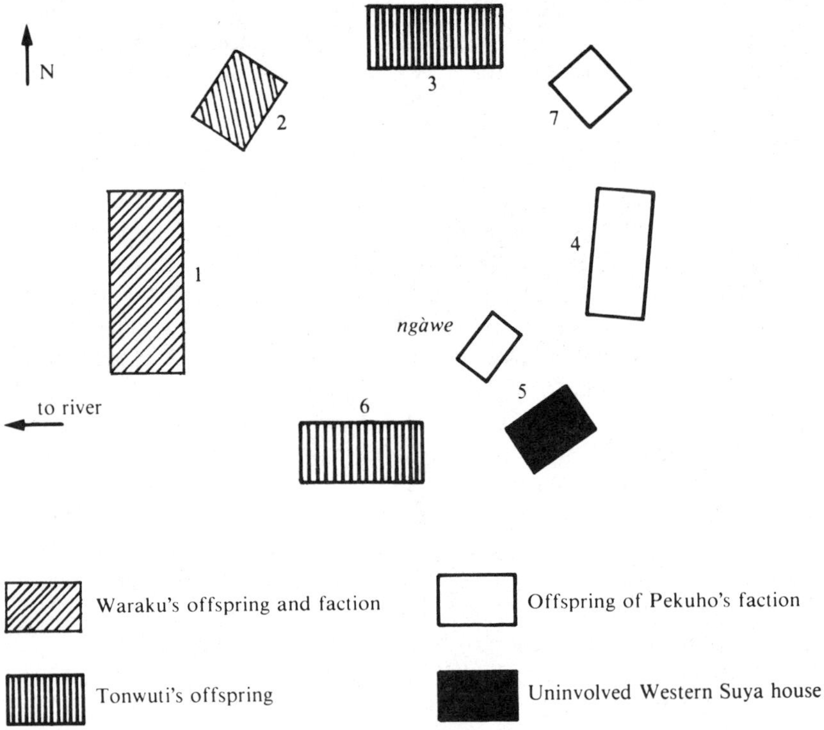

House 1: 203, 206, and children
House 2: 225 and married daughter and married son
House 3: 122 and family, his brother 115 and family, and 234
House 4: 232 and children, 227
House 5: Survivors of Western Suya group, not involved
House 6: 120 and family
House 7: Children of 243 (deceased)
ngàwe: Men's house
(A full village census is given in figure A.1)

Figure 9.3 *Suya village in 1972 showing factional alignment*

from his father's genitor through his father to himself. A man of the other faction, Takuti (227), whose sister was assassinated by Niokombedi and his brothers, affirmed that Waraku had never been a *mẽropakande*. He said that Waraku had merely been an aggressive man. Instead, it was Pekuho who had been the true *mẽropakande*.

In his oratory Niokombedi would ask rhetorically, "Was not my father a *mẽropakande*?" But in fact it was a point he was continually trying to emphasize, and not one that was accepted by everyone. That this was one of his legitimizing claims emphasizes the importance of a direct, genealogical relationship between the *mẽropakande* and past leaders.

Distribution. Niokombedi bases one of his claims to being a *mẽropakande* on his giving things to everyone. This is another important ideal for a leader. However, Niokombedi did not distribute food. He was not the owner-controller of any Upper Xingu Indian ceremony, and all distributions of food—whether parts of ceremonies or the division of meat after a collective hunt—were made by other men. But he did distribute the trade goods given to him by the Villas Boas and by visitors and anthropologists for general distribution. This distribution of trade goods was quite important, yet a two-edged sword.

One of the major and inevitable conflicts in Niokombedi's leadership was the jealousy of certain individuals over the amount he kept for himself and, even more important, the overwhelming amount he gave to his numerous relatives. One of the most outspoken complainers was Kokoti (230), a woman who was assassinated by Niokombedi and his brother as a witch in 1972.[10]

For the same reason Niokombedi's family feared witch attack from the Western Suya, who were generally given less and had fewer trade good possessions. The distribution of goods was always difficult, but it improved greatly during the years covered by our visits.

Coordination of collective activities. Niokombedi coordinated collective activities including hunts and fishing expeditions, plaza clearing, and occasional work at Diauarum.

Dispute settlement. Niokombedi claimed to act as a peacemaker. Except when his own interests were intimately involved, for example when he helped kill Kokoti, he prevented disputes from becoming violent. He would repeatedly reduce tension by interrupting, joking, orating, or otherwise dominating men's plaza meetings. He would also talk to the individuals involved and try to settle the matter out of the public arena. He could rely on the support of his numerous close kinsmen.

Two incidents show the combination of humor and implied force that he mobilized.

In the first, the Western Suya were all at Diauarum being treated for an epidemic of colds and pneumonia, and all the Eastern Suya had returned to the village. The Eastern Suya men were gathered in the men's circle one evening, and they were angry about Western Suya depredations on their manioc gardens. There was a real shortage of manioc in 1972, and the Eastern Suya were very sensitive about the continuing dependence of the Western Suya on their gardens even after the Western Suya gardens had begun to yield. Various men were doing quiet "angry speech," and someone suggested burning the Western Suya house (house 5). At that moment Niokombedi walked out to the men's circle, having rolled himself a cigarette in his house. He loudly addressed his joking relatives and said, "Jirrup, when the Western Suya come back, we'll screw all their women."[11] That was both funny and accurate. The Western Suya women were considered particularly desirable as sexual partners. His comment effectively stopped the serious conversation about the Western Suya for the evening and prevented any concerted action.

In another incident, Wetacti's wife (155) died in childbirth. One of the Western Suya feared that Wetacti was going to kill his wife, who was believed by some people to be a witch. When he found out about these fears, Niokombedi spoke to the Western Suya man and told him that there was no "bad speech" (*kaperni kasàgà*). Since Niokombedi and his brother had killed Kokoti the village was pretty good, and to kill anyone else would be bad. He added that Wetacti had few relatives and only one brother. Niokombedi told Wetacti that he and his brothers killed Kokoti because of a lot of bad speech and that she had been truly bad. Now, he said, there was no bad speech and people should not kill each other. Then he asked Wetacti, "Are you going to kill the man's wife?" Wetacti replied, "No." The matter was dropped.

The second case followed a typical pattern. Women gossiped about the accusation for several days. Then the men took up the matter. A direct confrontation in which one person agreed to keep the peace usually settled things for a while and the issue would be dropped without further discussion. The underlying conflict would not be resolved, however, and could be used to fire up emotions at another time. Wetacti was a classificatory son of Pekuho. Any retaliation for a death in his faction would be aimed at Niokombedi's kinsmen or against his prestige as a peacekeeper through an attack on the newcomers.

The implied threat of physical sanctions which Niokombedi could use against Wetacti is another important part of being a faction leader and *mẽropakande*.

Appropriate behavior. Niokombedi behaves as an example for the rest of the village. He hunts and fishes well. He takes rituals seriously and sings hard. He observes all his relationships with proper (or even exaggerated) decorum.

Family. Niokombedi was fortunate in having a large kindred, and he used the influence of the administration of the Xingu reserve as additional support for his leadership.

Pekuho's faction was considerably weakened by his failure to have more than one surviving male child, and that man a cripple. Both Waraku and Tonwuti were more fortunate in that respect. Niokombedi has two adult brothers and a number of adult sisters and female patrilateral cross-cousins. These are largely married to non-Suya, on whom he could count for support. In 1976 one of his sister's daughters married the eldest son of Takuti. Niokombedi himself made two excellent political marriages. His first marriage, to the daughter of Tonwuti, sister of the present leader of that faction, was arranged by his father when Niokombedi and the girl were very young. One of his wife's brothers is a *mẽropakande*; another is the ritual specialist (*mẽrokïnkande*). His second marriage, which occurred during 1972, was with the "niece" of a Kayabi Indian who was in charge of Posto Diauarum when Claudio Villas Boas was absent. This alliance cemented the ties between Niokombedi and the person in charge of the day-to-day operations of the post, who was in a position to help him in a number of ways. His third marriage, in 1976, to a Western Suya orphan does not seem to have been politically motivated, although it may have strengthened his ties to the Western Suya. This marriage caused considerable comment, as she had called him "father" until she moved her hammock next to his and began to accompany him on fishing trips. No children were born of the union, and in 1978 Niokombedi was talking about letting somebody else marry her.

Continuing a process begun by his father, Niokombedi tends to maximize the number of his close relatives. He does so by observing completely the diet restrictions for certain classificatory relatives for whom such restrictions are not usually observed and by tracing his relationship to people through consanguineal rather than affinal ties, when both are possible. The former strategy made some distant kinsmen into closer kinsmen. The second emphasized the relationship of physical substance over alliances by marriage whenever possible. Niokombedi, and his father before him, have reclassified large number of kinsmen in these ways.

Contact. Niokombedi was also strongly supported by the administration of the Xingu reserve. Waraku and, later, his son were quick to adapt to the presence of Brazilians. The first peaceful contact with the Suya occurred at Waraku's village. Waraku immediately proved himself to be the more cooperative leader. His son, Niokombedi, was groomed by the Villas Boas to be their representative in the Suya village. In itself, this support by the administration of the reserve was a resource because Niokombedi could count on the approval of the Villas Boas for most of his actions and because almost all trade goods were introduced to the Suya through the Villas Boas or their representatives and friends.

As a result of his manipulation of the traditional supports and resources as well as the recently introduced influence from outside, Niokombedi was the strongest of the three *mẽropakande* in 1977. He had virtually dominated the descendants of the members of Pekuho's faction, and he had allied himself with the descendants of Tonwuti's faction and Diauarum through marriage. Factional disputes continue to arise because every serious illness and every death are believed to be the result of witchcraft. Although Niokombedi and his family have little to fear from the bows and arrows of a united opposition, even a weak opposition can be fatal through the mechanism of witchcraft. Niokombedi therefore tries to be both the self-interested leader of a strong faction and the beneficent, ideal leader of all the Suya.

Mẽrokïnkande

The second important role among the Suya is that of the *mẽrokïnkande*, the owner-controller of Suya ceremonies. He usually decides when a ceremony should be performed. He orates in the plaza and exhorts the rest of the village to be good and to perform the ceremony correctly. He may organize the collective hunting and fishing expeditions prior to the ceremony. He decides which songs are to be sung at which times and leads their performance. He may also decide not to perform a given ceremony or to delay its performance. He is consulted on most aspects of ceremonial etiquette and song.

By Marc Swartz's definition of a leader as a person who formulates and implements public goals and events (1968, p. 2), the *mẽrokïnkande* is a leader. Ceremonies such as those associated with the initiation of young men, cutting gardens, or warfare are believed by the Suya to be necessary for the survival of their society.

While there are usually several *mẽropakande* in any Suya settlement, there is usually only a single *mẽrokïnkande*. There is no fixed rule of succession. Instead, becoming a *mẽrokïnkande* depends on interest, musical talent, and being a teacher of songs. The Suya say that a son may learn from his father, but such a relationship is not necessary. When a *mẽrokïnkande* dies, or a village fissions and a new ceremonial leader is needed, there is apparently no competition for the post. People ask the teacher of songs who knows the ceremonies best to lead them. From my genealogies, however, it appears that *mẽrokïnkande* are often classificatory brothers of a *mẽropakande*. They are not usually orphans (see figure 9.1). I have never heard of conflict between candidates for the post, and the strongest faction is not necessarily the one to which the *mẽrokïnkande* is allied. Nor does the office remain within the same faction over time. Although the person chosen may have prestige before becoming a *mẽrokïnkande,* the choice of one or another man does not appear to be a domain in which the factions are active.

Mẽrokĩnkande are always recruited from a group of men who teach songs and are called "men without spirits." The spirits of these men are believed to have been taken from them by a witch and hidden with some species of animal, plant, or fish. After a time, the man whose spirit has been stolen can hear and understand the speech and songs of the species with which his spirit is living.

The way a man becomes a "man without spirit" typically begins with an extremely successsful day of hunting, fishing, honey collecting, or other gathering. He brings the food back to the village and gives it to his family. A witch sees the food but is not given any and becomes jealous and angry. In the night the witch goes to the man's house, takes his spirit from his body, and hides it with the very thing that the man failed to give him. Thus if it was fish that he did not receive, the witch hides the man's spirit with the fish in the river.

After losing his spirit, a person becomes very sick. After a long illness he either dreams of his spirit or accidentally discovers its location. The present ritual specialist, Kaikwati (120), described his own experience as follows. He was sick for a very long time. When he recovered, he walked in the woods and heard the trees talking. He said he could understand the speech of the fish. He was walking in the woods, and he saw the trees dancing. A tree said, "Friend!" The man replied, "What?" The tree asked, "Where are you going?" and the man replied, "I'm not really going anywhere." Then he saw that the trees looked like people and heard them all singing and moving like dancers.

Under some circumstances the spirit of a "man without spirit" moves from one location to another and takes up residence with a different element, perhaps because of a personal crisis, another sickness, or the transformation of a man into a *wikenyi*. The spirit of Kaikwati fled to a different place. Kaikwati was accidentally shot in the thigh during the uproar after the assassination of Kokoti in 1972. He was shot by a ritual relation, one of his *ñumbre-krà-chi*, Màti (106). The man who shot him and his brothers were mortified and horrified at what they had done, for the relationship is one of intense shame. When he had completely healed, Kaikwati composed a new unison song (*ngere*), the first *ngere* to have been composed in some years. I was told that its significance was that Kaikwati's spirit had been so frightened by the bullet that it had run away from the trees and was hiding with the arrowcane and bullets. When I asked Kaikwati whether his spirit was still "with the trees," he replied that he still understood tree language and could teach their songs but that his spirit had moved away.

One old Western Suya, when he became a *wikenyi*, said that his spirit had moved from where it had been to a woman's vagina. Therefore he only sang songs of (and about) women's vaginas. These were obscene and funny, highly suitable for a *wikenyi*.

When there are ceremonies for which new songs are needed—and many ceremonies require a new *akia* for every man in the village and new *ngere* each time they are performed—men without spirits teach other men songs that their spirits hear as they live with the animals, fish, bees, and the like. In the older generation there were more teachers of songs than there are today. Although there is no idea that being without spirit is an inherited trait, my genealogies indicate that people without spirits are often the children of people without spirits. Captives often lost their spirits also. *Mẽropakande*, on the other hand, were rarely without spirits. During the period covered by my genealogies, *mẽrokïnkande* have always been considered relatives of a faction leader. Thus Ngàtuhrigi (280) was addressed as "brother" by Pekuho and was *mẽrokïnkande* in village 9a and, after its fissioning into two villages, in village 9b. Maikaiwa (201) was Waraku's wife's brother and acted as ritual specialist while the groups lived in separate villages. The present *mẽrokïnkande*, Kaikwati, was captured as a young child from the Waura, raised by Tonwuti as a son, and is brother to the inheritor of Tonwuiti's position as *mẽropakande* (122). Although knowledge is a prerequisite for being a *mẽrokïnkande*, and in spite of the lack of conflict over the position, those who occupy it have some status and are considered to be related to a political leader.

The present ritual specialist maintains that people without spirits are less socially complete than men with their spirits. They are bad because their spirits are living with animals, and they can never get them back. The contrast between complete men with their spirits and incomplete men who have lost their spirits was frequently made in discussing *mẽrokïnkande*.

Wayanga

The third important role among the Suya is that of the witch, or *wayanga*. Witches are potentially quite powerful. In contrast to the *mẽropakande*, whose leadership is legitimated and has a number of broad, social supports, a witch has illegitimate, unsanctioned, and individual power. He has this because of his marginal, antisocial properties and special attributes, including self-transformation. Witches may turn into animals at night, while their bodies lie sleeping. Their spirits may take the shape of bats to travel around the village or that of jaguars to travel long distances. Certain animals found in incongruous places are believed to be witches.[12] Witches are associated with the marginal color, black, and with darkness in general. In the witch village of the dead only "black" (purple) sweet potatoes are eaten. Witches are most active in the dark of night. Witches have exceptional faculties of vision, which they use for their night travels, taking the spirits of people with whom they are angry or attacking and preparing to kill other Suya. They can also use their extraordinary vision to look for spirits taken by other witches and thereby play the role of curers. Once a person has a witch-thing in his eye, he can never lose it; he always remains a witch. When he dies, his spirit goes to a village of the dead which is inhabited only by the spirits of witches. He does not join his relatives in the good village of the dead, where there are no witches.

One informant described the actual transformation in which a man became a witch as resembling a severe illness. A person becomes a witch because he has behaved immorally, disobeyed one of the Suya norms—often those against eating certain foods or having sexual relations in periods of restriction—and by close physical contact under certain circumstances. The informant related the following description.

> A person who gets a witch-thing in his eye because he has behaved wantonly (*añi mbai kïdi*) takes a while to get used to it. His extraordinary vision makes him very afraid. He is unable to sleep at night because he is always seeing other Indians. He can see in the dark. He looks down, and he can see fires under the earth, the fires of people who live there. He gets very thin and very weak. After a while he gets used to his witch-thing. He turns himself into a bat or a jaguar or an owl. He attacks people when he is angry with them, or takes their spirits and hides them, or takes the spirits of their belongings up to the sky.[13]

Witches are humans who have failed to observe the restrictions that preserve the social domain as the Suya define it and therefore become marginal and like animals. Because they do not observe periods of restriction, they are contaminated by the animals they eat or the women (or men) with whom they have sexual relations, and they are invaded by the witch-thing which lives in their eye. The transformation of a good human being (*mẽ tiri*) into a witch is due to the incorrect incorporation of a powerful animal or sexual power, especially those things classified as strong smelling.

I did not think to obtain a complete list of how each witch became one. Of three witches that I was told about, two were men who had sexual relations with women after they pierced their penises and one was a woman who had sexual relations repeatedly with a witch who took the form of her lover.

People who are suspected of being witches have a power over other people in the village. They may be provided with food when they might otherwise be forgotten. They are remembered in the distribution of trade goods, and they ask for things from people whom a Suya would normally never ask. A puzzling aspect of witches was that some of those accused of being witches really act as the Suya say that witches are supposed to act—selfish, demanding, and covetous. An example was Kokoti (230) before she was killed.

Kokoti (230) was believed to be a witch by most of the women in house 1 (Niokombedi's faction and his family). When Niokombedi's mothers (203, 205) were sick, Kokoti had advised them to avoid eating a certain fish (Portuguese, *pirarara*). Every time a *pirarara* was brought into house 1, Kokoti would come and stay until she was given some. Such behavior was extremely bad form for a Suya adult. She would also appear when honey was brought in, as well as certain game. She had power over people; when she wanted to gossip at night she would call to women who had already retired to their hammocks and insist that they come out to talk to her. She manipulated people to obtain what she wanted.

When the wife of one of the men in house 1 died, Kokoti was clubbed to death by the husband and his brothers, who were all sons of the two old women whom she had forbidden to eat *pirarara* and the husbands of people she had forced to come out and talk with her.

In my case histories it is evident that very strong, brave, belligerent men (*sàgri-kumeni*) were accused of being witches when they got old. Repeatedly I was told about famous warriors who loved to sing and were very belligerent. But the final sentences often described how they had become witches. It is quite possible that they exercised too much power, and people became resentful, or perhaps they threatened the leadership of a *mẽropakande*. Witches are the possessors of a power, and it can be the power of belligerence gone bad.

There was a positive role for a witch, that of a "good *wayanga*," or curer (*wayanga-mbechi; mbechi* good, beautiful, correct). These individuals could turn their extraordinary vision to social uses: for fighting enemies, curing illness, and helping *mẽropakande*.[14] This aid is usually given by the witch's spirit, which takes the form of an animal and uses its superior vision to look for things.

I was told that when the Suya were living to the west of the Xingu, they were being attacked by Indians. They wanted to move. One of their good witches went to sleep and saw the houses of the Upper Xingu Indians and the large river. He said "There is a big river to the east; let's go there." The Suya traveled east and settled in the Xingu. Good witches are also credited with making the Manitsaua Indians weak and peaceful. They could see whether enemies were nearby as well and could cure sick people, even after their spirit had left them. One informant told me that when someone was sick, people would send for a good witch who would look at the sick person and blow on him. The relatives ask him to look for the sick person's spirit, which has been taken by a bad witch. The witch curer goes away and goes to sleep. He looks for the sick person's spirit in the gardens, in the water, in the sky. When he finds it, he brings it back. The relatives are happy and give him presents. By repeated practice a good witch becomes valuable to people. He may use his extraordinary vision to tell which other witches are doing bad things.

Even a good witch turns bad if he becomes angry. No one admits to being a good witch because that is admitting that he is a witch. When someone dies, the witch could be held responsible. It is the relatives of the sick person who send for the witch.

The Suya maintained that there were no good witches living in the village when I was there. When they wanted the services of a curer, they went to Diauarum where they would engage a Kayabi curer and simultaneously take advantage of the medical care available there. Good witches were not famous. With the exception of the one that found the Xingu River, I was never told of a famous curer. When an important person became sick, however, the Suya tried all the suspected witches in the village for a cure. All were called to blow and rub leaves on the body of the patient. An example was the sickness of Niokombedi's infant son (012), which I take from my field notes.

> When the infant son of Niokombedi was sick there was suddenly fear of witch attack. Niokombedi (105) yanked the Western Suya girls living in his house out of their hammocks and made them blow on and rub the child. He went stalking out to another house while his mother (203) cried and complained about witches. Shortly Kontü (232) and Gaimo (a Western Suya accused of being a witch) came in to blow on the child and rub pungent leaves on it. Niokombedi's mother (203) placed a pile of piqui nuts next to Gaimo, telling her that the child was sick. Next the Western Suya adult man living in the house dragged his teenage daughter over to the part of the house where the child was. He threw her on the ground and kicked her. Then he kicked her out of the house. She was crying. He picked up his bow and arrows and stepped to the door but did not shoot at her. Women from all the houses and almost all the families within each house came and helped rub and blow, especially women from house 4, relatives of Kokoti who had been assassinated about six months before, when Niokombedi's brother's wife died. They were thus logical witch suspects, for they would want to make the child sick in revenge for Kokoti's assassination.

In this case all the suspected witches in the village were recruited to show their goodwill toward the child. It was also hoped that they might be curers. The relatives of the sick child were not sure that Gaimo was in fact a curer. She accompanied them to Diauarum with the child. When the child finally did get better, she was said to be something of a curer after all. When the child was sick, they were taking every precaution. The child was taken to Diauarum and treated by a Kayabi curer. Finally he was taken to Posto Leonardo where he was cured through extensive medication by a Brazilian doctor.

A good witch is able to cure and help in war because he can employ his extraordinary vision and his ability to transform himself into animals and travel long distances for social ends. Those very attributes that make him bad and animal-like also give him prestige in certain situations. This is a feature often repeated in Suya culture: animals possess powerful, useful attributes. Among the Western Suya only women, marginal and powerful, can become good witches. When a man becomes a witch, it is always for bad ends. But women, somehow marginal, can transform themselves into animals and bring back stolen spirits. Women are bad witches as well, and which women were which appears to depend largely on who is talking.

The Power of Descent, Knowledge, and Vision

The attributes of the political leader (*mẽropakande*), the ritual leader (*mẽrokïnkande*), and the witch (*wayanga*) are summarized in table 9.1. The *mẽropakande* is said to be an ideal man and at the same time to be frightening, to have a pungent odor and to be unpredictably bellicose and like a jaguar. The *mẽrokïnkande* is said to be less socially complete than other men because his spirit resides permanently with some species of animal, plant, or insect. The witch can turn himself into an animal and can see infinite distances. All three figures have natural attributes, and the reason for this not only clarifies the roles themselves but reveals the importance of nature's transformations in Suya society.

Among the most important supports for a political leader are his genealogical descent from a political leader and his bellicosity and oratory. The corporeal ties are attenuated by naming groups and severed by residence. The political leaders, however, continue to rely on their corporeal ties. Their factions are their brothers and sisters' husbands. Even in residence they may be exceptions to the general rule. In the Western Suya descriptions of their villages, the only exceptions to the uxorilocal rule were political leaders, who might live in the same residential segment as their fathers.[15] The emphasis on the ties of a political leader with his son, the ideology of conception and gestation, and the stress on the physical and animal-like attributes of the *mẽropakande* are all consistent with the power base on which authority is centered. His power is based on the control of a faction through the manipulation of his kinship ties and not through his ceremonial ties or, to as great an extent, his affinal ties. He organizes daily activities, which are primarily in the secular rather than the ritual sphere. When a man's father has maximized his kinship ties and the number of his kinsmen, the son is also in a good position to do so as long as he maintains his identity with his father and his father's allies. This is most easily done by remaining in his father's house, or in the same part of the village, and by stressing physical descent from him.

The pungent odor said to be characteristic of the *mẽropakande* has its origin in the same principles of ideology and social organization. Political leaders are adult men whose status is based on their biological relations; thus they do not lose all the odor they had when they are in-

Table 9.1 Comparison of chiefs, ritual specialists, and witches

Symbolic domain	Political leaders (*Mẽropakande*)	Ritual specialists (*Mẽrokïnkande*)	Witches (*Wayanga*)
Space	Associated with plaza, orates there, and is buried there	Associated with plaza in ceremonies and oratory, but spirit lives with natural species; buried in house	Associated with the periphery. May travel long distances at night. Killed outside village and usually not buried
Faculty	Associated with bellicosity and oratory, both related to mouth	Emphasis on hearing and on knowledge; memory associated with the ear	Have special vision and a witch-thing in their eyes
Odor	Said to be pungent smelling; if very belligerent, very pungent.	Like most adult men, no odor.	"Only witches know whether they have an odor." No outwardly perceivable signs of a witch other than general behavior and a swollen belly
Antisocial attribute	Pungent odor	Loss of spirit to natural species	Superhuman vision, can become animal, are responsible for all deaths, most sickness
Recruitment	Inherited patrilineally from genitor	Not inherited, but may be learned from father; achieved	Not inherited; the result of individual misbehavior
Activities	Generous distribution; officiates some ceremonies; orates on secular matters; coordinates secular activity	Does not distribute things; leads all other ceremonies; orates on ritual matters; coordinates ritual activity	Stingy and jealous; leads nothing; speaks bad speech; coordinates nothing

itiated. The attenuation of their natal ties is only partial. Their behavior is potentially dangerous (to members of other factions), and they are equated with more natural beings than are the rest of the adult men.

The ambivalence between the *mẽropakande* as an ideal adult man and also as a somewhat natural one is found in other Gê tribes (Seeger, forthcoming). Maybury-Lewis commented on the paradox of Gê leaders who must represent both a single faction and a whole village: "The qualities ideally required of him [the Shavante leader] and the behavior expected of him while he is in office are diametrically opposed to those of which he had to make use when he aspired to the chieftaincy" (Maybury-Lewis 1967 p. 204). The Suya are well aware of this conflict. The *mẽropakande* is beset by conflicting responsibilities, those to his kinsmen and faction and those to the entire village. The heart of this paradox lies in the characteristics of the *mẽropakande*, whose political and social powers derive ultimately from his biological kinship affiliations, which are associated with the periphery.

Just as political leaders are at once of the plaza and of the periphery, so are ceremonial leaders. Rather than being like an animal, every ceremonial leader and man without spirit is in direct and permanent contact with the animal domain; his spirit has taken up residence there. He can understand the speech of a natural species; this understanding is the source of his knowledge. It is precisely the association of the ceremonial leader with the natural domain that gives him his knowledge and makes him less than fully social.

The witch is the most natural of the three. He can become an animal at night and travel great distances in the forest. He is associated with the forest zones. His relationship with nature is neither metaphoric (pungent smelling) nor metonymic (part of him residing with an animal species); it is entire. The witch has powers of self-transformation: he can become an animal. He also transforms others. Only witches can cause death, only they can steal the spirits of people, an act that results in their becoming men without spirits.

A Suya village would be incomplete without all three kinds of individuals, different from the rest of the population because of their particular powers. Although their powers are different, the sources are similar. All three are mediators as well. The controller of the village mediates between men by settling disputes, protecting the village from enemy attack, and leading raids. More recently he has come to mediate between Brazilians and the Suya. The controller of ceremonies mediates between men and animals. His spirit lives with the animals whose songs he teaches to his fellow men. Society is perpetuated by this continual transference of songs from animals to men because new songs are always required. The witch is a creator of men who can understand the speech of animals, and they are mediators between the human and the spirit world—nature at its most distant. Witches can see great distances into the unsocialized distant forest. They can see invisible spirits and other things that normal people cannot see and are thus able to cure under certain conditions.

All the Suya leadership roles are apparently paradoxical. Political and ceremonial leaders are said to be ideal men, but they have definite animal-like, negatively valued attributes. The witch, negatively valued, can also use his powers for curing or seeing into the unknown. The paradox lies in the very nature of power itself. All power, in the Suya cosmology, comes from the natural domain. This same domain also threatens the existence of society, to which it is opposed. Power is necessary in society—in political leadership, in ceremonies (in which animal songs are sung), and in curing (in which animal metaphors are used in curing chants and witches use their extraordinary vision). Nature is transformative. Nature, with its power, does not always have a beneficial effect on men, however.

The ideology of power and the realities of political power are the same. The *mẽropakande* is at once a peacemaker, acting for the entire village, and the self-interested head of a kinship-based faction who is continually striving to consolidate his position. The attributes of odor and being like a jaguar as well as the patrilineal inheritance of the role are further indications that a political leader is an ambivalent figure. He is both social and natural, powerful and unpredictable. The opposition of the domains of nature and society, which is found in the cosmological beliefs of the Gê tribes and in their divisions of society into groups by sex and age and by birth and naming, is somewhat mediated by political leaders, ceremonial leaders, and witches. Their medial position expresses their power and also gives them their power: the power of faction leadership through inheritance, the power of leadership through knowledge, and the power of curing through antisocial vision. At once similar and complementary, these three roles express the importance of the oppositions of nature and society with their mediations and transformations in Suya social and political life.

10

Transformations in Myths, Curing Chants, and Dreams

THE PURELY SYMBOLIC MATERIAL of Suya myths, curing chants, and dreams reveals in more depth the ways in which the natural and social realms as defined by the Suya act on each other. Transformation and the relationship between the social and the natural appear in the three symbolic areas of myths, curing chants, and dreams, cultural domains in which there is a text rather than a context of behavior. All three reveal a concern with and manipulation of the realms of animal and social, the ambivalence of sexuality, and the power of the natural domain.

The Suya do not divide their oral narrative into genres of myth, tale, legend, and so on. All narratives are simply "what the old people told." I shall therefore include in this discussion everything that was so described, whether it is an origin myth or a children's tale. All are believed to have an equal reality, though they may have taken place more recently or further back in time.[1] I shall refer to them all as myths for convenience.

I was told thirty-four myths by the Eastern Suya, many of which I recorded, some of them several times. These were all the myths that the old men said they knew. I doubt the accuracy of this statement, because they remembered more as time went on and they recognized myths of the Western Suya which they said their fathers had told them but which they did not know well enough to tell, or which they had not thought of in a long time. Of the thirty-four narratives, there are four which I did not understand when I recorded them and in which the tape recorder malfunctioned to an extent that makes working with them now impossible.[2] That leaves me with a working corpus of thirty myths. Because of my interest in an eventual comparative analysis of myth I recorded several variants of the ones that were more interesting on a comparative basis, as much as possible from different tellers. In addition I recorded a fairly large corpus of myth from the Western Suya. However, that corpus is not complete, and my inability to follow easily the Western Suya dialect makes it difficult to work with. The near completeness of the Eastern Suya corpus makes it more valuable. It lends validity to my statements in a way that would not have been possible with a selected or incomplete group of narratives. In spite of the rich material I leave the discussion of Western Suya mythology to another work.

I have divided the myths into five groups on the basis of nature of the initial action, or imbalance: (1) improper sexual relations, (2) improper behavior toward affines and relatives, (3) obtaining a cultural item, (4) cannibal stories, and (5) miscellaneous. A complete list of myths and their initial and terminal situations is given in table 10.1.

Improper sexual relations. The group of myths whose initial actions are improper sexual relations is the largest of the five. The number of myths that begin with improper sexuality initiated by either a man or a woman is surprising when the Suya myths are contrasted with other corpora (Nimuendaju 1939, 1946; Schultz 1950). In a purely formal sense most of the myths that begin with an improper conjunction of the sexes end with a complete disjunction of the persons involved. The offending ones leave the village forever (myths 2, 3, 6, 7) or are killed (5, 8). The first group of myths is concerned basically with the contamination of male society by sexuality and the unfortunate results of that contamination (myths 2, 3, 5, 6, 7, 8).

Improper behavior toward affines and relatives. The second group of myths is not very different from the first, but the opening moves are not explicitly sexual. A man's mother-in-law is not supposed to sneak over to her son-in-law and break wind in his nose at night to make him sick (9). Nor is a man supposed to kill his wife (10). No motive is given for the killing. The old woman who is not given any water by her *taumtwü* (11) is an example of the failure to observe the proper behavior toward relations and affines. All three myths end with the death of the offender.

Obtaining a cultural item. The third group is the group of origin myths. The beginning of each states that there was a lack of something or that something existed that does not exist now. At the end of the myth men have obtained maize, gardens, fire, fruit, and lost self-growing maize and immortality. Myth 18 can also be placed in this group, for it is about the obtaining of beautiful names. Since it begins with a raid on the Suya village by cannibal enemy Indians, I included it in another group. Similarly myths 25 and 26 can be considered origin myths. The first explains the origin of a certain song, the second explains a variety of things such as the establishment of the seasons. However, the initial and final

Table 10.1 Initial and final situations in Suya myths

Myth	Initial situation	Final situation
	Improper sexual relations	
1	A man has sexual relations with female name receiver.	He gets burned in leg by wife.
2	Girl has incognito sex with her brother.	Women secede from village; men get new wives from fish.
3	Young men have sexual relations with unwilling married woman at improper time.	Eventual flood in which many people die.
4	Woman always bleeding from vagina; her brother thinks her husband is abusing her.	It was a long-armed monster which was almost killed but escaped.
5	Menstruating woman allows her husband to have sexual relations with her.	He sharpens his leg, eventually kills her, and her brothers (WB) and is killed.
6	Old men pierce their penises and have sexual relations with a woman.	Dance up into sky, leaving village forever.
7	Man has sexual relations with wife of *wayanga* in a ceremony (savannah deer ceremony).	He becomes a savannah deer at the end of the ceremony and leaves village forever.
8	Woman has sexual relations with a tapir.	Tapir is killed by husband and eaten by woman. Husband returns to his mother's house.
	Behavioral impropriety to affines and relations	
9	Woman farts in son-in-law's face every night, makes him sick.	Son-in-law kills woman by shoving pointed stick up her anus.
10	Man does not like his wife, kills her, later WM.	Man is killed by his second wife, a relative of the first wife.
11	Old woman is thirsty, no relative will giver her water; her *taumtwü* (CC, BC) are especially remiss.	She causes great drought which kills many children.
	Obtaining of a cultural item	
12	Suya had no maize.	Suya obtain maize.
13	Suya taught to plant gardens.	Suya harvest gardens.
14	Corn grew by itself (man cut hand, got mad at corn husk).	Corn no longer grows by itself.
15	No fire[a] (*tuwuyi* sends *taumtwü* to get it). (MM, FM, FZ/BS, CS).	Collective theft of fire from jaguar; everyone has fire.
16	Men did not know to eat seeds and fruit. (*Tuwuyi* sends *taumtwü* to bring fruit and teaches him.)	Man learns about eating fruit and nuts.
17	No death. (Man tells relatives not to destroy his belongs. They destroy them.)	Everyone must die.

Table 10.1 Initial and final situations in Suya myths (continued)

Myth	Initial situation	Final situation
	Cannibal stories	
18	Boy is stolen from village by cannibals living under earth.	Suya kill cannibals. Learn naming ceremony from a captured survivor.
19	Cannibal monster (*kot pü*) captures man.	Man escapes.
20	Cannibal monster (*kot kwürüti*) attacks man in forest.	Man escapes.
21	Cannibal monster (*kot pü*) kills and eats father of a *ngàtu* (young adolescent).	*Ngàtu* kills cannibal monster.
22	Cannibal monster (*kot pü*) kills *ngàtureyi* (children).	Cannibal monster killed by *sikwenduyi* (men living in the men's house).
23	Child cries at night; cannibal monster grabs its liver and eats it.	Father kills cannibal monster. Its independently roaming upper body is later killed by adolescent girls (*hen sum hrü*).
24	Man marries cannibal woman, from cannibal tribe which is otherwise just like Suya (*mẽ sànyi*).	After considerable fighting, the two groups move apart and do not see each other any more. The man is eaten by his wife's brothers.
	Miscellaneous myths	
25	Old man of *atàchi* plaza group wants to die. (Eats meat of savannah deer known as *atàchi*).	After he eats the meat he dies. Origin of a particular song in the savannah deer ceremony which he sang when he died.
26	Sun and moon travel on earth. Sun does well, moon is ridiculed.	Moon always comes out a loser.
27	Baby born looking like a little bird.	He grows old living in the men's house and never marries.
28	Young men play with cornhusk toy in back of house (*atuknumu*).	As they play, they ascend to sky where the lip disk of one is the Pleiades.
29	Man living alone in forest with his wife becomes a snake.	He is killed and his wife returns with his slayer to the village.
30	Man born small and ugly.	He becomes a great log racer and his moiety begins to win again.

[a]The Eastern Suya did not remember the myth of the fire of the jaguar as it is told by other Gê groups, including the Western Suya from whom I recorded several versions. They had separated the macaw episode from the actual bringing of fire into the village by a collectivity of men-animals in a relay race. Instead of the macaw incident, the boy is sent by his *tuwuyi* (MM, FM, FZ) to look for fire. When he finds it, all the men go out and get it, killing the jaguar in the process.

acts are different. In any typology individual examples may not be clearly of one group or another. However, altering the classification of myths 18, 25, 26, and 28 would merely shrink the miscellaneous group and swell this one without altering my conclusions. Fire, maize, names, and gardens were all obtained from nonhuman creatures—fire by theft from the jaguar, maize from a mouse, names from the sole survivor of a cannibal tribe living beneath the earth. Suya society was established through the obtaining of these elements from animals or "extra-human" sources who then were deprived of them. Society itself was founded through the incorporation of elements of nature into society.

Cannibal stories. Myths 18-24 are stories about cannibals. Myths 19-23 are all similar to the European Märchen of evil and rather stupid giants. They are told especially to children. They are important in that the Suya believed that these monsters existed. Now they think that the monsters may have been killed by Brazilians who have encroached in the farther forests which were the particular domain of these creatures. The cannibals (with the exception of those in myths 18 and 24) are opposed to human society in a number of ways. They live in the distant forest alone, with their families but not in villages. They have no ceremonies. They are described as being very big, with bushy pubic hair and floppy penises. They eat human flesh. They speak Suya, but in a funny, distorted way. In terms of these attributes they are natural beings and pose a constant threat to human society. The cannibals in myths 18 and 24 are both village dwelling and have ceremonies. They are similar to the Suya with the exception of their taste for human flesh. Myths in this group are symmetrical. If a person is captured by a monster and escapes, the monster is unharmed. If the monster kills and eats a Suya, then the monster is killed but not eaten. The cannibal monsters are not animals but marginal beings which are always a danger to society, especially to children and men alone in the forest.

Miscellaneous myths. The last group is indeed a mixed group. Three of the myths are partly origin narratives. Myth 25 is the origin of a particular song in a ceremony and the example of the force of a particular food restriction. Members of the *atàchi* plaza group cannot eat meat of the *atàchi* species of savannah deer (black with a white stripe on face and chest). In myth 26, the story of the sun and the moon, the moon is repeatedly humiliated, and certain features of the world as it is now are originated. Myth 27 is the story of a baby who was born looking like a baby bird and was so valuable to his parents that he entered the men's house but never married. When he wanted to marry, his parents said that he was too young. Finally he was bald and old and still had not married. Myth 29 is the story of a man who without explanation turned into a snake. Myth 30 is a Suya success story about a small boy who grows up to become a great log racer. He beats the fastest runner in a solo race, and his moiety begins to win races for the first time in many years.

A brief survey of the content and opening moves of the corpus of Eastern Suya myths thus reveals a comparatively large emphasis on sexual relations and improper behavior toward affines and relatives as a motivating element in myths. These are summarized in table 10.2. Sexuality is considered dangerous to men in times of transition, and yet enjoyable. The Suya concern with sexuality and its ambiguity finds expression in their myths. Sexual relations have bad results when they occur at improper times, in improper places, or with improper persons. Affines, defined by a relationship of sexual relations between two persons, are also dangerous, as are certain old people. Cannibal monsters, marginal beings which are neither human nor animal, are also dangerous. They, too, have some association with sexuality, for they have big floppy penises. They are greedy and stupid and live in the forest, which is an antisocial place. The men who turn into monsters effect their transformation in the forest. Then they attack the village or people from it. The marginal, be it location, sexuality, or mixtures of human and animal, is all dangerous to society, as the myths illustrate.

Animals classified as strong smelling are important figures in the myths. The jaguar had fire which men stole. The tapir carried it into the village and had sexual relations with a human woman. All human beings

Table 10.2 Initial movements in Suya, Apinaye, and Kraho myths[a]

Type of Myth	Suya	Apinaye	Kraho
Improper sexual relations	8 (26.75%)	2 (13.25%)	3 (15.0%)
Behavioral impropriety toward kinsmen and affines	3 (10.0%)	1 (6.75%)	2 (10.0%)
The obtaining of a cultural item	6 (20.0%)	1 (6.75%)	6 (30.0%)
Cannibal stories[b]	7 (23.25%)	2 (13.25%)	1 (5.0%)
Miscellaneous	6 (20.0%)	9 (60.0%)	8 (40.0%)
Total	30 (100.0%)	15 (100.0%)	20 (100.0%)

[a]The Apinaye myths are the corpus presented by Nimuendaju (1939). The Kraho myths are the corpus presented by Schultz (1950).

[b]Among the Apinaye and Kraho these are stories about animals that eat men rather than about marginal beings that eat men, as are found in the Suya myths.

were similar to animals at one time. That is the subject of the origin myths. When men went to get fire, they took the form of animals. Human society was not as separated from natural society in the beginning of the myths. At their conclusion, however, the jaguar no longer has fire, the mouse no longer has gardens, and the Suya have both fire and gardens full of all kinds of crops. They know which fruits to eat and have names and a naming ceremony. Suya society was completed and differentiated from nature and animals in the origin myths.

A cursory examination of the first and last situations in myths shows that the Suya myths elaborate the tension between the natural and the social as it is defined by them. The threat to society posed by strong, strong-smelling, and otherwise marginal animals, human beings, and monsters is repeatedly portrayed. The contrast with the myths of other Gê may be significant. A relatively large proportion of Suya myths begin with improper sexual relations or involve cannibalism. The sample is admittedly small,[3] but I would argue that the differences in the Northern Gê myths in this respect are due to differences in the definitions of natural and social and in the conflicts that are considered important. There are, of course, many similarities among the myths of the Northern Gê.

Curing Chants

Herb medicines play a secondary role in the prevention and cure of illness, accident, and disease. More important and more prestigious are the *sangere*. Up to now I have referred to this genre as curing chant. In fact *sangere* are neither exclusively for curing nor exactly chants. They resemble the herb medicines in that they are used to stimulate quick growth, give strength of body, strength of wind, and so on, as well as cure fevers, swellings, pain, and convulsions. They influence the properties of the body to give the patient (the person for whom the *sangere* is performed) the desirable attributes or to cure him. The actual performance of the *sangere* uses tonal qualities so different from the other melodic genres that I have called them chants primarily to separate them from songs.

The efficacy of the *sangere* is through what Victor Turner calls "the associative link . . . of contagion—to borrow a useful term from Sir James Frazer which indicates that the symbol has in fact been part of the object it signifies or has been in close physical contact with it. Thus, as part of the *materia medica* employed to cure tuberculosis we find portions of the diaphragm of an antbear (*itandantulu dachibudi*). This animal has a strong chest and *mpelu* taken from it will, so it is believed, strengthen the chest of the patient" (1967, p. 305).

The important element in the *sangere* is the metaphoric naming of a certain animal that possesses a desired attribute. For example, the *sangere* for a child with high fever and convulsions names the cayman (*Caiman crocodilus*), which lies very still in the water without a tremor and does not get hot. The implication is that through the *sangere* the child will gain the attribute of the cayman and cease his convulsions. When the attribute desired is quick growth, the wild banana plant is the subject of the *sangere* because it grows quickly and tall above the other plants. All *sangere* exhibit a basically similar metaphoric structure.

Several considerations are important in determining which *sangere* should be used. One of these is the age of the patient. Children, especially those younger than three or so, are the primary objects of *sangere* to make them grow, to prevent the ill effects of eating solid food, and to prevent convulsions and fever. Boys from about three until early puberty, are also the objects of a number of *sangere* whose purpose is to make them strong. Different *sangere* are performed for adults and for women of childbearing age. Another consideration is the desired effect. If the patient is sick, the object is the curing of the symptoms. If he is healthy, then *sangere* are employed to instill strength, good wind, easy birth, or some other desired attribute. Finally, certain *sangere* are sung at certain times. Some *sangere* are sung before and after bathing. These are usually *sangere* to make a child grow or a woman pregnant. Others are sung at the time of the crisis of symptoms, at the moment of fever or pain. Which *sangere* a person performs depends on these factors and some more idiosyncratic ones—such as which *sangere* he knows best and whether he has one of his own which he believes has special efficacy. Some complaints have no sangere: burns, stingray wounds, and spider bites are some of the most obvious ones.

The Suya say that in the past everyone knew a large number of *sangere*, but only married persons (with children) performed them. In general men knew more than women. When I was in the village only the older adult men performed *sangere*; I knew of at least one man in each house. It is important to sing them correctly. If they are performed incorrectly the patient can get worse. People who were not sure they knew them preferred not to perform them. I think that most adults knew a few, and when one specialist died another would take his place.

Sangere are occasionally composed, in which case the person who composes them has control over them. There was once a *sangere* for spider bites, but the owner-controller prized it so highly that he died before he taught it to anyone. Certain other *sangere* are very valuable and are taught to another person only in exchange for large gifts. The person who performs a *sangere* for a patient is given presents by the relatives of the patient when he recovers. When a man is the owner-controller of a *sangere* that no one else knows, its value is relatively higher. It is also worth a considerable number of valuable gifts to learn the *sangere* that makes a person get thin and die or to make a recalcitrant lover have multiple births. Knowledge is power in Suya society, and it is quite consistent with the emphasis on oral forms that verbal means of curing are more prestigious and effective than herb medicines. No presents are given for herb medicines, and the Suya maintain that everybody knows them. As a consequence, perhaps, they are not valuable.

In performance the *sangere* is unlike any other oral genre. It is recited very rapidly under the breath so that it is difficult to hear. Unlike the song genres, the *sangere* has a very wide range and makes extensive use of glissando. In itself it seems to unite the extremes of vocal range, which are usually distinct in Suya music. With a few exceptions the singer stands directly over or close to the patient and blows on him as he sings, especially at the beginning, middle, and conclusion of the *sangere*.[4] When I heard *sangere* being performed over a patient, they were usually too rapid and quiet for anyone but the patient and perhaps the person nearest to him to understand. When I recorded them, I had to do so at extremely high volume and obtained the best results away from the village where the only background noises were birds and insects.[5]

Sangere efficacy rests on the contagious association between a particular attribute of a species of animal, plant, or element and a human being. Animals and plants are by far the largest groups represented. Only two *sangere* rest on a human metaphor: the ritual relation of shame so that sickness leaves the body, and the quick flipping of a manioc cake for quick, easy childbirth. The others appear with the following frequency: mammals (nine), plants (seven), insects (seven), birds (six), reptiles (five), fish (four), and a few other items such as cool streams, rock, fire, and wind.

The object of the *sangere* is to introduce into the patient the desired attribute of the species named. This is done through blowing and through metaphor.

SANGERE FOR CHILDREN WITH FEVER: THE WHITE CAYMAN

1. Blowing over the patient; both long and short exhalations with friction between lips for women, lip and lip disk for adult men.
2. *Ngo* *iaseri* *kande* (blow once) *Ngo* *iaseri*
   Water still controller Water still
   (without ripples)
   kande (blow once)
   controller
   Ngo *iaseri* *kandeeeee* (blow once) *Ngo* *iaseri*
   Water still controller Water still
   kandeeeee (blow)
   controller
3. *Wa iõ ngo seri kande, mĩ- saka- chi kò kurã- chi*
   our water still controller cayman white aug. skin rough aug.

Si kra wiken-ti, si kra kït- chi ani-tòòòòòò
His hand spread out his hand (?) aug. How come?

4. *Mbru tõ, mbru tõ, ta kure ne nò*
Animal some species animal some species (that) to hit lie there

5. *Wa iõ ngo seri kande mĩ- saki- chi, ngo*
Our water still controller, cayman white aug., water
tu kande
shallow controller
[Repeat 2-5]

6. *Ngo iaseri kande* (blow once) *Ngo iaseri*
Water still controller Water still
kande (blow once)
controller
Ngo iaseri kande (blow several times)
Water still controller

This can be freely translated:

1. Blowing.
2. Controller of the still waters, controller of the still waters,
Controller of the still waters, controller of the still waters.
3. Controller of our still waters, rough-skinned white cayman,
His hand is spread out without shaking. Why?
4. Animal, animal, that lies there still.
5. Controller of our still waters, controller of shallow waters,
white cayman
[Repeat 2-5]
6. Controller of the still waters. Controller of the still waters.
Controller of the still waters.

Each of the numbered sections of the *sangere* is an integral part of the whole. There can be considerable variation in the ordering of the sections. The middle sections—3, 4, and 5—can be repeated in order several times before the complete repetition which includes 2. In spite of the variation, every *sangere* has these distinct parts, and they are always repeated all the way through once, as in this example. The structure of *sangere* is similar to that of Suya song in general (Seeger, 1979).

The blowing is an important feature of this kind of cure. It begins and concludes every *sangere*. Good witch curers also blow on their patients before looking for their spirits. The word "to blow," *sako*, is apparently the same word for lip, *sako*.[6] The word for lip disk is *sakoko*, possibly meaning the "round thing in the lip." The importance of speaking among the Suya is paralleled by the importance of blowing in curing. Though without semantic meaning, the blowing is one of the defining features of the *sangere*. In some *sangere* an animal call is given in this section as well as the blowing. The *sangere* that names the large otter begins with a sound like an otter; one about a wild pig (queixada) begins with grunts. *Sangere* that begin with onomatopoeia are a small minority. The call is a means of indicating the animal involved.

The lines in the second part are the repetition of the phrase "controller of still waters." The first two times there is no alteration of the syllables, but there is a blown breath after each phrase. The second two times that it is repeated, the last syllable of the phrase is drawn out with a glissando in the voice. These lines introduce what I call the "opening metaphor" for the animal that is the subject of the *sangere*. This metaphor indicates the attribute of the animal that is desired for the patient. The "controller of still waters" is a metaphor for the white cayman. The metaphor rests on the Suya observation that the cayman can lie so still in the water that there are no ripples at all. This contrasts vividly with the shaking of a child with a high fever. What is desired for the child is the stillness and coolness of the cayman. That is the subject of the opening metaphor for the animal. The opening metaphor is usually symptom specific. When the tapir is invoked in the case of a toothache, the metaphor is "big eater" because the tapir eats things that are hard to chew and does not get toothaches. The opening metaphor is always interspersed with blowing, which may help the attribute enter the body of the patient, though I failed to get exegesis on this point.

The lines in the third section name the animal and give additional metaphors for it. In addition to "controller of our still waters," the white cayman is described as "rough skinned' and as having a "wide-spread hand." I was told that the spread hand refers to the ability of caymans to sleep with their hands open but without shaking at all. Human hands shake noticeably when they are held spread out, especially humans with fever. It is another way of metaphorically referring to the stillness desired for the patient. The lines in this section conclude with the word *añi-tò*, which in general means "What do you mean?" or "why?"

The first words of part four of any *sangere* are one of the most important variables. If the subject of the *sangere* is a mammal, then the phrase there is "animal, animal" or, literally, "some animal, some animal." If it is a fish, the words are "fish, fish"; if a bird, "bird, bird." But an insect, cool water, or a small plant are just "thing, thing" (*tà tõ, tà tõ*). When I was hearing these chants performed over a patient, the first words of part four were often the first indication of what the subject of the *sangere* happened to be. *Sangere* are sung so rapidly and quietly and with such metaphoric elaboration that I often missed the object of the *sangere* and was only clued in at the start of this section. It was a regular structural feature of all *sangere*.

In this *sangere* the fifth section repeats "controller of our still waters" with the addition of a new metaphor "controller of the shallow waters."

The amount of repetition allowed after the fourth part varies considerably. In this *sangere* this section consists of only one line. In other *sangere* there is considerably more variation and repetition before the repeat of the entire *sangere*.

The repetition may include a few additional metaphors in the repeat of the third section. Otherwise it is simple repetition of the entire *sangere* from section two through section five. Then it moves to the conclusion.

The *sangere* ends as it begins, with the repeated opening metaphor interspersed with blowing.

In their entirety *sangere* are quite symmetrical, beginning and ending with blowing and a single metaphor. Their central section names the referent of the metaphors and gives several different metaphors for it, not all of which are necessarily associated with the desired attribute, as the opening metaphor always is.

I collected about fifty *sangere*. Most of them transfer an attribute possessed by an animal, insect, plant, bird, fish, or object to a patient. (Sometimes they operate on other objects, such as rain clouds, but only in a few cases.) *Sangere* all have a similar structure, and they transfer a relatively small number of attributes. Strength, quick growth, freedom from convulsions, and the ability to eat food without ill effects (an element from the natural domain) are all important attributes, especially for children. In addition six *sangere* are related to fertility and five to keep lightning from striking. There are none for improving social relations: no love chants to attract the attention of a woman, none to make a mother-in-law more agreeable, and none to settle quarrels. Nor should we expect to find them, since the natural domain does not possess these social attributes. Animals and plants are not characterized by social relations. But they are strong, fast, quick growing, fecund, and powerful.

Strength, or hardness, is the attribute most often sought in *sangere*. This is strength to run fast without getting winded or strength to grow rapidly. By far the greatest number of animals involved in this category are land mammals, and the group is heavily weighted to strong-smelling animals: jaguar (one *sangere*), deer (three), tapir (one) and large otter (two). Other mammals represented are the wild pigs (queixada) (two *sangere*), peccary (one), and the porcupine which are all pungent. The smaller armadillo, which is bland, is represented in two *sangere*.

Reptiles and mammals account for nearly all of the *sangere* for strength. Mammals are also important in the *sangere* that enable people to eat certain foods. Mammals eat the same foods as men. The attributes of fish are associated mainly with childbirth, and one species is associated with growth. Birds are quite scattered because each species has a different attribute. Insects are important largely for rain. Plants are for pregnancy (palm nuts are equated with plentiful offspring) and growth (because of the rapid growth of certain plants).

The greater portion of *sangere* are for children. They concentrate on the attributes of strength, stillness (the absence of convulsions), ability to eat food, and size and growth. For adults the emphasis is on strength as well as the ability to eat certain fruits, avoid head itching, and heal wounds quickly. A few *sangere* are for women of childbearing age. The *sangere* for old age are specifically for strength.

Suya *sangere* are another example of the importance of the natural realm as a powerful force which can act on the social realm. Animals are thought to be particularly strong and to have certain powers of strength, stillness, size, and growth. These can be used for healing, though the most powerful animals may never be eaten. The flesh of most of these animals may not be eaten during sickness or during early childhood. But through the *sangere* strength is incorporated in a controlled manner. The juxtaposition of a natural species and a sick or young human being is symbolic and specific. It is possible only through carefully controlled metaphor, perhaps explaining why the incorrect performance of a *sangere* will not merely fail to improve the patient, but actually make him worse. The power in the natural world must be controlled. The selective application of the power of animal and extra-village elements is typical of the *sangere.* The specificity is the result of the opening metaphor, which specifically alludes to that attribute of the animal that is desired for the patient. Eating the flesh of the animal introduces undesirable elements. But metaphor selects them out and concentrates on the desirable ones.

Through the creation of new metaphors new *sangere* may be composed. Within the historical past they were composed by Waraku (412) and Ropkugachi (222). The knowledge of *sangere* is one type of power that a man may obtain. The relatives of the patient give presents to the controller of the *sangere.* I also noticed the Suya performing *sangere* on Indians of other tribes at Diauarum.

In the hierarchy of Suya curing the *sangere* is midway between the herb medicines, which are common knowledge and for which gifts are not given, and witch curing, which is restricted to people with the witch-thing in their eyes. Like the *sangere* curer, the witch blows on the patient, but then his spirit looks for the patient's spirit using the extraordinary vision enabled by the witch-thing. The *sangere* curer is not necessarily bad, and his spirit may live in his body. His control of the natural world is not through the extraordinary vision of the witch but through the knowledge of and control of metaphoric *sangere.* Through these he seeks to instill the strength and exceptional attributes belonging in the natural realm into a patient, thereby strengthening the social individual. The transformation of the child into the strong adult, or the sick into the well, is through the use of this metaphoric process.

Omens and Dream Symbols

Sangere are not alone in the importance of metaphor. Many ritual objects are used with similar intention. The jaguar or savannah deer legbone is used to pierce a man's lip so that he will run fast like the animal whose bone is used. Some omens and dream symbols also work through a metaphoric association. Others are more complex and may truly be said to be symbolic. The mechanisms in portents and dream symbols are different.

My attention was first drawn to Suya omens by an article of Roberto Da Matta, "Les Présages Apinaye" (1970). Many parts of Da Matta's analysis hold for the Suya. Omens are widely invoked to explain death and hunting success. A person need not be a specialist to understand dreams. Omens do not exercise much effect on actual behavior after they have been interpreted—with the possible exception of going hunting after a favorable hunting omen. They also have a characteristic vagueness which lends them validity. After all, someone will die eventually. Since nearly all Suya are classificatorily related, the chances are that any death will be of some relative.

Da Matta maintains that the study of omens may help an investigator analyze aspects of the cosmology of the Apinaye: "But we do not simply intend to respond to the challenge posed by the study of the Apinaye omens: we believe they can help us to understand—at least in a preliminary way—certain structural characteristics of these Indians" (Da Matta, 1970, p. 77, my translation). This is also true for the Suya.

There are some important differences between the omens of the Suya and the Apinaye. The Suya have favorable omens, most of which involve dream symbols. Good dreams (*tàptiri mbechi*) and bad dreams (*tàptiri kasàgà*) are almost equally represented in the fifty-five dream symbols that I obtained. The representation of favorable omens in visible portents is much less. Only two out of twenty-nine visible portents were favorable in those that I collected. The four categories used by Da Matta in his analysis are also unequally represented in the Suya corpus. There is only one example of "the abnormal functioning of certain parts of the human body." The other groups, "certain events concerning animals," "the abnormal functioning of certain objects or the interrupted or improper development of certain normal continuous activities," and "dreams concerning certain elements or certain situations," are present (Da Matta, 1970, p. 81). My analysis owes much to the analysis of Da Matta, but the omens are investigated in terms of the relationships between the natural and the social domains in Suya culture.

For the purposes of this discussion I distinguish between dreams (*tàptiri*) and visible portents, which I will call signs (*watàhwĩri*).[7]

The Suya believe that every death and most serious illness has a cause.

The cause is always a witch.[8] Certain signs precede death and illnesses, just as signs precede certain types of success—war raids, hunting expeditions, and childbirth. The omens are not causal; they merely warn a person of the future and are used to explain the present. A man does not say, "I saw a giant catfish; therefore I am going to die." He says, "When I am going to die, I or one of my close relatives will see a giant catfish or another omen." There is nothing that can be done about a bad omen, for the omen is not the cause but merely the sign. Often a dreamer or witness of a bad presage will be sad for a while, but there is no avoiding the portended event or attempting to manipulate events to escape the portents. The portents are usually suitably vague and may be used to explain several events. An example was the omen of death, a ring around the sun, in the autumn of 1972. For several days there was a very striking ring around the sun, which is an omen of death. When a Northern Kayapo child died in Diauarum a Suya told me, "See, the sun had a halo and now the child is dead. It is always thus." However, a week later that man's wife died in childbirth, and one of the wife's brothers said, "See, the sun had a halo and now the girl is dead and we are digging a grave just like the ring around the sun [a round grave for the daughter of a *mẽropakande*]."

Dream elements are said to symbolize a future event (*kodo*) while signs tell (*saren*) of a future event. The events in dreams are more ambiguous than signs, but even those may have several possible interpretations as to who will die.

Three important mechanisms are at work in dreams and signs and determine the meaning of an omen. One of these is the establishment of a metaphoric relationship between the animal world and the human world. For example, dreaming of killing a jaguar on a raid means that someone will kill an enemy Indian. These metaphors play a prominent role in dreams and signs, and nearly all are based on a perceived similarity between the attributes of the animal and those of a human being.

The second mechanism that gives meaning to an omen is the sudden occurrence of an unusual event or an event that interrupts the continuum of daily life. An example is dreaming that a canoe is sinking instead of floating. Similarly, a lunar or solar eclipse does not occur in regular, periodic, daily life, where the behavior of sun and moon are predictable. Snakes are not frequently seen. To see one is a portent of death. Unusual events may be taken as presages of a future social event, most often the death of a relative. To some extent unusual events also establish a metaphoric relationship between the cosmic universe and the social universe. An interruption of the proper functioning of one universe symbolizes a death in the other. What is emphasized in portents of this kind, however, is their very rarity and unpredictability.

The third mechanism of omens is the use of social metaphor. In this case both symbol and referent are part of the social world.

Good dreams, bad dreams, and signs differ in their use of the three mechanisms. Table 10.3 summarizes my data in this area.

The nature-to-society metaphor is overwhelmingly important in the good dreams (68 percent) but falls to a relatively small percentage in signs (21 percent). Social metaphors are completely absent in signs but make up a considerable proportion of the good dreams (28.5 percent). Apparently there is nothing in the social world that can be a sign of impending death. Only animal metaphors and unusual events can portend death. Unusual events are overwhelmingly important in the signs but completely absent in good dreams, supporting the idea that sudden interruptions of normal functioning can be equated with the interruption of the social fabric in a death. An unusual event cannot presage anything good. While the numbers are, as always, small, the percentages are revealing and portray a considerable difference in the ways that the future is portended in good dreams, bad dreams, and signs. Bad dreams lie midway between signs and good dreams. Animal metaphor is less overwhelmingly important, and dreams of unusual events are present.

The social metaphors employed in dream symbols but absent in signs are of two kinds. One makes a direct metaphorical connection between an event and death by referring to death customs. For example, a house burning, purposefully broken belongings, soft flesh, and Upper Xingu Indian body paint are metaphors of death. The first two refer to the destruction of property after the death of a person, the third refers to the rotting flesh of the corpse, and the fourth is based on the association of alteration in the coloring of a corpse—a darkening of the temples and

Table 10.3 Mechanisms in three types of presage

Presage	Nature vs. society	Social metaphor	Unusual event	Miscellaneous	Total
Good dreams	19	8	0	1	28
(*tàptiri mbechi*)	(68%)	(28.5%)	(0.0%)	(3.5%)	(100%)
Bad dreams	10	9	6	2	27
(*tàptiri kaṣàgà*)	(37%)	(33%)	(22%)	(8%)	(100%)
Signs (*watàhwĩri*)	6	0	22	1	29
	(21%)	(0.0%)	(76%)	(3%)	(100%)
Total	35	17	28	4	84
	(42%)	(20%)	(33%)	(5%)	(100%)

chest in Upper Xingu body painting. Other metaphors associate personal belongings—bow, hammock, manioc strainer—with a person.

Another relationship between signifier and signified is unique to the social metaphors: an inversion. The following are examples: plaza speech—sexual relations; abstention from eating in dream—good health; singing—crying (keening); high singing (*akia*) in log race—crying (keening); log race, fish race—death (keening); eating food in dreams—bad health.

Da Matta writes that "the announced reality is the inverse of the dream content" (1970, p. 91). That is not true for Suya dreams, in which the majority employ metaphoric relationships rather than actual inversions.[9] Only these six involve actual inversion. The Suya say that dreaming of a log race is symbolic of crying. This is because *akia* resemble keening in melodic structure and style of performance. The ritual realm and the realm of mourning are opposed in a number of ways (kin-nonkin; happy-sad), and there is an inversion because one does not sing *akia* when one is sad. The examples of eating and abstaining from food in one's dreams reflect the importance of abstinence. The least dangerous foods in life (fish and manioc cakes) become dangerous in dreams. Food is often restricted, and to eat in dreams is a bad sign.

Most puzzling of the inversions is the dream in which angry plaza speech is symbolic of sexual relations (*hron kodo*). The two are, however, related. Angry plaza speech is an aggressive masculine assertion of strength and belligerence employed only by adult men. Sexual relations are also an activity of adult men. There is thus a kind of metaphoric association between plaza speech, verbal activity, and sexual activity. Singing and orating are to some extent associated with sexually active status. There is also an inversion. Plaza speech is literally of the plaza, while sexual relations are usually undertaken in the *atuknumu*, or the gardens. The dream can be interpreted only in the entire context of the meaning of the signifier (angry oratory) and the various meanings of the signified (sexuality).

The four miscellaneous presages are honey—honey (a good dream); high bank—shortness of breath (a bad dream); falling tree—sickness and death of a relation (bad dream); red halo around the sun—death through bloodshed (sign). The peculiar place of honey in South American Indian cosmology detailed by Lévi-Strauss (1964, 1966a) is amply supported by the unique nature of honey in the portent system of the Suya. A dream of honey means that the dreamer will eat honey. This alone, among all dream symbols, is not symbolic of anything except itself. A dream of sweet potatoes is symbolic of eating fish, and dreams of eating food are an omen of sickness. Honey is honey.

Whether or not one accepts the analysis of myths through which Lèvi-Strauss arrives at his structures, there can be no doubt about their importance in Suya society. The ambiguous position of honey with respect to the natural and the social domains of the Suya cosmology is merely another example. "In Indian thought, the idea of honey covers a multitude of ambiguities; first because honey appears to have been 'cooked' by the processes of nature; then because of its various properties of being sweet or sour, wholesome or poisonous; and lastly because it can be consumed in either the fresh or the fermented form" (Lévi-Strauss 1971, p. 296).[10]

The sign in which a red halo around the sun portends a violent death, usually from enemy attack, is based on a color symbolism in which the redness is symbolic of blood (*kambro kodo*). The omen is not merely an unusual event; it is also metaphoric in its color symbolism and combines elements of both metaphor and unusual event. A falling tree, here a symbol of impending sickness and death, is also dangerous to children. Men with pregnant wives should avoid felling large trees. The association of shortness of breath with a high bank is that one is out of breath after climbing such a bank. Labored breathing is a symptom of a number of serious illnesses, especially pneumonia.

Dream symbols are sometimes fairly simple metaphors. At other times they are both metaphors and symbols. In fact there are different degrees of symbolic complexity. Some portents in dreams are like signs: a man's dream of fire means that he will get a fever. Others are different. Probably the most complex is the dream of a woman before a hunt.

When a man dreams of a woman who flirts with him, it means that he will kill some game the next day, especially tapir, deer, capybara, paca, or monkey. This dream symbol has several meanings. First, the Suya say that if the dream woman is very seductive, the animals will be very tame and will not flee at the approach of the hunter. The seductiveness of the woman is paralleled by the tameness of the animal, and women are implicitly equated with game animals. Second, the smell of sex secretions in humans and of women in general is strong smelling. The animals that a hunter may hope to kill are among the strongest-smelling edible animals in the Suya classification: tapir, deer, and capybara. The smell of the woman, who is sexually active in the dream, is the same as the strong smell of the animals that the dream indicates may be killed. Third, in terms of the opposition of the center and the periphery, men are of the center and women and animals are of the periphery. Sexual intercourse rarely if ever takes place in the plaza; it usually occurs in the gardens surrounding the village. The location of most sexual intercourse and the location of animals are thus both found outside the plaza. Finally, on some occasions women are explicitly referred to as game, especially in certain rituals in which men enter a house and bring out a woman to participate in a ceremony. This extends to sexual joking; a man will say, "I am going to cut open my game," a pun on "pierce the woman I have brought out" in the ceremony. In some special situations there is an equation between women and game which is reflected in the symbolism of the dream. These four referents make the dream woman more than a sign. Her explicit sexuality, her smell, the animals associated with the dream, the peripheral location of game and sexual relations, and the parallel between women and game are all important significata.

The dream is more complicated still. A man who dreams of a woman trying to seduce him must refuse to engage in sexual relations in the dream. She propositions him, but he refuses. According to one informant, if the man has sexual relations with the woman, he will kill only a monkey when he goes hunting, because the monkey is like a woman. This could mean that a seductive woman is like the game animals in a number of ways. But if she actually becomes a sex object, the dream reduces its significata to "just a woman." One of the referents of the symbol is made more important, and the others less so. Once the dreamer interacts with the dream object as a woman, he "humanizes" her and will kill only a monkey.

Elements in dreams can have a variety of referents, and the Suya use the word *kodo* to describe the functioning of the dream elements. They use the word "to tell" (*saren*) to describe the signs, which are less ambiguous.

In good dreams, bad dreams, and signs, animals and other elements of the natural domain presage future events. The metaphoric relationship between the natural and the social makes up 41.5 percent of the dreams and omens that I collected among the Suya. Twenty-seven of the thirty-five metaphoric dreams and signs involve animals. Fourteen of them involve animals of the strong-smelling class. The jaguar is by far the most important, followed by the tapir, the hawk, the large otter, and the sloth. The jaguar has the following metaphoric meanings: a belligerent child, an enemy Indian (in four different ways), an enemy Indian child captive (baby jaguar), a dead Suya (dead jaguar). In dreams and omens the jaguar represents a nonsocialized human: an enemy, a troublesome child, a dead man. The dead jaguar is like a dead Suya because death is considered a transformation into a more natural, less human state. Jaguars are symbolic of marginal, less than fully human, aggressive beings.

The other strong-smelling animals found in dream symbols and omens are the tapir, otter, sloth, and hawk: a canoe pulled in by all the village—tapir killed on hunt; tapir—enemy Indians; dead tapir—dead Suya; large otter—huge appetite for fish in child; (sign) sloth—sickness followed by death; (sign) hawk—belligerent Suya; (sign) hawk—belligerent Suya. The tapir, because of its size and strength, may be equated with enemy Indians. Dragging a canoe is an appropriate symbol for the very heavy tapir, which is very difficult to carry back to the village. A dead tapir may be equated with a dead Suya. The tapir, like the jaguar, is marginal to but associated with men. The carnivorous diet and large appetite of the otter are stressed in the dream symbol, as is the belligerence of the hawk. The sloth looks dead all the time and resembles a very sick, very weak person.

Animals of the pungent class appear in five dreams, with the following associations: wild pig (queixada)—enemy Indians; many non-Suya Indians—herd of wild pigs; giant armadillo (*aseiti*)—corpse in hole; giant armadillo (*aseiti*) hole—grave; macaw—beautiful hair on child. The wild pig is associated with wild Indians because it travels in large bands. The metaphor is frequently used and is reversible. The giant armadillo must be dug out of its hole by the sinking of large holes somewhat like graves, according to the Suya. The macaw has beautiful tail feathers, equated with head hair.

The eight remaining animals mentioned are from the bland class of animals. The monkey is considered to be closely associated with humans because of its anatomy and its cries. Baby turtles and young birds are raised as pets and appear as metaphors for children and captured children in dreams. An adult pet bird is a metaphor for an adult woman captive. The remaining eight dream symbols and signs that rely on a metaphor for nature to society are not animals but elements such as stone, fire, rain, pepper, and wasps which are belligerent like enemy Indians and whose stingers pierce like arrows.

The metaphors utilized in dream symbols and in signs equate an animal with a less than social human being. Enemy Indians, dead bodies, children, huge appetites, and the like, are not fully social in the way that adult men are. In this respect the dreams and omens differ from the curing chants, which select a particular trait of a given animal and through metaphor and blowing seek to instill that trait in a patient.

The dream symbol and sign employ the juxtaposition of an animal and a human being. The result is to indicate the natural qualities of the human being. Dream symbols and omens that employ a nature-and-society metaphor present both signifier and signified as marginal to the central social core of the society. Dream symbolism and omens again reveal the use of animals to indicate an imperfect state of social being. Or an imperfect state of social being (sexuality) is used to indicate tamed animals which are easily killed. The conjunction of nature and society in dreams and signs always indicates an altered state in the signified. The domains are not simply opposed but imply the transformation of each other.

Human beings may be transformed from fully social beings into natural or less than social beings by natural attributes or by strong-smelling aspects of their own society. This transformation is the inverse of that described for the socialization of a male from childhood to adulthood. Becoming a witch, falling seriously ill, and getting old involve transformations in which the individual takes on animal-like characteristics. Witches transform themselves into animals. Sick persons lose their spirits and either die or continue to live while their spirit resides with some natural species outside the village. Old people (*wikenyi*) are without shame about eating and sexuality. They are often thought to be witches. Similarly, being a political leader or becoming a person who teaches songs involves a transformation, a less than fully social attribute.

Eastern Suya myths reveal regularities in their opening and closing situations. A large percentage begin with improper sexual relations or improper relationships between affines and kinsmen. Sexuality at the wrong time in the wrong place or with the wrong person is followed by a series of unhappy events and an eventual resolution of the close association by the separation of the partners. Similarly, cannibals are a frequent subject of Suya myths. These evil beings intrude on social life in the village and are either tricked into leaving or killed.

Suya curing chants, *sangere*, have a similar structure and style of performance. Their efficacy rests on the use of metaphor in which a desirable attribute of a particular species of plant or animal is named and blown into the patient. These curing chants, like the herb medicines, are used for prophylactic purposes as well as to cure sick persons. The *sangere* instill the power of a natural species to form or cure a patient. The ingestion of an animal by a human is carefully avoided in times of illness and transition, but the curing chants are effective because of the use of metaphor and symbol to juxtapose the natural and the social.

Dream symbols and signs are also largely metaphoric. Three mechanisms are at work. One is the establishment of a metaphor between something outside the village, or natural, and something social. The second is the sudden and unusual occurrence or experience which always presages sickness or death. The third is the establishment of a social metaphor in which social signifiers signify social events. In dreams and omens an element in nature with a metaphorical significance always signifies something less than fully social in the social world. Animals are symbolic of enemy Indians, dead bodies, children, sickness, or death. Metaphor and symbol are employed in the deciphering of the dreams and omens by the Suya.

The Suya manipulate the natural and the social domains in their own cultural productions. The times of transition from social states to less social states, the myths, the curing chants, and the presages illustrate the pervasive presence of the nature-society contrast in Suya culture. The Suya use the contrasts in their oral literature, metaphors, and symbols. The contrasts are useful in analyzing a variety of cultural productions.

11

Nature and Society in a Broader Perspective

THE CONTRASTING PRINCIPLES of nature and society operate in a number of domains in Suya cosmology and social organization. The fundamental unity of Suya society and cosmology is revealed in their concepts of space and time, the body and its faculties, the classification of animals, some plants, and human beings, the processes of the life cycle, concepts of leadership, and finally genres of oral performance: myth and curing chants.

The same principles operate in other important areas. Perhaps the most important of these is that of music and ceremony. I am in the process of writing a book on Suya music which will examine in detail the way that social transformations are effected through the conjunction of natural and social entities under specific circumstances (Seeger 1977, 1979). Singing is a very important, virtually ignored, feature of lowland South American societies in general and of Gê-speaking societies in particular. The social, rather than purely aesthetic, importance of the music has prevented ethnomusicologists from giving the musical systems the attention they deserve; the musical emphasis of social life has similarly received insufficient attention from anthropologists.

Another important area that has been largely neglected in this book is the Suya perception of their relationship to the national society. An understanding of their cosmology helps to understand their reactions to Brazilian society. The Suya emphasis on the importance of the body as demonstrating identity, of body ornaments as defining social groups, and of body painting as establishing the equivalence of members of name sets and moieties is present in their talk about "becoming" whites. The first words for non-Indians were "people of the big skins," the "big skins" referring to the clothing worn by the early explorers. For the Suya, to "become" Brazilian is to wear clothes and ornaments such as watches (which no one can read) or "watches" made of straw, to cease to paint the body, and to cease to use body ornaments. This identification is consistent with their expression of identity through body ornamentation and painting: if one wears the body ornaments of a Brazilian, one is a Brazilian. Similarly, Suya emphasis on performing rituals, painting their bodies, and singing is seen as part of an attempt to avoid "becoming" Brazilian.

An example of the influence of Suya constructions of their own world on their perception of the industrial society that has already influenced their lives was the reaction of Niokombedi, the strongest leader, to a squatter settlement in Rio de Janeiro. In 1978 Niokombedi, one of his wives (117), and his youngest son were our guests in Rio de Janeiro. He asked us that year to take him to a city so that he could learn more about Brazilian life. After twenty months of living in his house, we welcomed the opportunity to act as hosts. The experience of being the subject and the informant of an intelligent, sympathetic observer was indeed challenging. As part of the varied program we put together (trips to the zoo, the National Museum to see the Suya material culture I had collected, to a soccer game, to the beach) he visited one of the squatter settlements called *favelas* that are built on the hills that jut up around the city and are built over tidal mud flats. He went to one of these, with a resident of the *favela*, and conversed with a number of people there. He came back horrified by the odor of the *favela*. He called the *favela* "the white's rotten-smelling houses" (*karaí kikre kraw*). He walked into our apartment, stripped off his clothes and shoes, washed them all (giving special attention to his shoes), and took a very long bath. Then he worried for hours whether he would get sick from inhaling so much rotten air and wondered how people could live in a place like that.

Other visitors to the *favelas* have been particularly struck by the malnutrition, ill health, poverty, poor housing, and other signs of marginalization. Niokombedi's perception of this marginality was through the odor that people had to live with and the "rotten water" they had to wash with and drink. Paradoxically, the odor of *favelas* is not mentioned in the sociological literature (Heye 1979). One of Niokombedi's comments to his wife, which I overheard as we drove through heavy traffic, was the following: "Some of us Suya, living in the forest, want to become whites. Now that I have seen all this I know that it is not worth it. We will go back and say it is not worth it: it is better to be Suya."

Ceremonies and the perception of Brazilian society are only two of the domains that I have not discussed much. But the same principles revealed in analyses of other domains are operating in these areas. The main principles of Suya cosmology continue to be used to incorporate new events and new experiences as well as to reconsider former ones. Important changes are occurring, and many of their institutions and beliefs are once again being reformulated. Far from impeding their interpretation and evaluation of new situations, the general principles of their cosmology allow for perception and evaluation. The evaluation of certain elements of their cosmology and social system has changed, but the principles organizing them are being used creatively and constructively as part of, and in defense of, Suya identity.

The Suya and the Northern Gê

Although this book is specifically about the Suya, a brief examination of some features shared with the Northern Gê clarifies the Suya case and suggests comparisons that might fruitfully be undertaken. Any structural analysis must face two questions. One is how a society changes. The second is how the Northern Gê societies differ, if they all present the opposition between nature and society. The possibilities for controlled comparison among these groups will help answer these questions.

At one level Suya society is constantly changing, as are all the tribal societies in lowland South America. These changes occur because of historical circumstances such as contact with the Upper Xingu societies or massacre by Brazilians, or because of individual inventiveness, or because of conflicts in the social organization itself. Without a written tradition to fix language and traditions, modification in a small-scale society such as the Suya is quite easy. Nor do the Suya have a mythology of founding culture heroes that inhibits change; they have a rather pragmatic attitude toward new technology and ideas.

An instructive example of these changes is the differences between the Eastern and the Western Suya. They consider themselves part of the same group, but over the course of the two hundred years since their separation they have both changed. There are dialect differences in their languages. The changes are largely phonetic, and many of them apparently occurred after Von den Steinen's visit to the Eastern Suya in the late nineteenth century. His word list shows that the Suya on the Xingu River pronounced words at that time as the Western Suya now pronounce them. The Eastern Suya attribute the change to their linguistic contact with Upper Xingu captives. Other features of their society have also changed: subsistence techniques, the specific moiety affiliation of several names, and the general monogamy of the Northern Gê. But these are minor compared with the overall similarities in their social organization and cosmological views: the same moieties and recruitment to them, the same men's house organization, initiation ceremonies, and songs (although they have somewhat different vocal styles, some songs are recognizably identical), and the same ways of classifying animals and humans.

When the Eastern and Western Suya are compared with the other Northern Gê, their basic similarity is immediately apparent. Table 11.1 presents a few of the principles that are important for the Suya with their occurrence in other Northern Gê groups as far as it is possible to discern them. The table points out instructive similarities and contrasts.

Self-identification and the symbolism of body ornaments (features 1, 2, and 5). The Suya identification of themselves as a group by their body ornaments has some salience. Their language is more a continuum than a way of establishing contrast with other Gê-speaking groups. Their subsistence style is not much different from the other Gê with the exception of the fairly recent acquisitions of the Eastern Suya. But their body ornaments clearly distinguish them from the other groups.

The different Northern Gê tribes have different body artifacts. The Eastern Timbira wear large ear disks somewhat like those of the Suya, but they are worn only by men. The Apinaye, like the Suya, pierce the ears of both males and females, and they wear disks in them that resemble those of the Eastern Timbira and Suya. In addition, they perforate the lower lip of adolescent males, but they do not use lip disks, instead they use a small labret. The Northern Kayapo do not use ear disks, but both men and women have large holes in their earlobes from which they suspend bead earrings. The men wear lip disks similar to those of the Suya, but without the design of the Pleiades on the underside. The Northern Kayapo in addition use penis sheaths, which are not found among any of the other Northern Gê, but appear among the Shavante, a Central Gê society.

The alteration of an organ is related to the social emphasis on the faculty associated with it. Ear disks are associated with hearing-understanding-knowing and Suya morality. Lip disks are associated with an emphasis on oral productions—oratory, speaking, curing chants, and blowing. Among the Kraho, where only the men wear ear disks, oral performance may not be as highly stressed, though music is important (Maria Manuela Carneiro da Cunha, personal communication). The Apinaye, who have both male and female ear disks, but only a labret, have ideas about hearing-understanding-knowing and morality that are similar to the Suya, but place less emphasis on oral performance (Roberto Da Matta, personal communication). The Kayapo have a somewhat similar configuration of ideas about morality, and there is an emphasis on speech and oral performance. In this context the question is why the Kayapo have large holes in their ears but do not use ear disks and why they use penis sheaths. The explanation may lie in the symbolic equivalence of the penis sheath with the ear disks.

According to Terence Turner (1969), the penis sheath restrains rather than emphasizes male sexuality among the Kayapo. It is given to young men at their initiation and stresses social control (T. Turner, personal communication). Among the Suya control over sexuality is one of the aspects of hearing-understanding-knowing. Furthermore, the Suya pierce a boy's or girl's ears at about the same age that the Kayapo give the boys penis sheaths: at the beginning of sexual experimentation. I would argue that the control of sexuality among the Suya is achieved by the perforation of the ear and the concomitant emphasis on morality. The Northern Kayapo, who pierce the ears of both sexes shortly after birth, mark this social control in men by giving them the penis sheath and place less symbolic emphasis on the ear as the source of moral teaching. There is thus a certain equivalence between penis sheaths and ear disks. But there is a difference: penis sheaths are by definition bestowed only on men. Kayapo village fissioning is usually blamed on adultery and on women. Within the Suya village fissioning is blamed on witchcraft, which is associated with not hearing-understanding-knowing. The faculty controlled through ornamentation at puberty seems to be the one blamed for the malfunctioning of the society, and these two vary with the society.

The appearance of an artifact is not random. Variation in body ornamentation among the different Northern Gê tribes is related to other features in these groups.

The village (features 3 and 4). Northern Gê villages are quite similar. They are all circular, and residence is uxorilocal. The Apinaye and Eastern Timbira villages lack the men's houses that appear in Northern Kayapo and Suya villages. Only the Suya have named houses. The apparent similarity of the Eastern Suya and the Kayapo villages—ideally they both have two men's houses—disguises an important difference. Kayapo men's house groups are political factions, while Suya men's house groups are determined by name-set identity, which is similar to the Eastern Timbira naming system. Factions are organized on a different basis.

Kinship terminology and naming systems (features 6 and 7). All the Northern Gê societies have kinship terminologies with generational skewing. What is striking is that they alter the generational terminology in different ways. Thus the Suya have an Omaha-type cross-cousin terminology in which the sons of a mother's brother (*ngedi*) are also addressed as "mother's brother" (*ngedi*), while the children of a father's sister (*tuwuyi*) are addressed as "sister's child" (*taumtwü*). In the Eastern Timbira groups with a Crow-type skewing the situation is reversed. The daughter of a father's sister is also addressed as "father's sister" while the son of a mother's brother is addressed as "child." The Apinaye are inconsistent. The same person may use both Omaha and Crow principles. Different analyses of this apparently contradictory situation among the Gê appear in Maybury-Lewis (1979). This work has not had the benefit of the suya data, which challenge its predictions.

Table 11.1 A comparison of some aspects of Suya society with other Northern Gê groups

Feature	Eastern Suya	Western Suya	Northern Kayapo	Apinaye	Eastern Timbira (Canela, Kraho)
1. Language	(taken as base)	Dialectical differences, recognized as the same language	Can be understood by the Suya if spoken slowly and on topics familiar to the listener.	Suya have never heard Apinaye, but seems very similar to author	Less similar to Suya than Apinaye to author; Suya have never heard it
2. Subsistence	Upper Xingu style of manioc processing is linked with Gê style of cooking and eating of most animals	Typical Gê subsistence style: less emphasis on manioc, dry season treks	Typical Gê subsistence	Typical Gê subsistence	Typical Gê subsistence
3. Village	Circular village with ideal of two men's houses	Circular village with a single men's house	Circular village with ideal of two men's houses	Circular village without men's house	Circular village without men's house
4. Houses	Uxorilocal residence; houses are named	Uxorilocal residence; houses are named	Uxorilocal residence; houses are not named	Uxorilocal residence; houses are not named	Uxorilocal residence; houses are not named
5. Body ornaments	Ear disks (M, F), lip disk (M)	Ear disks (M, F), lip disk (M)	Earring of beads (M, F), lip disk (M), Penis sheath	Ear disks (M, F), hole in lip for feathers, no disk (M)	Ear disks (M), no lip ornament
6. Kinship terminology	Omaha-type cross-cousin terms	Omaha-type cross-cousin terms	Omaha-type cross-cousin terms	Mixed use of both Omaha- and Crow-type cross-cousin terms	Crow-type cross-cousin terms

7. Ideology of conception	Fetus formed by semen alone	Fetus formed by semen alone	Fetus formed by combination of semen and blood	Fetus formed by combination of semen and blood	Mixed ideology; some informants gave ideas similar to those of Suya, others similar to those of Apinaye and Kayapo (Kraho)
8. Naming system	Male names pass in fixed sets from MB to ZS, female names from FZ to BD	Male names pass in fixed sets from MB to ZS, female names from FZ to BD	No fixed name sets, obtain names in rituals. Divided into "beautiful" and "common"	Male names pass in sets from MB to ZS, female names from FZ to BD. A given person may have more than one name set, unlike Suya and Timbira.	Male names pass in fixed sets from MB to ZS, female names from FZ to BD, like Suya.
9. Leadership	Two types. Political leadership should pass from father to son	Two types. Political leadership should pass from father to son	One type. Political leader also officiates rituals. Should pass from MB to ZS[a]	Two types. Political leadership should pass from MB to ZS	Two types. Political leadership should pass to son or near kinsman
10. Marriage	Polygynous, MBD preference, exchange of siblings	Monogamous, MBD preference, exchange of siblings	Monogamous, no preference	Monogamous, no preference	Monogamous, no preference
11. Animal classification	According to odor	According to odor	"Good" and "common"	"Tame" and "wild"	No information

[a] Recent research by Vanessa Lea indicates that the N. Kayapo may have two clearly distinguished leadership roles, resembling the Suya.

The ideology of conception (feature 7). The ideology of conception is important as the basis of the kinship groups in all the societies listed in table 11.1 and is apparently related to ideas about succession in political leadership (feature 9) and possibly to marriage (10). In all the Northern Gê societies close kinsmen observe diet restrictions for one another. But the ideology of conception varies. The Suya say that the fetus is formed by semen alone. The Northern Kayapo and Apinaye say that it is formed by the mixture of blood and semen. The Kraho are divided: some give the Suya version, other maintain that of the Kayapo and the Apinaye.

Among the Suya a political leader should be the genealogical son of a political leader. This idea of physical relatedness appears in a different form among the Kayapo and the Apinaye: the political leader should be the sister's son of a political leader. The Kraho, whose members do not agree on an ideology of conception, simply say that a political leader should be some close relative of a previous political leader.

In all the Northern Gê societies there are cases of sons having succeeded their fathers. But only in those societies that have a consistent ideology of conception as a mixture of the substances of both parents is the sister's son considered an especially appropriate candidate for succession, again suggesting the importance of the biological formation of the body as a symbol for the formation of kinship groups and factions.

The classification of animals (feature 11). There are some clear differences in the way that the different Northern Gê tribes classify both animals and men. The Suya classify animals on the basis of their odor. Groups of people (arranged by age and sex) are classified by the same criterion. The Northern Kayapo classify all animals as either beautiful or common. All human names are also so classified. People with beautiful names should restrict themselves to eating only beautiful animals. People with common names may eat both (Bamberger 1967). According to Da Matta (1970, p. 85n), the Apinaye classify animals as fearless and timid. He believes that this distinction plays a fundamental role in the system of animal classification among the Apinaye. It is impossible to say how animals are classified among the Timbira because anthropologists who have worked with these groups have tended to restrict themselves to the numerous social groupings—the abundant moieties, plaza groups, and age sets—rather than discussing animals.

There is enough information to suggest that animal classification is related to the classification of human beings in all the Northern Gê societies. The Suya classification of animals by their odor is important to their classification of other domains and events. The use of odor as a classificatory device, however, does not seem to be as important in the other Northern Gê societies, where other principles are used.

The differences among the Northern Gê animal and human classification have yet another important feature. The Suya occasionally discriminate between two groups of animals, one being good or beautiful and the other bad or ugly, similar to the distinctions made by the Northern Kayapo. They also refer to some animals as tame and to others as wild, in the fashion Da Matta reports for the Apinaye. But in the first case the Suya do not apply the same distinction to names or to diet restrictions. In the second case it is usually within a given species that certain animals may be tame and others wild. One deer will walk right into the arms of the hunter while another deer will elude him. The differences in the cosmologies of these groups are characterized by the degree to which one of these principles and not another is generalized and applied to the social domain and to which domains it is applied. In the case of the Suya it is the classification by odor that is extended widely to human beings.

Animal classification again shows that although the opposition of nature and society appears in all the Northern Gê, what specifically characterizes the social and the natural varies among the groups. A society's vision of nature is related to its vision of itself; nature and culture are part of the same symbolic construct. This point, which is applied to Western society by Sahlins (1976b), demonstrates the importance of analyzing societies as a whole. Although the Suya use a number of distinctions in talking about animals (including those found among the Northern Kayapo and Apinaye), only odor is widely used to determine dietary restrictions, to talk about sex and age groups, and to discuss political leaders. The others are secondary. Completely separate analyses of the natural and the social domains of Suya society would mask an important feature: the unity and interrelatedness of the many domains. Without an analysis of the social domain it might be hard to distinguish which of the principles of animal classification is most important to the Suya, the Kayapo, and the Apinaye.[1]

The brief comparison of the features in table 11.1 clarifies the particularity of the Suya within the general Northern Gê pattern. There is a great deal more to be done in the comparative study of the central Brazilian societies; although an increasing number of ethnographic studies of individual societies are appearing, comparative treatment has not gone much beyond Lévi-Strauss's suggestions of 1952. This comparative look at the Northern Gê also supplies an important link to Lévi-Strauss's *Mythologiques*. The cosmologies of the Northern Gê societies are similar in general structure. The contrast between nature and society appears in all of them, but the features used in the contrast (odor, body faculties, and so forth) are differently stressed, implying that the native categories in lowland South America are not freely interchangeable. An observation about odor among the Suya does not necessarily apply to the Kayapo, nor does one about naming or about men's houses. Perhaps instead there is a pool of ideas (and institutions) which are appropriated and developed by the Northern Gê and applied differently in different domains. These variations deserve close attention, for they may lead to a better understanding of the individual societies. A more detailed comparative analysis of the Gê, and one that contrasts them with other lowland South American societies, would be extremely rewarding.

The Suya and Anthropology

Documenting the way of life of a small, threatened Indian society may have some importance in itself, but few anthropologists would consider the endpoint of their analyses to be simply an adequate description of a society. This is even more so in the case of the Suya Indians, whose population totals about 140 individuals, among whom I have lived for more than twenty months and about whom I have been thinking and writing and imagining and singing for nearly a decade. Anthropologists want their societies to say important things about societies in general, and their analyses to say something about anthropological analysis in general. The final question to be considered is thus, What has analyzing the Suya in terms of their perception of, and creation of, the universe done that another form of analysis would not do? What is the contribution of this analysis to the study of lowland South American societies in particular and to human societies in general?

I believe that this analysis does make a more general contribution, along with a few recent analyses of central Brazilian societies (for example, Da Matta 1976; Carneiro da Cunha 1978; Viveiros de Castro 1977; Da Matta, Seeger, and Viveiros de Castro 1979). The Suya construction of their world and this analysis of it can contribute to our increasingly sensitive understanding of certain aspects of many human societies.

The history of anthropology has been more than making available to ourselves "answers that others, guarding other sheep in other valleys, have given, and thus to include them in the consultable record of what man has said," as Geertz (1973, p. 30) has characterized it. Rather than revealing a shelf full of uniform "consultable records," the history of anthropology reveals a shelf full of uneven analyses of different societies with a clearly increasing sensitivity to certain aspects of society that previously (in the ninteenth century, for example) went unperceived. Anthropology has been refined by, and in fact constructed with, the substance of the thought of the peoples studied by anthropologists. Native concepts have repeatedly been adopted by anthropologists and reified into analytic concepts. This occurred in the cases of *mana*, *tabu*, the contrast between witches and sorcerers, the Roman *Gens*, and many others. Each of these concepts, specific to a given ethnographic reality, has thrown light on other more or less distant societies.

Anthropology is not simply the application of theory and method to various peoples. It is also the reapplication of the ideas of other peoples to our own and to yet other societies. Basic to much anthropology is the belief that certain societies, by dramatically throwing certain ideas and institutions into relief, help us to understand better our own society and those of other peoples. Suya society does throw certain ideas into relief. My analysis of the Suya can provide tools for analyzing certain kinds of human behavior that have not yet been served by anthropological analysis.

A clear example of the inadequacy of anthropological concepts to deal with the ethnographic realities of lowland South America (and especially the Gê) is the concept of lineage. This has been the subject of special symposia in the American Anthropological Association Meetings in 1975 and the International Congress of Americanists in 1976 (*Actes* published in 1977). The importance of the concepts of descent and lineage is signaled early in Henry Maine's *Ancient Law* (1861), and the concept of *gens* was used by L. H. Morgan in 1871.

The concepts of lineage and descent were useful in parts of Melanesia and Australia and applied well to the African societies studied by a number of British anthropologists (among them Evans-Pritchard 1940; Fortes 1945, 1949). Radcliffe-Brown claimed that nearly all societies are matrilineal or patrilineal (Radcliffe-Brown 1935). It seemed to be so, until people tried to use the lineage concept in New Guinea. The now-classic article of J. Barnes on the difficulty of applying African models of descent in the New Guinea highlands rings true for lowland South America. But perhaps the most important suggestion of Barnes is that even in Africa the lineage principle does not explain everything. The experience in New Guinea could help anthropologists reconsider the ethnography of Africa (Barnes 1962, p. 9). Subsequent analyses of both New Guinea and Africa stress decision making and alternative alliances as well as rules of descent. Perhaps lowland South America can similarly render anthropological analyses more sensitive.

Many erroneous reports on South American descent systems have been published. The misreported *kiye* system of the Apinaye, described by Nimuendaju in 1939, was analyzed by Alfred Kroeber, Robert Lowie, George Murdock, Jules Henry, David Maybury-Lewis, and Claude Lévi-Strauss. The ethnographic record was set straight only by Roberto Da Matta (1968). The Siriono data were similarly mined for support of a theory of marriage alliance by Rodney Needham, who was refuted on the same data by Harold Scheffler and Floyd Lounsbury (1971). Murdock (1960) has called the social organization of the lowland South American groups "quasi-lineages." Curt Nimuendaju tended to find descent and marriage regulation where there was none (Nimuendaju 1939, 1941). Robert Murphy's characterization of the Mundurucu as "strongly patrilineal" has been criticized as an oversimplification by Alcida Ramos

(1978). Clearly the lineage model runs into impossible difficulties in Central Brazil, just as it does in New Guinea. In much of lowland South America there are no resource-controlling social groups through which to reconsider social organization, as there are in Melanesia and New Guinea. Nor are there any clearly defined spouse-exchanging groups as there are in parts of Asia and the Pacific (Lévi-Strauss 1949). Rethinking lowland South American social organization demands a specificity of its own.

Instead of puzzling over the absence of Roman descent systems, or African ones, we should turn our attention to what *is* characteristic of the lowland South American societies. Social organization is based not on descent or on corporate groups jointly controlling certain resources but on naming and on small groups of people believed to share a physical identity. The unity of kinship groups is expressed through an idiom of physical identity and through observation of diet restrictions, joking behavior, and other forms of behavior. Identity is not *corporate* in the juridical sense but *corporeal* in the physical sense (Seeger 1975b). The body is important; it is a focal symbol of several systems of classification. It is formed by one or both parents; it is repeatedly altered through ornamentation, scarring, and painting; and it appears as the basis for many other concepts, such as morality. Analysis of the symbolism of the body and its faculties will yield rich insights into many domains, as was demonstrated for the Suya.

The population of central Brazilian societies is relatively small, and their economic systems are quite different from those typical of African lineage-based societies or those of highland New Guinea. It is often quite hard to reach generalizations about their behavior that fit into the framework of analyses developed in these other societies. As a result it is often written that these societies are "flexible." This may be translated as meaning that given the rules we can devise, there are still many things that are apparently pretty random. But the "flexibility" of lowland South American societies may be an anthropological fiction. They may appear to be flexible because we are using the wrong approaches to their analysis.

One of the best antidotes to the careless use of alien analytic frameworks is the analysis of the native's own perception of his society. At least his own concepts should fit the ethnographic data relatively well. In the case of the Suya, the corporeal and name-based identities of a person are quite illuminating with respect to the social organization, as are the odor classifications of sex and age-based groups. Such categories can be used as the basis for a more ample comparative approach to lowland South American societies than is possible with concepts such as lineage and descent.

I have not tried to apply a predetermined classificatory scheme to the

Suya. Rather than building up to the discovery of what Suya society is *almost*, or is *not* (and it is not many things, including Talensi, Javanese, French, American, or even Northern Kayapo), I have tried to present what it *is* in its own terms. I have described to the best of my ability the principles that operate in the social organization and cosmology of this Gê-speaking group.

The analysis presented here makes some suggestions for lowland South American ethnography in general. First, the concepts of nature and society developed by Lévi-Strauss in the *Mythologiques* and by other anthropologists who studied the Gê are quite useful in analyzing many other aspects of these societies in addition to cosmology. Second, ideas about the body, its formation, its faculties, its ornamentation, its fluids, and its forces may provide a useful approach to the social organization of these societies. Third, ideas about what makes a person human and the formation of the social identity through naming, ornamentation, and body painting are also important features to be analyzed. The importance of this work for the analysis of other lowland South American societies is that although the domains of nature and society may be found in them all, these domains are differently defined and their relationship differently expressed. The analysis of the domains and their appearance in the social organization and cosmologies of these groups can be an important tool for the analysis of a single society or for their comparative analysis.

All this is not to say that lowland South American societies can be analyzed only in lowland South American terms. Taken to its logical extreme this would argue the absurd position that only Suya concepts can analyze Suya society. Far from presenting the radical position that every society needs its own theoretical constructs, I am arguing that every society can help anthropologists refine the concepts with which they approach other societies, including their own. This has already happened in cases too numerous to mention. If anthropology may be said to have cut its teeth in Oceania, learned its ABCs in Africa, tried out advanced mathematics in parts of Asia and New Guinea, and now to face the theory of relativity in its own backyard of industrial societies, urban environments, and emerging nation-states, then it is also true that the interaction of anthropological theory with lowland South America is only beginning and may refine anthropologists' analytical tools as well. It is not that we need different anthropologies for different societies, but that different societies will refine different aspects of anthropology's analytic and theoretical approach to society.

Joana Kaplan, in her call for papers for the Forty-Second Congress of the Americanists in 1976, noted that South Americanists are often accused of being idealist by their more "empirically" minded or materialist Africanist or Southeast Asianist colleagues. A similar accusation of creating perfect structures whose existence is not quite believable has been leveled at Lévi-Strauss on more than one occasion (Geertz 1973, p. 18). But what are taken for mere "ideas" are in fact sociological principles as "real" as lineages, castes, classes, taboos, witches, and preferential cross-cousin marriage. The analysis of the natural and social domains and of the body with its odors and properties has been shown to be important in societies with other types of social organization (for example, Douglas 1966). But they do not necessarily constitute organizing sociological principles of the same order as in lowland South America. What the lowland South American societies can contribute to anthropology is to show that the principles relegated to lesser importance in societies hithertofore analyzed are the basic organizing principles in some societies. By their clarity, their singularity, and the breadth of their application, the analysis of the use of these principles in South America can contribute to our understanding of these aspects of our own and other societies. That is, undoubtedly, the hoped-for end of this analysis. If the Suya way of thinking and acting as described in this book has made the reader reconsider some aspect of his own experience in society, then it has been at least partly successful.

The Suya, the people of the circular villages, are at once unique and yet similar to other people in other societies. My own analysis of them is at once unique and yet similar to others. The Suya, and my analysis of them, should suggest possibilities for the analysis and understanding of other societies as well.

Appendix A
Eastern Suya Genealogical Charts and Village Census
Appendix B
Animal Names in English, Suya, Portuguese, and Latin
Notes
References
Index

Appendix A

Eastern Suya Genealogical Charts and Village Census

This appendix provides detailed information on Suya genealogical relationships, naming relationships, and the residence patterns in 1972. These data should be particularly helpful for careful examination of the discussions of history and politics given in the text. The genealogical chart (figure A.1), spanning four generations, is especially useful for tracing naming relationships and political alliances. The summary of the residential census (figure A.2) indicates which Suya were residing in each house, but shows neither ancestors nor immature children.

Each individual in figure A.1 has two forms of identification. To the left of the sex-specific symbol is a series of letters and numbers that give moiety and name-set affiliations as well as the identifying number used in the text for that person. To the right of the symbol is the name by which the person is addressed. In addition, if the individual was not born a Suya, or was captured or killed by a raiding tribe, or was assassinated as a witch, that is also noted on the right side of the symbol.

The symbols used in the diagrams are as follows:

△ = male
▲ = deceased male
○ = female
● = deceased female
— = genealogical siblings
═ = marriage bond
| = genealogical descent (*Pater* in case of males)

The letters and numbers to the left of the symbols are as follows:

1. The first capital letter indicates the moiety affiliation, or lack of it, for the

name set of which the individual is a member.

A *Ambàn*
K *Kren*
F Female name set without moiety affiliation

The *Ambàn-Kren* moiety pair is the more frequently used in Eastern Suya ceremonies, but every male name set is also part of another pair of moieties. The affiliation of each name set in these other moieties is given in table A.1.

2. After the dash that follows the capital letter, there is a lowercase letter that indicates to which name set within the indicated moiety the name belongs. All the individuals who share the same set of letters share the same name set. Thus all individuals with A-e are members of the *Ambàn* moiety with the name set that includes the names Kahrantoti, Tebnti, and so forth. They are also all members of the group *Ponirekunawti* which is associated with the *Saikokambrigi* moiety in other ceremonies. All individuals with K-e are *Kren* moiety members who share the name set including the names Pentoti, Niogo, and so forth, as well as being members of the *Saikokambrigi.* While A-e and K-e are of opposed moieties in one pair of moieties, they are part of the same moiety—the *Saikokambrigi*—in the second pair. Although different name sets are associated or opposed in the different moiety systems, the members of a given name set are always together. Table A.1 shows the moiety affiliations of the name sets for the Eastern Suya.

TABLE A.1 EASTERN SUYA NAME SETS

AMBAN MOIETY		KREN MOIETY		FEMALE, NO MOIETY AFFILIATION	
a	Domba[1]	a	Botesi[1]	a	Angrondiyi
b	Dombedi[3]	b	Kowo[1]	b	Gaihwati
c	Hwaintü[1]	c	Ndemonti[3]	c	Gaihwü
d	Hwatïgi[3]	d	Ntoni[4]	d	Gaikono
e	Kahrantoti[2]	e	Waraku[1]	e	Gaimbedi
f	Kogrere[1]	f	Temokati[3]	f	Gaisoti
g	Niokombedi[4]	g	Temwensoti[1]	g	Gaitemti
h	Moti[3]	h	Tonwuti[3]	h	Gaiti
i	Kaikwati[1]	i	Wengrodnti[2]	i	Kokoti
j	Ropti[1]			j	Kokoyango
k	Wetacti[3]			k	Kuyayu
l	Pekuho[1]			l	Kwükwüni
				m	Nikiti
				n	Sireti
				p	Sokso
				q	Wekwoiti
				r	Gaidombedi
				s	Gaitemti

1. Members of this name set also belong to the *Saikokambrigi* moiety.
2. Members of this name set also belong to the *Ponirekunawti* group affiliated with the *Saikokambrigi* moiety.
3. Members of this name set also belong to the *Saikodnto* moiety.
4. Members of this name set also belong to the *atàti* group affiliated with the *Saikodnto* moiety.

3. The moiety and name-set affiliations are set off from the three-digit identifying number by a slash (/). Individuals are referred to by these numbers through the text. The first digit indicates the generation of the individual. Arbitrarily the youngest generation is labeled O. The fourth ascending generation is very small because few adult informants could remember their own third ascending-generation kinsmen.

4. The second two digits identify the individual within his generation and indicate where he is to be found on the chart. The numbers are roughly consecutive in each generation. Where an individual is listed in two places, one of the listings merely refers to the other number in parentheses.

The names and comments to the right of the symbols are as follows:

1. *The name.* The name is usually written in the augmentative, or formal, form. For the ascending generations I have recorded them as they were given to me. Any differences in the use of what seems to be the same name may be resolved by looking at the name-set affiliations.

2. *Non-Suya.* When an individual is known to have originated in another tribe, this is indicated by placing the name of that tribe in parentheses ( ). All persons from other tribes in generations 2–, 3–, and 4– were captured by force and raised by the Suya. All those in generation 1– married into the tribe. Not all such couples resided in the village, and this information may be discovered by referring to figure A.2, which records residence.

3. *Capture and death.* When I was told that an individual was taken or killed by enemy Indians, I have entered that fact in order to give an idea of the scale of the raiding that was occurring. The list is probably not exhaustive, but it is indicative of the rate of attrition. When an individual was assassinated as a witch, that fact is indicated by the word "witch" in parentheses.

Figure A.2 summarizes the data of my village census in 1972 and shows the residence patterns when I was in the field. Suya residence in 1972 did not meet their own norm of uxorilocality and was considered abnormal. Houses 1-4 were headed by widows living with their married sons and daughters. In house 6 were a man and his wives and children. House 7 consisted of a man and his two widowed sisters. A number of non-Suya spouses were residing in the village, which exacerbated the trend toward mixed residence. Over the eight years during which I have followed the Suya residence patterns, there have been a number of changes as houses were built or torn down. Figure A.1 gives the residence at a single moment, the one during which much of the political activity described in chapter 9 occurred, without attempting to follow the changes that occurred.

The house numbers here are the same as those in figures 2.2 and 9.3.

House 1. Two widows, formerly co-wives of a strong faction leader, live here with their married and unmarried sons and daughters. In addition, the brother's daughter of one of the widows lives here with her Juruna husband, several Western Suya orphans have been adopted by the various families, and the anthropologist and his wife reside here.

House 2. A widowed Northern Kayapo captive lives here with one of her married daughters and her married son as well as an orphaned grandchild.

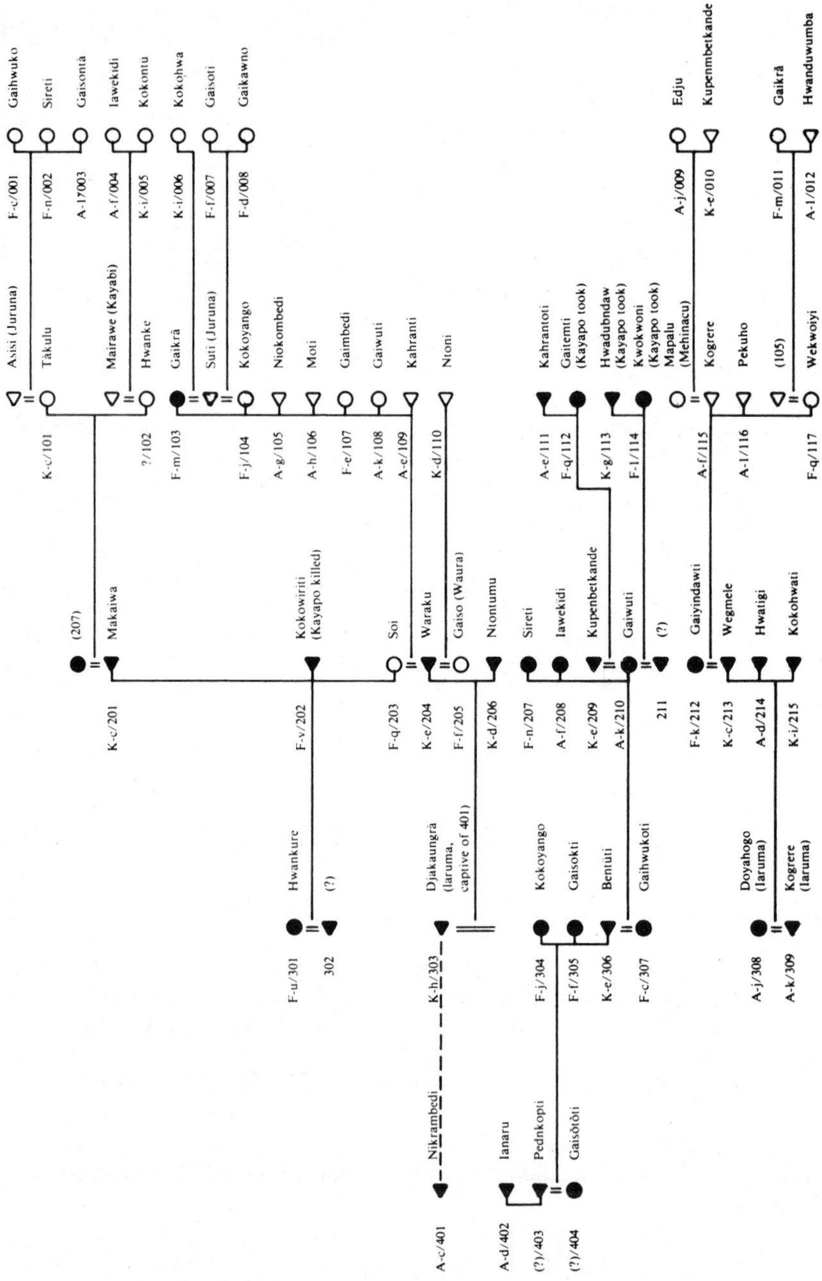

Figure A.1 *Eastern Suya genealogical chart*

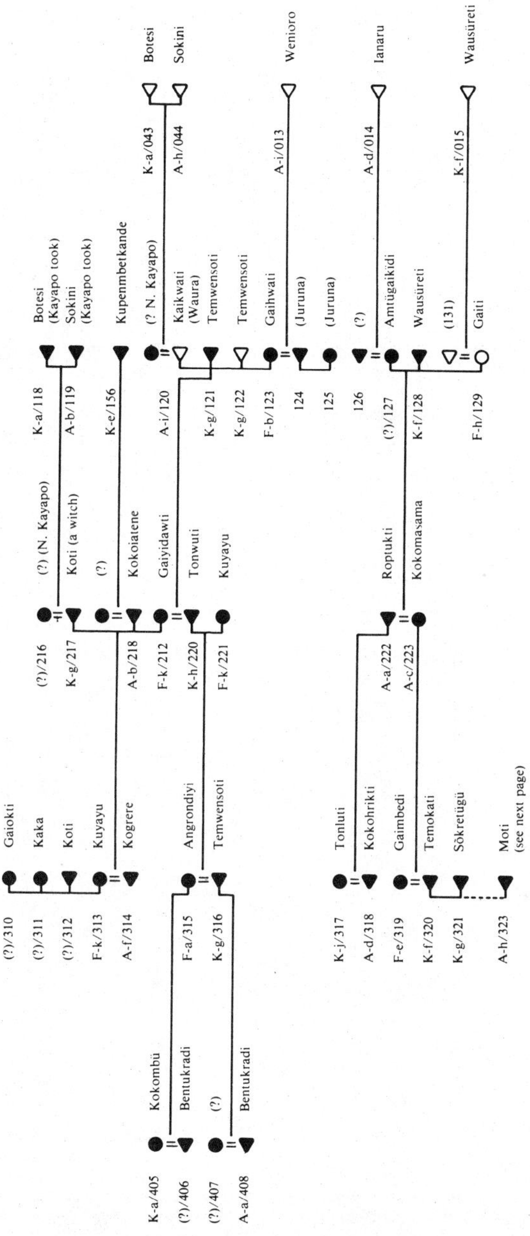

Figure A.1 *Eastern Suya genealogical chart (continued)*

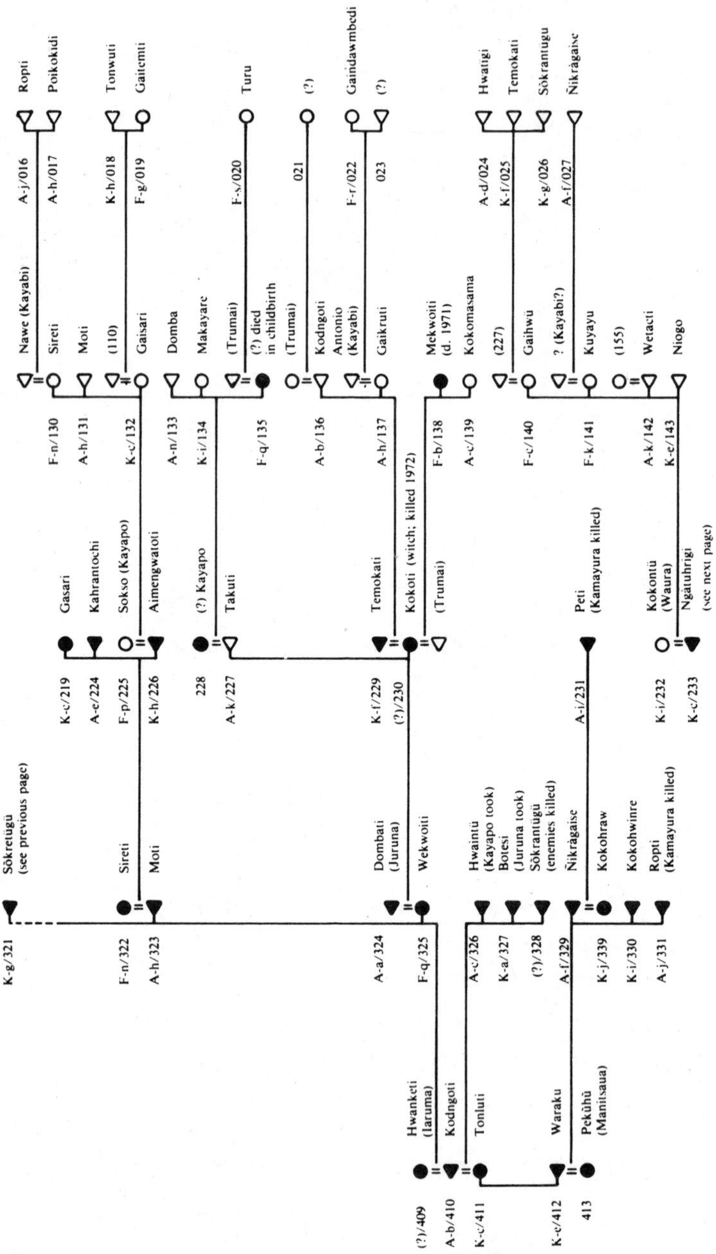

Figure A.1 *Eastern Suya genealogical chart (continued)*

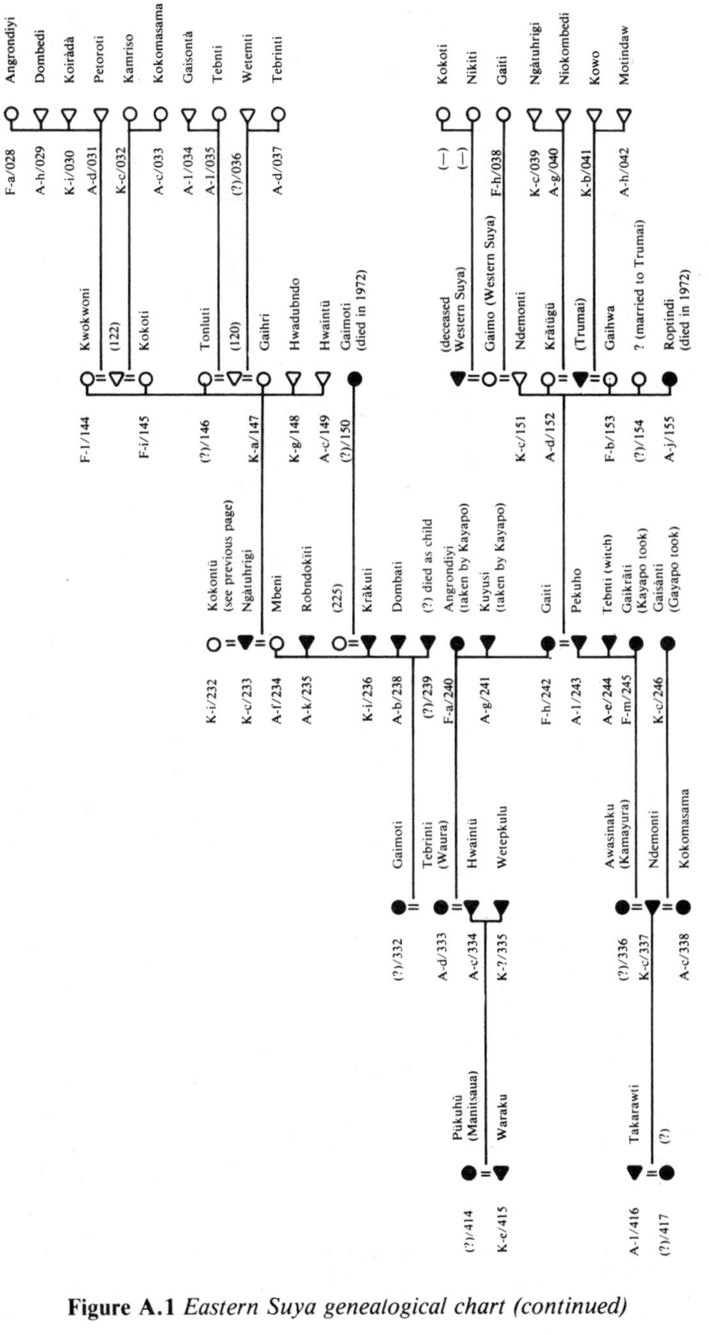

Figure A.1 *Eastern Suya genealogical chart (continued)*

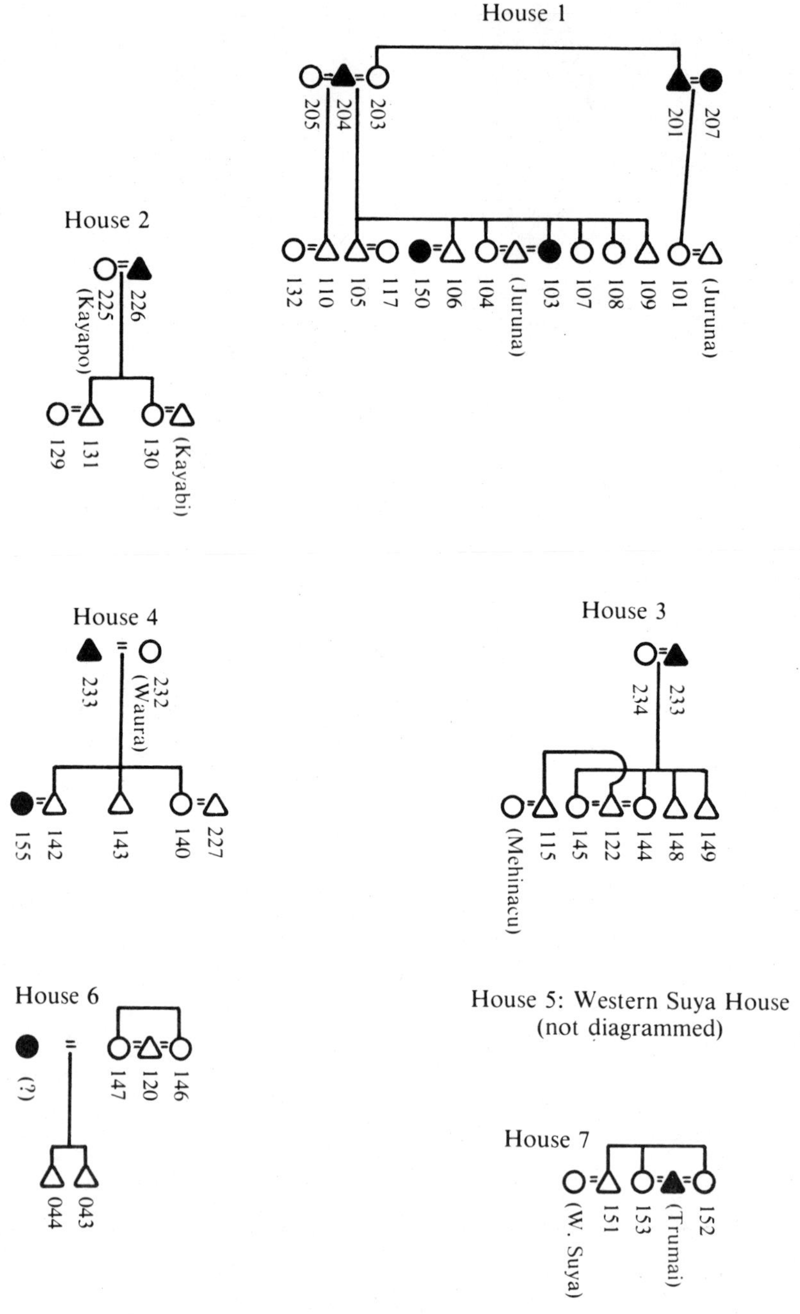

Figure A.2 *Summary of 1972 village census*

House 3. A widow lives here with two of her married daughters (the other two live in house 6), her unmarried sons, and her daughters' husband's brother who lives there with his Mehinacu wife. A Western Suya family lives with them.

House 4. A widow, formerly co-wife of the widow in house 3, lives here with her married daughter, her married but childless son who had started to build house 8 when his wife died, and her adolescent unmarried son. In addition, a Western Suya couple live with them.

House 5. The residents of this house are a number of Western Suya who had previously lived with Eastern Suya in the other houses and had only recently constructed a house of their own. Eventually (by 1978) almost all Western Suya lived in this house. I do not list the residents because they do not appear in the discussions of politics or history.

House 6. A man married to two sisters lives here with his adolescent sons by a previous marriage.

House 7. A brother and two sisters, widows of a Trumai man, live in this house with their children.

Appendix B

Animal Names in English, Suya, Portuguese, and Latin

English	Suya	Portuguese	Latin[a]
Mammals			
tapir	kukrudu	anta	Tapirus terrestris (Linnaeus)
giant otter	nde-ti	ariranha	Pteronura brasiliensis (Zimmermann)
capybara	kutumu	capivara	Hydrochoerus hydrochaeris (Linnaeus)
red deer	karàn-ti	cervo	Blastocerus dichotomus (Illiger)
coati	swakon-ti	coati	Nasa nasua (Linnaeus)
mouse	amto	gambà	Didelphis spp.
howler monkey	kupüdü	bugio	Allouata belzebul (Linnaeus)
weasel	krokrogà (Western Suya)	irara	Tayra barbara (Linnaeus)
capuchin monkey	kukwoiyi	macaco prego	Cebus cay (Olfers)
bat (fruit, vampire)	ntewe	morcego	Chiroptera spp.
jaguar	rop kambrigi	onça parda	Felis concolor (Linnaeus)
spotted jaguar	rowo	onça pinteda	Felis onça (Dinnaeus)
black jaguar	rop tugü	onça preta	Felis onca Linnaeus f. melanica
porcupine	groisi-ti	ouriço	Coendou spp.
paca	gra-chi	paca	Cuniculus paca (Linnaeus)
sloth	hwàt-kasàgà	preguiça	Bradypodidae sp.
collared peccary	angro	queixada	Tayassu pecari (Link)
white-lipped peccary	angro-mbedi	caitetu	Tayassu tacaju (Linnaeus)
rat	amto	rato	Muridae spp.
	kukwoimbedi	sagüim	Hapalidae spp.
anteater	hwàt-chi	tamanduá bandeira	Myrmecophaga tridactyla (Linnaeus)
anteater	hwàt-kutü-chi	tamanduá colête	Tamandua tetradactyla (Linnaeus)
giant armadillo	asei-ti	tatu canastra	Priodontes giganteus (E. Geoffroy)
armadillo	toni (ton-ti)	tatu peba	Euphractus sexcinctus (Linnaeus)
armadillo	ton-mbedi	tatu galinha	Dasypus novemcintus (Linnaeus)

English	Suya	Portuguese	Latin[a]
forest deer	niatü-ti	veado mateiro	Mazama americana (Erxlehen)
savannah deer	baw-ti	veado campeiro	Ozotocerus bezoarticus (Linnaeus)
Birds			
macaw	bodlàn-ti	arara azul, arara caninde	Anodorhynchus hyacinthinus (Latham) & Ara ararauna (Linnaeus)
hummingbird	judnti	beija-flor	Trochilidae in general
stork	kamrikasàkti	carara	Anhinga anhinga (Linnaeus)
rhea	moti	ema	Rhea americana (Tostchild and Chubb)
	sokon-ti	garça-branca-grande	Casmerodius albus egretta (Ihering)
stork	kamri tuk-ti	soco, maguari	Ardea cocoi (Ihering)
	kürükürü	corocoro	Phimosus nudifrons (Ihering)
	poi-ti	bigua, corvo-marinho	Phalacrocorax olivaceus (Ihering)
	kenkoi kasàgà	jacana, piacoca	Jacana spinosa jacana (Ihering)
	ken koikasàgà	frango d'agua azul	Porphyrula martinica (Ihering)
	kenkoye	saracura	Aramides cayennensis (Ihering)
	kwu-kwu kaisàkti	quero-quero	Belonopterus cayennensis (Ihering)
	nda kande	batuira, macarico	Aegialitis collaris (Ihering)
stork	kamritük-ti	tuiuiu, cabeca de pedra	Tantalus americanus (Ihering)
stork	kamri-ti	jaburu	Mycteria mycteria
stork	kamri-ndaw-kregno-ti	jaburu-moleque	Euxenura maguary
duck	husumkasàkti	marreca, ananai, irere	Dendrocygna autumnalis discolor, Nettion brasiliense, Dentrocygna viduata
muscovy duck	husum mbut iakacidà	pato-do-mato	Cairina moschata (Ihering)
	tete-gaisakti	frango-d'agua	Gallinula chloropus galeata (Ihering)
	kikik-ti	matraca	Megaceryle torquata torquata (Ihering)

ENGLISH	SUYA	PORTUGUESE	LATIN[a]
hawk	sàg-ti	variety of gavião, carnivorous birds, hawks	Tarasaetus harpyia
hawk	sikru-ti	gavião-tesoura	Elanoides forficatus
hawk	sàg-ti-ndo-ti	uraçu, gavião real	Morphnus guyanensis (Ihering)
tinamou	atoro-ti	macuco	Tinamus tao (Temminck)
tinamou	atoro	jaó	Crypturellus undulatus subsp.
	sàg-kiki-ti	tem-tenzinho	Falco albigularis (Ihering)
king vulture	kukrüt-ti	urubu-rei	Sarcorramphus papa (Linnaeus)
common vulture	nton-hò-ti	urubu cacador, comum	Coragyps atratus foetens (Lichtenstein)
	sàg-saka	quiriquiri	Cerchneis sparverius eidos (Peters)
curassow	keingoro-ti	mutum penacho	Crax fasciolata (Spix)
curassow	muteng-ti	jacubim	Pipile cumanensis subsp.
curassow	muteng-ti	jacupemba	Penelope superciliaris (Wied)
pigeon	tut-ti	pomba de bando	Zenaida auriculata (Salvadori)
pigeon	tut-ti	pomba trocal	Columba speciosa (Gmelin)
owl	hoho	corujâo	Bubu virginianus nacurutu
	sipeti		
toucan	gron-ti	tucanaçu, tucano	Ramphastos, monnilis and toco (Mueller)
	kïd-mbedi	juruva	Momotus momota (Linnaeus)
	piri-to	surucura	Aramides cajanea (Mueller)
	kürükürü	corocora	Mesimbrinibis cayennensis (Gmelin)
song bird	jao	tesoura	Muscivora Tyrannus (Linnaeus)
		aratinga curea	
small parrot	soie	suiá	Poinus menstruus (Linnaeus)
parakeet	kïdi	piriquito	Periquitos em geral (Carvalho)
parrot	kroi-ti	papagaio verdadeiro	Am. aestiva

English	Suya	Portuguese	Latin[a]
parrot	kroimbedi	papagaio	Am. amazonica
	sipeti	mochinho	? (Carvalho does not list Latin equiv.)
	kopkop-ti		
Fish			
	kwòran-ti	pintado	Pseudoplatistoma (sp) (Carvalho)
	sinkacoti	barbado(?)	Pirinampus sp. (?)
	ambàn-ti	piranha	Pygocentrus and Serrasalmus sp (Carvalho)
	ambàn-tügü	piranha	Pygocentrus and Serrasalmus sp (Carvalho)
	komdutendepti	pirarara	Phractocephalus sp. (Carvalho)
	samdaw-ti	tucunaré	Cichla ocellaris (Bloch and Val.)
	hwiriti	pacu manteiga	Characidae sp. (Carvalho)
	tepsoati	cachorra	Raphiodon sp. (Carvalho)
	sikambrigi	matrichan	Characidae sp. (Carvalho)
	gron-ti	piau	Leporinus sp. (Carvalho)
	wari	tamboata	Callicthys sp.
	waikòchi	camrinha	Triglideos gen. Prionotus (Ihering)
	kuga-ti	piau	Leporinus sp. (Carvalho)
	ambe	sarapo	Gimnotidcos giton fasciatus (Ihering)
	krüt-ti	trairâo	Hoplias sp.
string ray	komdu-ho	arraia	Elipisurus strogylopterus (Schomburgk)
electric eel	mbok-ti	poraquê	Electrophorus electricus (Linnaeus)
mussel	ngàwà	molusco bivalvo de agua doce	Anodontitis sp.
snail	ngàp-siweji	caracol	Strophocheilus sp, Helix sp.
crab	mbai-sü	caranguejo d'agua doce	Trichodactylus fluviatilis

English	Suya	Portuguese	Latin[a]
Amphibians			
toad	piri	sapo	Bufo marinus (Linnaeus)
toad	piri-whai-haw	sapo de agua	Pipa pipa (Linnaeus)
tadpole		girino	
Reptiles			
cayman	mïjï (mï-ti)	jacaré	Caiman crocodilus (Linnaeus)
land turtle	kong-ti	jaboti	Testudo tabulata (Linnaeus)
river turtle	kahrankukre	tartaruga	Podecnemis expansa (Schweiger)
river turtle	kahran-ti	tracajá	Rodocnemis unifilis (Troschel)
all lizards	wede		
Snakes			
anaconda	roti	sucuriju	Eunectes murinus (Linnaeus)
rattlesnake	kangã-ti	cascavel	Crotalus terrificus (Laurentius)
bushmaster		surucucu	Lachesis muta (Linnaeus)
	kangã-tuk-ti	cobra azul	Pseudobea cloelia

[a]Carvalho 1951.

Notes

Introduction

1. I use the term "Brazilian" to refer to any non-Indians of Western, African, or mixed descent who are citizens of Brazil. They are not always "white," nor can they always be called "civilized" in view of their behavior toward the Indians they encountered in the interior. Since the terms "brancos" and "civilizados" are therefore inaccurate, the term "Brazilian" distinguishes people who are culturally not Indians from those that are—even though in a manner of speaking the Indians are also Brazilians.

2. The number inside the parentheses refers to the genealogical chart of the Suya village in appendix A. Although I have kept the number of Suya names given in the text to a minimum, the chart should prove helpful because it shows the relationships of the Suya mentioned in the text.

1. Suya Cosmology

1. Of course, the completeness of the analysis is only relative, since undoubtedly for some I have neglected the key piece as well. Since I have undertaken a number of comparative analyses, however, I have an especially acute appreciation of the difficulty (Seeger 1974, 1975 a, b, 1977b).

2. This contrasts with the common use of binary columns, for example in Needham (1973). What is crucial is the relationship between the opposed poles. It is interesting that the Suya, and other Gê, apparently have no right hand-left hand opposition—one that might be difficult to mediate.

2. A First Encounter with the Suya

1. The Eastern Suya account is similar to the report in Villas Boas (1973, p. 36). However, I take issue with the hypothesis that the Eastern Suya and the Txukahamae were one group at any time in their migration. The discovery of the Western Suya militates even further against such a hypothesis.

2. The lack of walls indicates that the house was like the present Suya men's house, and not a house in which sacred flutes could be hidden from women, as among the Upper Xingu tribes.

3. This could be taken as support for Terence Turner's hypothesis (1966) that a village with two men's houses is unstable. The Suya case is unfortunately inconclusive. There were two villages with two men's houses in the Suya history on the Xingu. Neither of them fissioned. One suffered an epidemic, the second a massacre. It is therefore impossible to tell what the nature of the fissioning might have been. What fissioning there was does not seem to have been along moiety lines, but could have been by factional alignment.

4. The role of the administration of the Xingu reserve is described in Junqueira (1973) whose conclusions hold to some extent for the Suya. See also Viveiros de Castro (1977).

4. The Human Body and Modes of Perception and Expression

1. The design of the artifacts varies somewhat on special occasions, particularly among the Western Suya from whom I was unable to gather satisfactory information on variation. My remarks are based on my observations and information from the Eastern Suya.

2. *Añi mba* is the approximate equivalent of *ku-mba*. The difference is that it appears to have a particular reflexive reference and may refer to the body of a person. Thus *añi sogo* is body paint, *añi hraw tà* is blanket (thing that covers the body). I have refrained from translating the word *añi* as "body" because it would imply a division of body and spirit (*mẽgaron*) that I am not at present prepared to defend for the Suya.

3. Harald Schultz (1960-61) is incorrect when he says that only married men can wear lip disks. The relationship is the other way around. A Suya can marry only after his lip was pierced and his initiation completed.

4. Those who have described "primitive" peoples' ceremonies as being repetitive and unchanging have not been watching carefully. There is much that is new, spontaneous, and variable in Suya ceremony. The songs are the most obvious of these features. While body painting emphasizes the identity of certain ritual groups, individuality is forcibly expressed through the singing of *akia*, since every man has a different one and they all sing them at the same time (Seeger 1979).

5. The Classification of Animals and Plants by Odor

1. Unlike the Kayapo, the Suya do not perform the same ceremony after killing a jaguar as after killing a man. There is, however, an association between jaguars and enemy Indians, further investigated in chapter 10.

6. Sex, Age, and Odor

1. *Wa*, our; *iõ*, indicator of possession; *kasàgà*, bad. This can also be translated as "that of ours which is bad" or "our bad possessions."

2. The Suya contrasted their attitudes with those of the Northern Kayapo, where accusations of adultery may result in a club duel involving two factions and may lead to village fissioning. The Suya villages tended to fission because of witchcraft accusations.

3. The Suya men insisted that sexual relations with a sister were usually initiated by the woman, as is the case in a myth about the subject. The phrase used in discussions of sex with sisters is that the woman "chooses a male lover" rather than that the man "chooses," as is usually the case. This is yet another example the men's representing women as subverting the ideal, ceremonial, social order.

7. The Principles of Kinship and Naming

1. The social organization of the Gê tribes is one of the most intensely studied features of these groups. David Maybury-Lewis (1960, 1967) and Roberto Da Matta (1968, 1976) have written extensively on kinship terminology and ideology. Terence Turner (1966) and Lux Vidal (1977) have written on the age-grade system that is so important among the Northern Kayapo. Jean Lave (1967) has provided an interesting analysis of Krikati naming systems. These are features of rich and puzzling variations among the Gê-speaking societies. These closely related groups have terminologies with Crow, Omaha, and Dakota cross-cousin terms. Some have name-set based moieties while others do not. Interesting attempts are being made to explain this variation (Maybury-Lewis 1979). Anthropologists who have not done fieldwork with the Gê have also been fascinated by the reports of their social organization, and they provide rich material for comparative analysis. Harold Scheffler and Floyd Lounsbury's book on the Siriono kinship system is an interesting attempt to deal with problems of kinship in a small-scale endogamous band organization using what the authors call "structural semantic analysis" (Scheffler and Lounsbury 1971). The vague and often incomplete data collected by Alan Holmberg, however, at times reduce them to inference and speculation (see especially Scheffler and Lounsbury 1971, pp. 39-40). The Gê material will provide a much better source of data and would challenge any attempt to analyze their terminology in a complete way. My own analysis here owes much to an insightful article by Melatti (1976) and to Da Matta's work on the Apinaye (1971, 1976).

2. For brevity, I shall use a standard abbreviation for genealogical relationships. These are abbreviations of genealogically specific usage in English: F, father; M, mother; B, brother; Z, sister (Z distinguishes this term from S for son); D, daughter; S, son; C, child; P, parent.

3. I am indebted to Roberto Da Matta for suggesting this technique to me.

4. The Suya distinction between *gitumu* and *ngedi* is made incipiently by some of the Eastern Timbira. Among the Krikati the terms *kit* (MF, FF, MB) and *tui* (MM, FM, FZ) are both naming relationships and kin terms (Lave 1967, p. 223). The Kraho term *keti* (MB, MMB, MF, MFB, FF, FFB) is paralleled by the term *ikratum*, which Melatti reports is used less but which "seems to cover all of the referents of the term *keti*" (Melatti 1970, p. 123). The Suya term *i-krã-tumu* means "my name giver" and denotes only naming relationships. A *ngedi,* not a *gitumu,* is supposed to be the ideal giver of names, an ideal that is statistically supported. Similarly, marriage with the daughter of a *ngedi* is ideal, although the marriage with the daughter of a *gitumu* is also permissible.

5. An example of using distant sisters to make the exchange occurred when 105 married 117. 122 had married 144, who was a classificatory sister of 105 because his father had been sleeping with 234 and claimed to be the father of 144. During

my visit 105 was maximizing his sibling relationship with 144, observing *sangri* for her even though he would not normally do so for a distant sister (*muhai kandikwoiyi*). This behavior made 105's own marriage an exchange of sisters.

6. Some informants maintained that in the past a man did not actually have sexual relations with a brother's wife or wife's sister. One informant said that in the distant past they used different terms for those affines, similar to the system of the Northern Kayapo, whose terms he was familiar with from a trip to a Kayapo village. He attributed the change in terminology to encounters with the Upper Xingu Indians. I doubt that this was the case, since the terminologies of the Eastern and the Western Suya groups are identical in this and other respects even though the Western Suya had never seen the Upper Xingu Indians before 1969.

7. Among the Apinaye, *tukàya,* wife's father; *tukà,* daughter's husband; *tukà-ti,* sister's husband (Nimuendaju 1939).

8. The word *whai-yi* has several referents, one being a traditional Gê bed, another being a rack for roasting meat over a fire. Although the image of "growing up" on a mother's bed and of transforming meat from raw to cooked on a roasting rack makes a suggestive metaphor, I hesitate to take it with much seriousness at the present stage of my investigations. The Suya explicitly denied the association.

9. These two moiety sets are clearly distinguished, so that about half of the name sets in the *Kren* moiety belong to the *sàiko-kambrigi,* while the other half belong to the *sàiko-dnto,* and the same is the case with the *Ambànyi.* The same balance holds for the associated groups: of the two *ponirekunawti* name sets, one is an *Ambànyi* name set, the other a *Krenyi* name set. There are three *atàti* name sets, one of them *Ambànyi,* the other two *Krenyi.* Men with the same names always perform together in ceremonies. Different name sets perform together in different ceremonies.

10. These ceremonial relationships have been described by Da Matta (1976) for the Apinaye and by T. Turner (1966) for the Kayapo. They are less important among the Suya, for they play only a small role in establishing the social identity of the individual.

11. In the first case, *chi* is an augmentative, while *ngedi* indicates a greater age (*hen kwï ngedi* means "already old"). The terms, however, are used even when ego is quite old and the *kràm-ngedi* is only learning how to walk.

8. The Process of the Life Cycle

1. Another example of the association between the bowstring and the umbilical cord occurs when the father of a very young child avoids stringing his bow tightly. It might cause the child's cord to swell and perhaps pop out.

2. I never observed the bathing, but I was told it should occur. One man killed a giant armadillo after he stopped his diet restrictions. He threw it down in front of his wife's house (the wife's mother had picked the baby up), and it was distributed to the entire village.

3. Among the forbidden animals are some whose odor is bland, and among the recommended ones are some whose odor is pungent. Certain traits are considered especially related to infancy, especially convulsions in high fever caused by

malaria. Any animal with strong death spasms, regardless of odor classification, is thus prohibited to the parents of newborn children. The specificity of diet restrictions is always related to the specificity of the situation itself: whether *sangri* are being observed for a sick person, a young child, a dead person, and the like.

4. Western Suya women with only women's names also had some ceremony when the child could walk.

5. A very similar ceremony, described as defunct, is reported by Nimuendaju among the Eastern Timbira (Nimuendaju 1946, pp. 207-208).

6. *Pe* is another term for *pebyi*, who are the equivalent of the *Peb* of the Timbira and the *Bemp* of the Northern Kayapo; *hrò* means covered, and refers to the seclusion of the boys intended to make them grow fast, literally to "grow old with many children" (*kwï ngedi*).

7. *Pe*, rubber tree (possibly the same as the root of the word *pebyi*); *sog* from *sogo* or sap; *tagü*, to hit up in the air. Thus the game of hitting the sap of the rubber tree (and of the initiates on whom it is spread) up in the air.

8. A ball was made for me. It was of solid rubber and quite heavy. No paddles were made especially for the game, however, as are made among the Apinaye (Nimuendaju 1939, p. 63).

9. *Bokàyi* is a plaza group whose membership is determined by name set. They appear in ceremonies concerning the *pebyi*.

10. *Iaren* are a group of ceremonies involving a special heightened oratorical style. The *iaren kande* is the person who speaks the special oratory.

11. Before the Suya left Diauarum all the *sikwenduyi* slept on the ground. Each boy's mother would bring out a sleeping mat.

12. Apparently two boys were initiated in this particular performance of the ceremony.

13. *Tep swasiti* is the *peixe cachorra* in Portuguese. All *akia* of any ceremony contain the name of an animal. Since this was the "fish ceremony," the animal named is a fish. *Tutwä* is an ornament held in the hand by the dancer and moved up and down. An example made for me out of a toucan's beak has mother-of-pearl eyes. A man's lip is pierced to make him belligerent. At the point of entering the men's house, the boy is indeed in the process of becoming belligerent, and it is particularly appropriate that he sing these words at the time.

14. The importance of hearing and the bad effects of sexual relations on hearing-understanding-knowing have been discussed in chapter 4.

15. The *pebyitugü* has a number of parts in which different groups are important. In the moiety dancing they also wear headdresses and have large rattles painted according to plaza group membership.

16. This may be the same girl who chewed food and gave it to him in his entry into the men's house, but I am not sure.

17. "Our wife" is the formal form of "your wife."

18. This is a special body paint design worn only by men who have killed enemies.

19. Nimuendaju reports a similar circumstance for the Apinaye; old men accompanied the hunt of the young men to eat the heads of the animals they killed (Nimuendaju, 1939).

20. The liver was highly desired and was not usually given to old people.
21. *Whiasàm*, shame; *kïtïli*, negative.
22. The meaning of this word was examined in chapter 6.
23. I was told of a number of important and belligerent men who became witches when they got old. But the Suya are not consistent, for at least one of the people who was assassinated as a witch in the past (Tebni, 244) was a *sikwenduyi*.
24. The village of the dead is described as being very large and as having, variously, two and four men's houses. The newcomer is taken to the men's house of his moiety.
25. A person who dies at night is buried at dawn; one who dies in the day is buried at dusk.
26. This is similar to the hair style of Northern Kayapo women and men in some ceremonies (see T. Turner 1969, photographs).
27. There was no physical violence to themselves among the mourners, as Nimuendaju describes for certain other Gê tribes (Nimuendaju 1946, p. 133).
28. In the preceding description the girl was the daughter of a *mẽropakande*, but she had never taken a village-wide role in anything. So she was buried in a *mẽropakande* type grave inside her house. Since she had no *kràm-ngedi*, her hair was cut by a *tuwuyi*, her father's sister.
29. The Eastern Suya differ from the Western Suya and all the other Gê on this point. I suspect that they may have learned to bury corpses with their feet to the east, rather than their heads, from the Upper Xingu Indians at the same time that they started to bury chiefs sitting up. But I have no real evidence to support this.
30. I never heard of this actually happening, but my informants all said that it could. Widows generally lived as widows and took on lovers. There were neither young widows nor adult men without wives during my stay, however, which may explain why this did not occur.
31. This is, of course, schematic. The processes vary from individual to individual depending on his particular situation. Furthermore, some of the power of political leaders comes precisely from denying this process.

9. Political Leaders, Ritual Specialists, and Witches

1. *Sàgri,* belligerent, bellicose, aggressive, a state of belligerence classified as strong smelling.
2. *Wa*, first person possessive singular or plural; *ro* (?); *pa*, village; *kande*, owner, controller. This differs from a *mẽropakande* only slightly.
3. The office of the *gaiontòni* is somewhat similar to the Kayapo *ben-iaduòrò* described by T. Turner (1966, p. 85) who sing special falsetto songs in certain ceremonies.
4. *Mẽ*, Suya; *sise*, periphery of village; *kande*, owner, controller. *Sise* means curved in general but here refers to the village.
5. When the Suya speak of a chief, they say that he has become a chief (*kwï mẽropakande*). A *mẽropakande* becomes one because of his hereditary right and because the village accepts him as one. He usually becomes one only when the previous incumbent dies or is incapacitated. Before that he is only a potential *mẽropakande*, being called that but without the rights or obligations of office.
6. One man is *kande* of an Upper Xingu women's ceremony, and he provides food to the women.

7. The Western Suya *waropakande* seem to have done some food distributing, but not on the same scale. The Eastern Suya themselves took this as the distinctive feature of the *mẽropakande*.

8. I have not used the names by which the participants are at present addressed but have substituted a different name from their name set. The numbers refer to the genealogies and correspond to those in Seeger (1974).

9. This was generally agreed upon and was confirmed by the direct son's son of Ndemonti (151) as well.

10. One of the reasons given for Kokoti's killing of Niokombedi's brother's wife, the accusation that precipitated Kokoti's assassination, was that she was jealous because Niokombedi and his family were getting so many of the trade goods we brought. Conversely, one of the tensions between myself and Niokombedi was that I reserved some things to distribute as I saw fit rather than giving everything to him to distribute. During the early parts of our stay, most of these items went largely to his relatives and affines.

11. "Screw" means "have sexual relations with" in this context.

12. Occasionally a small bird would fly into the house and not be able to fly out again. It would fly around the ceiling, get caught in the huge spider webs, fight free, and fly into others. The women in the house would start shrieking, and a man or boy would be sent to kill the bird by knocking it down with a pole or catching it. These birds were believed to be witches from other tribes who were coming to harm the Suya.

13. All things, animate and inanimate, have *garon*, or spirits, souls, shadows, reflections. The spirits of men go to the village of the dead. There men hunt and plant and eat the *garon* of animals and crops. When a man's belongings are destroyed at his death, their *garon* go to the village of the dead for him to use. However, witches sometimes take the *garon* of a person's belongings up to the sky so that he will want to join them and die soon. There was quite an uproar in the village in 1973 when one witch told some people that another witch was doing just that.

14. That there are good witches in no way detracts from the contention in chapter 4 that all witches are fundamentally bad because they all have done something immoral and have a witch-thing living in their eyes.

15. A Western Suya leader, and later his son, lived in houses of the same name in the same part of the village in spite of a rule of house exogamy. A similar patrilocal tendency is also found among the Mundurucu, where the chiefs were the only men who did not marry outside their natal village (Murphy and Murphy 1974, p. 121) and may be a general tendency in uxorilocal societies with the inheritance of leadership through the patriline.

10. Transformations in Myths, Curing Chants, and Dreams

1. Myths learned from captives were not given equal validity, and I was usually told that a specific story was an Upper Xingu story. Since a number of women were captured, and they told the stories they heard as children to their own children, there may have been some mixing of myths. In general I do not think it was very great. When I was collecting Western Suya myths I discovered that myths that I had thought were Upper Xingu from their content were in fact shared by the two Suya groups, one of which had not had contact with the Upper

Xingu tribes. In this discussion I do not treat stories that were called Upper Xingu Indian stories, but only those called "what the old people told."

2. I recorded some myths before I understood Suya well, in the hopes that I would eventually be able to understand them. That was possible except when the recorder malfunctioned.

3. It is possible that other collectors were interested in different myths. That is why I chose two different collections for comparison. It would be interesting to see the myths of other fieldworkers on this point.

4. The exceptions were the pregnancy song for all the women of the village, which was sung as they went to bathe, and the *sangere* to make a person die, which could be sung anywhere, usually in the woods, and still be effective. *Sangere* to give a reluctant (female) lover multiple births were sung at night either at the head of her hammock or just outside the house.

5. I found some small individual variation among my informants in how quietly they sang, how intelligibly they enunciated, and how much range they employed, but not enough to comment on with any specificity.

6. *Sako* is third person singular and plural of lip. First person possessive is *iako*; second person, *ñako*.

7. *Wa*, our; *tà-hwĩ*, synonym for death; *ri*, possibly diminutive suffix. This is very similar to the Apinaye name for omens *akupĩ-re*, which is also rooted in the word for death (Da Matta 1970, p. 78).

8. A few diseases are not believed to be caused by a witch, but the rule generally holds for all diseases not introduced by Brazilians and all deaths, including those in warfare.

9. Not all the dreams listed in Da Matta's list are inverted. For example, in his dream 13 where to dream of fledgling parakeets and macaws is a sign that a man will have a child (Da Matta 1970, p. 91), actually makes a parallel between domestic pets and children. It is true that the Apinaye dreams employing social metaphor show an inversion. Dreaming of a log race indicates that one will carry a corpse to the graveyard (5). Dreaming of an argument with a father or brother signifies that one will have an argument with another person (12). There is indeed inversion in these examples as well as in several of the Suya dreams.

10. It would require an entire chapter to investigate the place of honey in the Suya cosmology. In this context, I can merely summarize a few points. Honey is associated primarily with sexual relations. It is a lover's food; like the act of sex, it is called sweet. Honey is never fermented or associated with fermented things, which are not thought of as sweet. When a woman initiates a relationship, she will often request honey of the man. That will begin a sexual relationship, and honey is given by a man to his lovers whenever possible. It is usually collected by a man with his family, as much as they desire being eaten at the tree. This contrasts with fish and game, which are brought back to the village before distribution, cooking, and consumption. Honey, along with fish and game, is one of the foods for which there are male collection expeditions. The honey is divided by a *mẽropakande* at the tree and brought back for the women. There are many species of bee. Each makes a different flavor of honey. Each honey is thought to have its own properties, and they are selectively restricted in periods of diet restriction. Some species are particularly good for people observing these restrictions; others may not be eaten at all. Honey does not appear in Suya myths, but a ceremony which is

ideally performed before the cutting of the gardens is called the bee ceremony. In this ceremony all the men sing bee songs and rush from house to house like swarms of bees. As the only very sweet element in the Suya diet before the introduction of sugarcane in the last few years, honey is important in everyday conversation as well as in most interpersonal relations.

11. Nature and Society in a Broader Perspective

1. In the case of the odor classification of animals, there is no danger of its importance being overlooked even in a study of the animal domain alone. But confusion might possibly arise in other domains. A similar argument is made by Witherspoon (1977), who criticizes linguistic analyses of the Navajo language that ignore other features of Navajo thought.

References

Bamberger, J. 1967. Environment and Cultural Classification: A Study of the Northern Kayapo. Ph.D. dissertation, Harvard University.

Barnes, J. African Models in the New Guinea Highlands. *Man 62:5-9.*

Basso, E. B. 1973. *The Kalapalo Indians of Central Brazil.* New York: Holt, Rinehart and Winston.

Basso, K. 1976. "Wise Words" of the Western Apache: Metaphor and Semantic Theory. In *Meaning in Anthropology*, ed. K. Basso and H. Selby, pp. 93-123. Albuquerque: University of New Mexico Press.

Bohannon, L. 1952. A Genealogical Charter. *Africa* 12:301-315.

Carneiro da Cunha, M. 1978. *Os Mortos e os Outros.* São Paulo: Hucitec.

Carvalho. J. C. M. 1951. *Relações entre os índios do Alto Xingu e a fauna regional.* Publicações Alvulsas do Museu Nacional no. 7. Rio de Janeiro: Graphics Office of the University of Brazil.

Charlin, J. 1950. Notas preliminares sobre la dispersión continental de um adorno del labio en los pueblos aborigines, el bezote labret, o tembeta. Ovalle, Chile.

Clastres, P. 1962. Echange et pouvoir: philosophie de la chefferie indienne. *L'Homme* 2:1.

Colette, J. R. F. 1934. Le Labret en Afrique et en Amerique. *Bulletin de la Societe des Americanistes de Belgique* 13:5-61.

Crocker, J. C. 1967. The Social Organization of the Eastern Bororo. Ph.D. dissertation, Harvard University.

Da Matta, R. A. 1968. Ume breve reconsideração da morfologia social Apinaye. In *Proceedings of the Thirty-seventh International Congress of Americanists,* Stuttgart, 3:355-364.

______ 1970. Les presages Apinaye. In *Echanges et communications: melanges offerts à Claude Lévi-Strauss,* ed. Jean Pouillon and Pierre Maranda, pp. 77-99. The Hague: Mouton.

______ 1971. Apinaye Social Structure. Ph.D. dissertation, Harvard University.

______ 1973. Poe e Lévi-Strauss no campanário: ou, a obra literária como etnografia. In *Ensaios de antropologia estrutural,* ed. Roberto Da Matta, pp. 93-120. Petropolis: Vozes.

______ 1976. *Um mundo dividido: a estrutura social dos índios Apinayé.* Petropolis: Vozes.

Da Matta, R., A. Seeger, E. Viveiros de Castro. 1979. A construção de pessoa nas sociedades indigenas Brasileiras. Rio de Janeiro: Bulletin of the Museu Nacional, N.S. Anthropology 32.

Douglas, M. 1966. *Purity and Danger.* New York: Frederick A. Praeger.

______ 1970. *Natural Symbols: Explorations in Cosmology.* London: Barre and Rockliffe.

Dumont, J. 1976. *Under the Rainbow: Nature and Supernature among the Panare Indians.* Austin: University of Texas Press.

Dumont, L. 1966. *Homo hierarchicus.* Paris: Gallimard.

______ 1977. *From Mandeville to Marx: The Crisis and Triumph of Economic Ideology.* Chicago: University of Chicago Press.

Durkheim, E., and M. Mauss 1903. *Primitive Classification.* Reprint. Chicago: Phoenix Books, 1963.

Eggan, F. 1954. Social Anthropology and the Method of Controlled Comparison. *American Anthropologist* 56:453-473.

Evans-Pritchard, E. E. 1940. *The Nuer: A Description of the Modes of Livelihood and Political Institutions of a Nilotic People.* Oxford: Clarendon Press.

Fortes. M. 1945. The Dynamics of Clanship among the Tallensi; Being the First Part of an Analysis of the Social Structure of a Trans-Volta Tribe. London: Oxford University Press.

______ 1945. The Web of Kinship among the Tallensi; The Second Part of an analysis of the social structure of a Trans-Volta Tribe. London: Oxford University Press.

Fustel de Coulanges. 1864. *The Ancient City.* Reprint. New York: Doubleday Anchor, no date.

Galvao, E. 1953. *Cultura e sistema de parentesco das tribos do alto rio Xingu.* Rio de Janeiro: Bulletin of the Museu Nacional, N.S. Anthropology 14.

Geertz, C. 1973. *The Interpretation of Cultures.* New York: Basic Books.

Griaule, M. 1965. *Conversations with Ogoteméli.* London: Oxford University Press.

Hanbury-Tenison, R. 1973. *A Question of Survival for the Indians of Brazil.* New York: Scribner's.

Hugh-Jones, S. 1974. Male Initiation and Cosmology among the Barasana Indians of the Vaupés Area of Colombia. Ph.D. dissertation, Cambridge University.

Junqueira, C. 1973. The Brazilian Indigenous Problem and Policy: The example of the Xingu National Park. AMAZIND/IWGIA document no. 13. Copenhagen.

Kaplan, J. 1975. *The Piaroa: A People of the Orinoco Basin.* London: Oxford University Press.

Labouret, H. 1952. A propos des labrets en verre de quelques populations voltaiques. In *Bulletin de l' Institut Français d'afrique noire* 14:1384-1401.

Lanna, A. D. 1967. La division sexuelle du travail chez les Suyá do Brésil central. *L'Homme* 8:67-72.

Lave, J. E. C. 1967. Social Taxonomy among the Krĩkati (Gê) of Central Brazil. Ph.D. dissertation, Harvard University.

LEACH, E. R. 1966. Two Essays Concerning the Symbolic Representation of Time. In *Rethinking Anthropology*, ed. E. R. Leach, pp. 124-136. New York: Humanities Press.

LEVI-STRAUSS, C. 1955. *Tristes tropiques.* Paris: Plon.

______ 1963. *Structural Anthropology.* New York: Basic Books.

______ 1964. *Le cru et le cuit.* Paris: Plon.

______ 1966a. *Du miel aux cendres.* Paris: Plon.

______ 1966b. Overture to le cru et le cuit. *Yale French Studies* 36-37:41-66.

______ 1966c. *The Savage Mind.* Chicago: University of Chicago Press.

______ 1968. *L'origine des manières de table.* Paris: Plon.

______ 1971. *L'Homme nu.* Paris: Plon.

MALINOWSKI, B. 1922. *Argonauts of the Western Pacific.* New York: Dutton.

MAYBURY-LEWIS, D. 1960. Parallel Descent and the Apinaye Anomaly. *Southwestern Journal of Anthropology* 16:191-216.

______ 1965. *The Savage and the Innocent.* Boston: Beacon Press.

______ 1967. *Akwẽ-Shavante Society.* Oxford: Clarendon Press.

______ 1979. *Dialectical Societies.* Cambridge, Mass.: Harvard University Press.

MELATTI, J. C. 1970. O sistema social Krahó. Ph.D. dissertation, University of São Paulo.

______1976. Nominadores e genitores: um aspecto do dualismo Krahó. In *Leituras de etnologia Brasileira,* ed. E. Schaden, pp. 139-149. São Paulo: Campanha Editora Nacional.

MURDOCK, G. P. 1960. Cognatic Forms of Social Organization. In *Kinship and Social Organization,* ed. P. Bohannon and J. Middleton, pp. 235-255. Garden City, N.Y.: Natural History Press.

MURPHY, R., AND B. QUAIN. 1955. *The Trumai Indians of Central Brazil.* American Ethnological Society Monograph 24. Seattle, Wash.: American Ethnological Society.

MURPHY, Y. AND R. MURPHY. 1974. *Women of the Forest.* New York: Columbia University Press.

NEEDHAM, R., ed. 1973. *Right and Left: Essays on Dual Symbolic Classification.* Chicago: University of Chicago Press.

NIMUENDAJU, C. 1939. The Apinaye. Washington, D.C.: Catholic University Press. Reprint. Oosterhout N.B.—The Netherlands: Anthropological Publications, 1967

______ 1941. *The Eastern Timbira.* University of California Publications in American Archeology and Ethnology, Vol. 41. Berkeley and Los Angeles: University of California Press. Reprint. New York: Kraus Reprint Co., 1971.

______ 1946. The Cayabi, Tapanyuma, and Apiacá. In *Handbook of South American Indians* 3:307-321.

______ 1952. Os Gorotire. *Revista do Museu Paulista (N.S.)* 6:427-453.

POCOCK, D. F. 1964. The Anthropology of Time Reckoning. In *Contributions to Indian Sociology* 7:18-29.

RADCLIFFE-BROWN, A. R. 1922. *The Andaman Islanders.* London: Cambridge University Press.

______ 1924. The Mother's Brother in South Africa. Reprinted in *Structure and Function in Primitive Society,* pp. 1-14. New York: Free Press, 1965.

RAMOS, A. R. 1978. Munducucu: Social Change or False Problem? *American Ethnologist* 5:675-689.

RAPPAPORT, R. 1968. *Pigs for the Ancestors.* New Haven, Conn.: Yale University Press.

REICHEL-DOLMATOFF, G. 1971. *Amazonian Cosmos.* Chicago: University of Chicago Press.

——— 1975. *The Shaman and the Jaguar.* Philadelphia: Temple University Press.

RIVERS, W. H. R. 1910. The Genealogical Method of Anthropological Inquiry. *Sociological Review* 3:1-12.

RIVIERE, P. 1960. *Marriage among the Trio.* London: Oxford University Press.

SAHLINS, M. 1976a. *Culture and Practical Reason.* Chicago: University of Chicago Press.

——— 1976b. *The Use and Abuse of Biology.* Ann Arbor: University of Michigan Press.

SCHEFFLER, H., AND F. LOUNSBURY. 1971. *A Study in Structural Semantics: The Siriono Kinship System.* Englewood Cliffs, N.J.: Prentice-Hall.

SCHNEIDER, D. M. 1968. *American Kinship, a Cultural Account. Englewood Cliffs, N.J.: Prentice-Hall.*

——— 1972. What Is Kinship All About? In *Kinship in the Morgan Centennial Year,* ed. P. Reining, pp. 32-63. Washington, D.C.: Anthropological Society of Washington.

——— 1976. Notes toward a Theory of Culture. In *Meaning in Anthropology,* ed. K. Basso and H. Selby, pp. 197-221. Albuquerque: University of New Mexico.

SCHULTZ, HARALD. 1950. Lendas dos índios Krahó. *Revista do Museu Paulista (N.S.)* 4:49-165.

——— 1960-61. Informações etnográficas sobre os índios Suya. *Revista do Museu Paulista (N.S.)* 13:315-332.

——— 1962. Brazil's Big-Lipped Indians. *National Geographic Magazine* 121: 118-133.

SEEGER, ANTHONY. 1974. Nature and Culture and Their Transformations in the Cosmology and Social Organization of the Suya, a Gê-Speaking Tribe of Central Brazil. Ph.D. dissertation, University of Chicago.

——— 1975a. The Meaning of Body Ornaments: A Suya Example. *Ethnology* 14:211-224.

——— 1975b. By Gê Out of Africa: Ideologies of Conception and Descent. Presented at the Seventy-fourth Annual Meeting of the American Anthropological Association, San Francisco, 1975. (Seeger 1980, pp. 127-135.)

——— 1977a. Porque os índios Suya cantam para as suas irmãs. In *Arte e Sociedade,* ed. G. Velho, pp. 39-64. Rio de Janeiro: Zahar.

——— 1977b. Fixed Points on Arcs in Circles: The Temporal Processual Aspects of Suya Space and Society. In *Actes of the Forty-second International Congress of Americanists,* vol. 2, pp. 341-359. Paris: International Society of Americanists.

——— 1979. What Can We Learn When They Sing? Vocal Genres of the Suya Indians of Central Brazil. *Ethnomusicology* 23:373-394.

——— 1980. *Os Índios e nos: estudos sobre sociedades tribais Brasileiras.* Rio de Janeiro: Editora Campus.

______ forthcoming. Physical Substance and Knowledge: Dualism in Suya Leadership. *In Leaders and Leadership in Lowland South America,* ed. W. Kracke.
SWARTZ, MARC. 1968. *Local Level Politics.* Chicago: Aldine.
STEINEN, KARL VON DEN. 1940. *Entre os aborígenes do Brasil central.* São Paulo, Journal of the Municipal Archives of São Paulo, nos. 34-58.
______ 1942. *O Brasil central.* São Paulo: Brasiliana.
TURNER, T. S. 1966. Social Structure and Political Organization among the Northern Kayapo. Ph.D. dissertation, Harvard University.
______ 1969. Tchikrin: A Central Brazilian Tribe and Its Symbolic Language of Bodily Adornment. *Natural History* 78:50-59.
______ 1973. Myth as Model: The Kayapo Myth of the Origin of Cooking Fire. Manuscript.
TURNER, V. W. 1967. *The Forest of Symbols.* Ithaca, N.Y.: Cornell University Press.
______ 1973. Symbols in African Ritual. *Science* 179:1100-1105.
UCKO. P. J. 1969. Penis Sheaths: A Comparative Study. In *Proceedings of the Royal Anthropological Institute of Great Britain and Ireland,* pp. 27-68. London: Royal Anthropological Institute.
VIDAL, L. 1973. *Put-Karôt,* grupo indígena do Brasil central. Ph.D. dissertation, University of São Paulo.
______ 1977. *Morte e vida de uma sociedade indígena Brasileira.* São Paulo: Hucitec and the University of São Paulo.
VILLAS BOAS, O., AND C. VILLAS BOAS. 1973. *Xingu, The Indians, Their Myths.* New York: Farrar, Straus and Giroux.
VIVEIROS DE CASTRO, E. B. 1977. Indivíduo e sociedade no Alto Xingu: Os Yawalapiti. Master's dissertation, Graduate Program in Social Anthropology, Museu Nacional, Rio de Janeiro.
WAGNER, R. 1972. *Habu: The Innovation of Meaning in Daribi Religion.* Chicago: University of Chicago Press.

Index